Valhalla's Warriors

A History of the Waffen-SS on the Eastern Front 1941-1945.

For Mandy and Hayley

First published by Dog Ear Publishing
4010 W. 86th Street, Ste H
Indianapolis, IN 46268
www.dogearpublishing.net

ISBN: 978-159858-445-5

This book is printed on acid-free paper.

Printed in the United States of America

Preface

This book is an exploration of the Waffen-SS, and by necessity of evil. The Waffen-SS are commonly regarded as the elite of Germany's armed forces during World War II. They gained much of this reputation whilst fighting on the Eastern Front in Russia. Germany's war against the Soviet Union in World War II, in particular the role of the Waffen-SS forms much of the subject matter of this book.

The death and destruction during this conflict would result not just from military operations, but also from the systematic killing and abuse that the Waffen-SS directed against Jews, Communists and ordinary citizens. This book provides a clear, concise history of the Waffen-SS campaign of conquest and genocide in Russia by looking at the actions both on and behind the front lines. By drawing on the best of military and Holocaust scholarship, this book dispels the myths that have distorted the role of the Waffen-SS, in both the military operations themselves and the unthinkable crimes that were part of them.

The conventional wisdom that the Waffen-SS in World War II fought a relatively clean fight, unsullied by the atrocities committed by the Nazis, is challenged—and largely demolished. Focusing on the Eastern Front, the book contends that the Nazi vision of a racial-ideological death struggle against Slavic hordes and their Jewish-Bolshevik commissars resonated with soldiers of the Waffen-SS, steeped in traditional anti-Semitic and racist dogmas. In doing so this book clearly shows that the Waffen-SS was an organisation that committed widespread atrocities, and were truly soldiers of evil.

Contents:

List of Tables:

Diagrams, illustrations or tables

Introduction

Why the Waffen-SS?

My interest in the Waffen-SS[1] was first sparked when I read a short history of the *Totenkopf* Division many years ago. It struck me that here was a magnificent fighting force, yet at the back of this image something darker lurked. The spectre of the atrocities apportioned to the Waffen-SS reared its head and served to intrigue me as to the real story behind the Waffen-SS. To this end a disturbing question arose. *Were the Waffen-SS just simple soldiers doing their duty or did they commit some of the most evil acts in recent history?* It is envisaged that this book will fill a large void in relation to examinations of the Waffen-SS and the perception of this organisation from a criminological and historical perspective. This examination is important for a number of reasons. First the analysis of the Waffen-SS allows close scrutiny of gross organisational behaviour within historical frameworks. Second the examination of the Waffen-SS becomes even more pertinent when one considers that there has been no meaningful and objective discussion of the criminal activities of the Waffen-SS. The study of this military formation allows a close examination of situational, dispositional and interactional factors that helped to promote the growth and occurrence of evil in the context of the genocidal barbarity of the Eastern Front. From this understanding I hope to be able to draw an accurate picture and reach a defendable analysis as to the actions of the Waffen-SS.

Since Stein's (1966)[2] seminal examination there have be some analyses of the crimes of individual units as well as a major work by Theile (1997) in defence of the Waffen-SS. The Waffen-SS has also been examined by a number of authors with its formation and structure being the main focus. However, the few studies available on the Waffen-SS point to a high frequency of crimes being committed by this elite force during the conflict on the Eastern Front (Christensen, Smith, & Poulsen, 2003:9). The purpose of this book is to draw upon these studies and other sources to explore the Waffen-SS within the framework of the criminal liability for actions undertaken on the Eastern Front. Wegner notes that:

> If one surveys the literature on the history of the SS and the Waffen-SS, it becomes obvious how immense the discrepancy is between the veritable avalanche of titles and the quite modest yield of credible and scholarly insights. The reason for this discrepancy is clear; more than a generation after the collapse of the Third Reich, the SS as a historical phenomenon has exercised a powerful emotional attraction. At the same time it demands that we come to terms with it morally, and both of these factors are the leitmotivs of public discussion. (Wegner, 1990:1)

This absence of real discussion in relation to the crimes and criminality of the Waffen-SS has allowed proponents both for and against the Waffen-SS to create various myths about who and what the Waffen-SS actually were.

> The Waffen-SS possesses a surprisingly wide cult following among military buffs. The status of a military elite within the German armed forces … the impressive combat record and aura of toughness that surrounded the force: all hold enormous fascination for modellers and collectors alike, as the huge volume of post-war photographic and illustrated material relating to the Waffen-SS attests. (Mackenzie, 1997:135)

It is for this reason that the Waffen-SS is one of the most frequently discussed and persistently controversial subjects of that era. Indeed the "… SS poses sociological and psychological questions to political science that go far beyond the still existing need to furnish documentary proof for the functions assigned to certain formations of the SS" (Paetel, 1959:34). One of the most pressing social and psychological questions is the "… extraordinary power to accomplish pure evil that helps to make the SS an endlessly fascinating subject to study" (Kren & Rappoport, 1976:87).

Since the close of World War II the veterans of the Waffen-SS have been actively involved in the denial of its involvement in and responsibility for atrocities on the basis that its members were simple soldiers with no links to the terrible actions that took place on and behind the front lines. This book will argue otherwise. Throughout this book I will use the term Waffen-SS apologists. This is a loose grouping of proponents supportive of a positive image for the Waffen-SS. By this term I am referring to those organisations, veterans and writers who have determinedly undertaken efforts to rehabilitate the image of the Waffen-SS and separate it from the SS organisation as a whole, and the crimes committed by such. The motivations of these apologists are many and varied, but the most common underlying theme would seem to be that the military achievements of the

Waffen-SS far outweigh any crimes committed by such, and therefore any elements that may tarnish the fighting reputation of the Waffen-SS should be discounted or ignored. It is not that this book is seeking to show that the crimes committed by the Waffen-SS were any more or less evil in comparison to other military formations during or since World War II. As pointed out by Knopp the Waffen-SS were "… not unique in their brutal behaviour, and the difference between the *Wehrmacht*[3] and the Waffen-SS was by no means as great as has been claimed" (Knopp, 2002:xiii).

The role of the Waffen-SS on the Eastern Front was something akin to a holy crusade; its purpose was to destroy those groups who were abhorrent to the ideals of the Nazi Party. These included Slavs, Jews and Bolsheviks. During the conflict the Waffen-SS were to prove themselves to be excellent soldiers and they became known as the *Fuhrer's fire brigade,* with the result that Waffen-SS units were rushed wherever the fighting was fiercest. In his extensive work on the war as a global conflict Weinberg (1994:458) describes the Waffen-SS on the Eastern front as follows; "… the armed formations of the SS. Fanatical in spirit, favoured over the regular army in delivery of weapons, and not always particularly obedient, these contingents were in the process of becoming a kind of fire brigade from critical points on the front". But this group was also employed in other roles. In fact, clear links can be drawn between the Waffen-SS, the concentration-camp system and the *Einsatzgruppen*[4].

This military formation was peculiar in that it was integrated into the overall system of violence that was the SS and as such did not possess the professional autonomy of the army. For this reason it cannot be seen as a pure military force, rather it had all the hallmarks of being a political tool of the Nazi regime. When Italy began to withdraw from the war after the fall of Mussolini, Waffen-SS units were rushed to Italy despite the fact they were desperately needed on the Eastern Front. Foremost among them being the 1st Waffen-SS Panzer Division *Leibstandarte SS Adolf Hitler.* The reasoning given by Hitler to his generals at a military conference on the 26th July 1943 was as follows:

> … I have to take units that are politically reliable… In Italy I can only accomplish something with crack formations that are politically close with fascism. If it weren't for that I could take a couple of army divisions. But as it is, I need a magnet to gather the people together … I must have units that come under a political banner (Gilbert, 1950:106-109).

These political aspects are important as they provide a background against which the actions of the Waffen-SS can be examined to determine the perceived liability for their actions. In order to examine the Waffen-SS it is necessary to limit the scope of the investigation to the specific actions of the Waffen-SS in the East. This is due to the enormity of the conflict itself and the need to examine a defined and specific group for the purpose of this book. To examine more is simply beyond the scope of this book. The Eastern Front, in particular the actions of the Waffen-SS, provide an excellent case study of the total war doctrine and genocidal actions. The examination of this selected and limited section of the German armed forces (the Waffen-SS), allows development of a more complete picture of the factors that can cause soldiers to commit acts of evil. To complete this examination the nature of the conflict on the Eastern Front is studied to place the actions of the Waffen-SS in an overall context. Lastly specific actions of the Waffen-SS are examined and analysed in the light of the post-war War Crime Trials.

The Eastern Front – An introduction

The formation of the Nazi Party and it's ascension to power under the guidance of it's leader, Adolf Hitler, was an event that would begin the German revolution and in a matter of 12 years bring to an end what was going to be the 1000-year Reich. World War II was one of the most pivotal events of the 20th century. The conflict on the Eastern Front was seen as the most important phenomenon of the conflict and its political repercussions lasted for decades after the war ended. But of even more importance is the impact that the Eastern Front had on the course of the war and its eventual outcome. It was a war that unleashed unparalleled genocidal barbarity and resulted in a death toll in excess of 30 million people. Indeed it has been argued that even before it began Hitler insisted it was to be a *Vernichtungskrieg*, or war of annihilation unlike any other in history. In his directive number 21 issued on the 18th of December 1940 to the armed forces, Hitler made clear that the aim of Operation *Barbarossa*[5] was to crush Soviet Russia in a rapid campaign. It was envisaged that the East would see a different kind of occupation from the type used in the conquered countries in the West. The occupation policies would see the brutal imposition of German interests. It was part of the plan that the conquered territory was to be resettled by Germans and the current population used as slave labour where possible.

The seeds for this barbarity stemmed from Hitler's rambling view of the world. His policies sprung from a political ideology that mixed the ideas of living space (*lebensraum*), racism, anti-Semitism, economic independence and the vision of Germany being a world power. Hitler perceived

Germany as a nation without space and she needed to conquer land in the East to obtain living space and extension of German resources. Certainly Hitler saw the conflict in Russia as being a war of absolutes with two outcomes, either victory or annihilation. Hitler invaded Russia to crush a political and ideological system that was abhorrent to the National Socialist ideals. Further he envisaged a Nazi style colonialism that would gain living space for the racially superior Germans and reduce the Slavs living in Russia to the status of subhumans with the result that in the military sphere too, the bloodiness and barbarity of the struggle owed much to its ideological character. This view of the Russian as a subhuman is reflected in the post-war comments of Waffen-SS general Max Simon:

> All have in greater or lesser degree the Asiatic characteristics of frugality, cunning, cruelty, hatred of foreigners and indifference to death. The fact that, as Asiatics, they have little or no will of their own, indulging only in mass thinking, but at the same time can face mass death, facilitated Communist education and uniformity. (Simon, 1953:4)

During one of his private conversations in August 1941 Hitler outlined his thoughts on the way in which these German colonists would live:

> The German colonist ought to live on handsome, spacious farms. The German services will be lodged in marvellous buildings, the governors in palaces. Beneath the shelter of the administrative services, we shall gradually organise all that is indispensable to the maintenance of a certain standard of living. Around the city, to a depth of 30 to 40 kilometres, we shall have a belt of handsome villages connected by the best roads. What exists beyond that will be another world, in which we mean to let the Russians live as they like. It is merely necessary that we should rule them. (Trevor-Roper, 2000:24).

The nature of the Russo-German conflict was distinct in that not only was it a battle of racial origins and ideology, but it was also seen as a war of economic survival. Hitler needed the land of Russia for three main reasons: living space for the German people, food to feed the German people, and resources to drive German industry. Without these Germany, in Hitler's view, would be unable to conduct a lengthy conflict and would be at risk both from a military and economic standpoint. Hitler was driven by strategic and ideological motives, which resulted in his perceived need to destroy the racially inferior Slavs and take their land while at the same time destroying the Jewish-Bolshevik threat to Germany. The International Military Tribunal (IMT) recognised that this conflict was to be conducted in a manner conducive to committing war crimes.

... war crimes were deliberately planned long in advance. In the case of the Soviet Union, the plunder of the territories to be occupied, and the ill-treatment of the civilian population, were settled in minute detail before the attack was begun. As early as the autumn of 1940, the invasion of the territories of the Soviet Union was being considered. From that date onwards, the methods to be employed in destroying all possible opposition were continuously under discussion.
(The International Military Tribunal, 1946 Vol 1:227)

During the trial of the major war criminals by the IMT it was held that Germany had conducted an aggressive war against Russia.

The plans for the economic exploitation of the U.S.S.R., for the removal of masses of the population, for the murder of Commissars and political leaders, were all part of the carefully prepared scheme launched on the 22nd June without warning of any kind, and without the shadow of legal excuse. It was plain aggression.
(The International Military Tribunal, 1946 Vol 1:215)

Hitler saw the opportunity of a quick blow against Russia as being imperative in 1941, as once Russia was out of the war it would allow Germany to focus on the still-defiant Britain, and America should it decide to enter the war. Upon his rise to power Hitler had always seen his destiny and that of the German Reich being decided in the East. For it was there that he saw his true enemy. At dinner on the 17th of September 1941 Hitler commented on the struggle in the East:

The struggle for the hegemony of the world will be decided in favour of Europe by possession of the Russian space ... the essential thing, for the moment is to conquer. After that everything will be simply a question of organisation ... The Slavs are a mass of born slaves who feel the need of a master. (Trevor-Roper, 2000:33)

The recent exhibition "The German Army and Genocide" by the Hamburg Institute for Social Research provided clear evidence that:

The war in the East was not simply a particularly ruthless, ideologically charged war, but it now appeared as a destructive war against entire populations – a war which aimed at the total annihilation of some groups of people and the decimation and enslavement of others. (Bartov, 1999:7)

For the purpose of this book the Eastern Front shall be deemed to include front-line actions and occupied areas that were to the East of the German Reich borders prior to the beginning the World War II. The time period being taken into consideration is from the 22nd of June 1941 until the taking of Berlin by Russian forces in May 1945. From a purely military standpoint conflict on the scale of the Eastern Front had not been seen prior to or since World War II. Indeed Operation Barbarossa, the invasion of Russia, pitted the largest national armies ever assembled against each other. On the 22nd of June 1941 Hitler unleashed three German Army Groups upon the Soviet Union. Army Group North eventually advanced to Leningrad and besieged that city for some 900 days, but failed to take the city. Army Group Centre advanced upon Moscow and came within view of the golden spires of the Kremlin. This was as close as the Germans would come to taking the city. Army Group South advanced into the Ukraine and Crimea until the disaster of Stalingrad in 1942 where an entire Army was lost. In 1943 the Germans gambled on a strategic victory at Kursk, but ultimately failed, being beaten by thorough Russian preparation for the offensive and German vacillation. From the end of the Kursk offensive, with few exceptions, the next few years would be ones of constant retreat by the German forces until their ultimate defeat before the gates of Berlin. As noted by *SS-Gruppenführer* Max Simon in a post-war statement:

> Very soon, we realised that we had underestimated our opponent … the flower of our shock troops had been irretrievably lost by then, and today I feel justified in saying that a complete misjudgement and underrating of the Russian power of resistance was one of the reasons for the failure of Germany's campaign against Russia. (Simon, 1949:3)

Sources of information on the Waffen-SS

To build a picture of the operations and nature of the Waffen-SS I have referred to a number of sources to give an accurate account. The primary sources include the military trials held after the war by the Allies, and later by Germany itself. These being the trials of the Major War Criminals conducted by the International Military Tribunal (hereafter referred to as the IMT – commonly referred to as the Blue series), a comprehensive 42-volume set of documents and testimony from the first war crimes trial at Nuremberg. In particular volumes IV and XX, which deal with various aspects of the Waffen-SS. As well as this, the eight-volume set of the decision of the International Military Tribunal against the defendants at Nuremberg (commonly referred to as the Red Series), summarises the crimes for which the defendants were put on trial and explains the Court's decision against each defendant. It also includes the dissenting verdicts and the sentences handed down to the criminals. This set was published in the United States by the Office of Chief of Counsel for the Prosecution of Axis Criminality. It is generally referred to as the Nazi Conspiracy and Aggression set.

The Nuremberg Military Trials (hereafter referred to as the NMT - The Green series) a 15 volume set of documents and testimony from the last 12 Nuremberg trials. This was a series of 12 trials for war crimes the U.S. authorities held in their occupation zone in Germany in Nuremberg after the end of World War II. The trials that I shall refer to include the Doctors' Trial, which examined medical experiments on concentration-camp prisoners. The *Einsatzgruppen* Trial, which looked at the actions of the SS mobile killing groups in the East, and the Pohl Trial, which examined the role of the SS Main Economic and Administrative Office (WVHA) in various crimes against humanity.

Further information was available from the war trials held in Germany after the war. The German post-war trials include those conducted in West Germany in the Federal Republic (here after referred to as the FR series) and; East Germany in the German Democratic Republic (hereafter referred to as the GDR series).

I have also utilised manuscripts prepared by former Waffen-SS officers for the Historical Division, United States Army, Europe.[6] The manuscripts deal with various facets of the armed conflict involving the Waffen-SS. The Studies consist of seven series as follows: ETHINT (European Theatre Interrogations) 1-80; A 855-1000; B 001-850; C 1-102d; D 001-431; P 001-217 and T 1a-123K3. There are 1,737 items in English and 2,169 items in German. Copies of the manuscripts are held at the National Archives, Washington (catalogue available on paper and microfilm).

There are also a number of SS publications referred to throughout the trials that provide an insight into the ideology and political outlook of the SS and its members. A number of these documents of this nature have also been translated into English and published in recent times.

I decided to include unit histories written by veterans and also interviews given by such veterans for video productions and books, etc. This is because it allows a view from below in contrast to the views of the command and control level, the difficulties with these being that while they provide first-hand accounts, naturally few of the veterans are going to disclose if any atrocities were committed. Indeed there has been a concerted campaign to rehabilitate the image of the Waffen-SS in post-war years. To this end organisations, such as the Mutual Aid Society of the Waffen-SS (HAIG organisation) have financed a multitude of memoirs and units histories that focus purely on the military role of the Waffen-SS (Mackenzie, 1997; Paetel, 1959; Sydnor, 1973). I have included these accounts because of their value as primary sources and second because direct quotes from some of the main actors give a clear insight into their intentions and reasons for their actions. As noted by former Waffen-SS officer Georg Maier in his history of the 6th SS Panzer Army: "Contemporary witnesses are able to provide essential insight for the course or events and evaluation of them. The can help fill in the obvious gaps and frequently bring important informative facts to light, clarifying them for the historian" (Maier, 2004:1). To this end I have utilised the accounts of many Waffen-SS veterans.

There has been an interest both in popular journalism and contemporary history as to the actions of the Waffen-SS. As noted by Sydnor there has been "… an outpouring of scholarly literature recording, and analysing the personalities, agencies, and institutions of the SS…" (Sydnor, 1989:249). However, one of the difficulties in dealing with the Waffen-SS is that often studies tend to be polarised in that they either portray the Waffen-SS as a terror organisation or they adopt an apologetic tone and focus purely on the military achievements of the Waffen-SS (Koehl, 1962; Wegner, 1985). As such:

> … its achievements on the battlefield are isolated from the context of the history of the SS and National Socialism and presented as it were in a historical vacuum. In this way members of the Waffen-SS appear to have been just like other soldiers. (Wegner, 1985:221)

As noted by one author, sensationalist journalism has been responsible for many stories about the SS where "… the emphasis is on the gory atrocity, the cloak and dagger story, the sexually abnormal, the idiosyncrasies of personalities and the fantastic plans and dreams of individuals" (Koehl, 1962:276). It is my intent to pierce this veil of military achievement and sensationalism to look at the systematic abuses that were committed by the Waffen-SS. Other sources have, however, become available to assist in any analysis of the Waffen-SS. In recent years a number of new books and scholarly articles have been published that assist with understanding and exploring the actions of the Waffen-SS on the Eastern Front and its association with other aspects of the SS state.

As well as this I have relied on such crucial sources of information as the private conversations of Hitler (Trevor-Roper, 2000) and the transcripts of Hitler's military conferences and the military directives issued from such (Gilbert, 1950; Heiber & Glantz, 2003; Trevor-Roper, 1964). From these varied sources I hope to be able to draw an accurate picture and reach a defendable conclusion as to the actions of the Waffen-SS and the application of the concept of evil. This book is also accompanied by appendices that will assist the reader in acquiring the knowledge required in such a specialised area such as the Waffen-SS.

Outline of the book

This book is structured in the following manner. Chapter 1 essentially examines who the Waffen-SS were and why they were created from an organisational standpoint. The chapter also studies the logic of the Nazis and the ideological purpose behind the Waffen-SS. In particular the role of Himmler's influence over the Waffen-SS is discussed.

Chapter 2 examines the structure, organisation, training, economic and sociological makeup of the Waffen-SS to some degree. From this discussion I hope to be able to give the reader a good understanding of who the Waffen-SS were as an organisation.

Chapters 3, 4 and 5 look at the actions of the Waffen-SS on the Eastern Front by looking at links to the concentration-camps, involvement in the *Einsatzgruppen*, anti-partisan operations and general combat actions. These chapters are essentially answering the what part of the question; that being, what crimes did the Waffen-SS commit? In these chapters I describe the violence and atrocity that were undertaken by the Waffen-SS.

Chapter 6 addresses the important question of group responsibility and collective guilt. This has often been an area where apologists for the Waffen-SS have based much of their argument that the Waffen-SS were just innocent soldiers. The argument that the Waffen-SS soldiers were demonic or evil is also rejected and the concept of demonisation is refuted.

In Chapter 7 I analyse the reasons behind the criminal and evil acts committed by the Waffen-SS. This is done so that one can understand *why* the acts were committed. I examine a number of areas that are relevant in explaining (without condoning) why the Waffen-SS committed the crimes they did. These issues include obedience to orders, the factors of devaluing the enemy, and responsibility of the individual soldier. The role of difficult life conditions on the Eastern Front is then explored as a background context to the actions of the Waffen-SS.

1. The origins and ideology of the Waffen-SS

The SS were initially formed as a bodyguard for Hitler who could no longer rely on the support or loyalty of the original SA[7] stormtroopers, who were the foot soldiers of the Nazi Party. From this handful of men the Waffen-SS became the largest branch of the SS. In doing so, apologists for the Waffen-SS argue that it became the defacto fourth branch of the German armed forces of World War II, the others being the Navy, Army and Air Force. During the course of this book I will show that the Waffen-SS was clearly not just another branch of the German Armed forces.

The Waffen-SS soldiers were unique in that they were the first of Germany's armed forces that swore a personal oath of loyalty to Hitler, and underwent a rigorous process of indoctrination to Nazi ideals and were trained to be a highly disciplined, motivated and successful military formation. For this reason the Waffen-SS has been viewed by some as a "… praetorian guard and elite" of the Nazi state (Wegner, 1985:220). Indeed, during a dinner conversation on the 1st of November 1941 Hitler remarked that "Within a hundred years or so from now all the German elite will be a product of the SS, for only the SS practices racial selection" (Trevor-Roper, 2000:106). The Waffen-SS gained considerable respect both from foes and friends due to the fact that The Waffen-SS possessed military qualities equalled by few others and surpassed by none. By war's end it numbered some 900 000[8] men.

Defining the Waffen-SS

One of the most contentious issues when dealing with the Waffen-SS is actually clearly defining what units and departments should be considered to be part of the Waffen-SS. As noted by Sydnor:

Attempts to define what the Waffen-SS was lead invariably to questions
about the extent to which the Waffen-SS was or was not an integral part
of the overall SS organisation, and the degree to which it was or was not
involved in the criminal acts attributed to the SchutzStaffel. (Sydnor,
1973:339)

On the 2nd of March 1940 Hitler accepted a proposal from *Oberkommando der Wehrmacht* (OKW) or Armed Forces Command that led to the
re-organisation of SS units and the use of the term Waffen-SS became official (Stein, 1966). As a result of this proposal the Waffen-SS was at that
stage to include the *Leibstandarte SS Adolf Hitler*, the *SS-Verfügungstruppe
Division*[9] (SSVT was the forerunner to the Waffen-SS), the *Totenkopf* Division, the *SS-Polizei* Division, the *SS-Junkerschulen* or training academies
and all replacement and training units. Of crucial importance is that the
proposal also recognised the SS *Totenkopfverbände* as part of the Waffen-
SS, with the qualification that "... the decision as to whether this duty
counts as military service is to be taken in the future" (Stein, 1966:49).

The proposal also acknowledged that there were additional sections of
the Waffen-SS that went beyond the armed fighting units. These included
"... seven administrative organisations handling recruitment, supply,
administration, justice, welfare, weapons development and medical services" (Stein, 1966:49). Service in such units was considered to be military
service. In addition to this the term Waffen-SS actually included all SS formations and offices borne on the budget of the Reich Minister of Finance.
In a memorandum dated the 11th of May 1942 Himmler, when referring to
the budget of the Waffen-SS, included the fighting divisions, schools and
the concentration-camps and other ancillary units as being part of the Waffen-SS (Butler, 2004; Krausnick, Buchheim, Broszat, & Jacobsen, 1965).
This order was to be:

> The most cogent argument against those SS apologists who claim that the
> Waffen-SS had nothing to do with the concentration-camps. On both the
> highest formal level and the lowest guard level Himmler had irrevocably
> bound the knights of his black order to the murkiest corners of his deadly
> empire. (Mollo, 1982:42)

This at least provides a starting platform as to what units or sections
can be considered to be part of the Waffen-SS. However, like most apparatus of the Nazi state this organisation was subject to revision as the war
went on. As I proceed through the following chapters I will discuss my
arguments in more detail as to why the units, which undertook anti-partisan

duties, and the activities of the *Einsatzgruppen* and the concentration-camps, were either part of, or heavily linked to the Waffen-SS.

It is my argument that the Waffen-SS was not just limited to the fighting formations at the front. A fighting unit relies on a supply and administrative apparatus to survive. It is not sensible to separate the combat units from the other units that were so necessary for their ability to undertake the duties placed upon them. During his testimony at Nuremberg, *SS-Oberstgruppenführer* Paul Hausser attempted to distance the Waffen-SS fighting units from the concentration-camp guards.

> HAUSSER: All persons who served at home and in the police had to be exempted from military service in the army by the Wehrkreis or district commander in order to carry out their police tasks. That did not apply when all guard units were designated as Waffen-SS, for these were a part of the armed forces. In the main offices in Berlin these units, in order to differentiate them, were designated nominal Waffen-SS. But all this I learned only here later.
>
> (The International Military Tribunal, 1946: Vol 20:366)

Hausser has outlined a major argument of Waffen-SS veterans and their supporters, that being "... except for organisational connections there were no fundamental ties between the SS and the Waffen-SS" (Kren et al., 1976:88). This is just simply not the case. Apologists such as Theile attempt to distance the Waffen-SS from the unsavoury parts of the SS organisation. In his study, Theile excludes from his discussion of the Waffen-SS the concentration-camps, the *Einsatzgruppen* and the main SS administrative offices (Theile, 1997). As noted by Stein, the *SS-Totenkopfstandarten* (Death's Head units formed from concentration-camp guards) "were eventually incorporated, unit by unit, into the larger field formations of the Waffen-SS" (Segev, 1987; Stein, 1966:50). The Death's Head units were used to form various Waffen-SS formations, which some describe as a second Waffen-SS. This was due in the main to the appalling reputation of the *Totenkopf* units; it suited the apologists to distance these groups for the other fighting units. This second Waffen-SS is similar to the expression used by the SS in their defence at Nuremberg where some members were described as *nominal*. This is a flawed approach; it seems that the argument is that those parts of the Waffen-SS that appear tainted should be excluded from account. This is simply not the case; these formations were part of the Waffen-SS and as such should be included in the examination of the Waffen-SS organisation as a whole just as much as the front-line fighting units.

The actions of officers and men attached to such as the above raised problems for the defence of the Waffen-SS at Nuremberg. To try and circumnavigate this problem the defence coined the term nominal members of the Waffen-SS, which they almost exclusively applied to those members of the Waffen-SS who were not in the combat units or who committed atrocities in places such as the camps. The argument of nominal Waffen-SS members was a constant theme used by the SS defence witnesses. It is of concern that at the time of the trials, the defence and witnesses never presented any documentary evidence that, indicated that the Waffen-SS command had protested against the inclusion of such officers or men within the ranks of the Waffen-SS. Certainly there is no evidence that officers like Hausser attempted to resign their commissions or leave the Waffen-SS in protest at such actions that they claimed were an insult to their honour.

In essence the witnesses were trying to say that these other people were Waffen-SS, but not Waffen-SS. The difficulty in including such units can be seen by the answers given by Waffen-SS officers such as Robert Brill when questioned by the Russian prosecutor:

> MR. COUNSELLOR SMIRNOV: Will you tell us, please, who was in charge of the command within the concentration-camp. Was it not the Waffen-SS?
>
> BRILL: No, they were not commands of the Waffen-SS. Certain members of the nominal Waffen-SS were with the commands; but there is a clear order of the High Command of the Armed Forces which I have already mentioned. It is included in the Army circular of December 1940, and states that members of the Death's Head units do not do any military service in the sense' of the Waffen-SS -Members of the Death's Head units.
>
> MR. COUNSELLOR SMIRNOV: I would like to ask you to be more concise. So you contend that the commands in concentration-camps were not Waffen-SS commands?
>
> BRILL: The commands were not under the High Command of the Waffen-SS; but I wish to point out that members of the Waffen-SS were with the commands. This is the difference.
>
> (The International Military Tribunal, 1946: Vol 20:352)

This would appear to be an inaccurate statement. The question needs to be asked at what point did these members of the Waffen-SS become nominal? Was it before they joined the fighting divisions of the Waffen-SS, or was it after they left them and took up duties in the camps? At what point did Max Simon, commander of the *Reichsführer-SS* Division, or Georg Bochmann, commander of the *Gotz Von Berlichingen* Division, consider themselves to be merely nominal Waffen-SS members? Simon and Bochmann both served at Sachsenburg and Dachau (MacLean, 1999a).

One purpose of separating the Waffen-SS from these other organisations is that it allows the reputation of the Waffen-SS to be rehabilitated to some degree, and this has often been the aim of post-war apologists. As stated by Wegner when he began his study of the Waffen-SS:

> Initial investigations soon revealed that the analysis of the Waffen-SS solely in terms of its military characteristics would not be historically relevant because this approach would have hidden the central fact that the Waffen-SS, as a result of its integration into the all-encompassing system of organised violence that was the SS, neither possessed the professional autonomy of the army nor could it be defined as strictly military in the traditional sense. (Wegner, 1990:3)

This study rejects the notion of the nominal Waffen-SS member as it was rejected at Nuremberg. It is my contention that the Waffen-SS needs to be examined as a whole organisation, rather then just isolating certain sections of the organisation. It is beyond the scope of this book to perform a full analysis of the SS organisation. The main departments as they relate to the Waffen-SS only have been included in this book; as such it is not a complete representation of the SS state. Further discussion of specific Himmler and Führer orders will shed more light on the relationship between the Waffen-SS and other departments of the SS.

The Nazi ideology and the creation of the Waffen-SS

> I swear to you, Adolf Hitler, as Leader and Chancellor of the Reich, loyalty and bravery. I pledge to you and the superiors appointed by you, obedience unto death. So help me God.

"Loyalty is my honour", this was the oath of allegiance of the Waffen-SS man. It was with this oath that the members of the Waffen-SS bound their destiny to a man who committed some of the worst atrocities in history and embarked on a path of murder and mayhem that would result in the destruction of the Nazi state and the deaths of millions. The purpose of this chapter is to basically explore *who* the Waffen-SS were from an ideological standpoint. That the Waffen-SS was a prodigy of the Nazis is beyond doubt; Wegner states that "… there was an intimate connection between the development of the Waffen-SS and the whole of the SS as a party organisation" (Wegner, 1990:62). Indeed the Waffen-SS as an organisation was prepared to surrender its moral responsibility to the Nazi state. The following pages will outline how this occurred.

The SS was initially formed in 1925 as a protection squad for Hitler and other leading Nazis. It was formed from only the most active and reliable party members and was seen to be an integral part of the party structure. Upon the election of Hitler to the office of Chancellor, *SS-Reichsführer* Heinrich Himmler and the SS took up a number of official administrative, police and military functions. It was in these roles that the SS would become the ultimate terror machinery of the Nazi state. Indeed at the International Military Tribunal (IMT) the prosecution described the SS as below:

> For the SS was the elite group of the Party, composed of the most thorough-going adherents of the Nazi cause, pledged to blind devotion to Nazi principles, and prepared to carry them out without any question, and at any cost, a group in which every ordinary value has been so subverted that its members can ask, "What is there unlawful about the things we have done?".
>
> (The International Military Tribunal, 1946: Vol 4:161)

From its initial beginnings the SS developed into three main manpower sections. Initially there was the political arm, the General or *Allgemeine SS*, from which grew the *SS-Totenkopfverbände* (Death's Head units) or camp guards, and finally the Waffen or fighting SS. At the outbreak of war in 1939 the Waffen-SS emerged from a few regiments to some 38 divisions[10] by war's end. The General SS by war's end would cease to be a significant force and the Death's Head units would be absorbed into the Waffen-SS. As noted by the Nuremberg Military Tribunal (NMT):

> After the outbreak of war, units from both the Special Service Troops and the Death's Head Formations were used in the Polish campaign. These troops came to be known as the Waffen or armed [Combat] SS. By 1940 the Waffen-SS contained 100,000 men, 56,000 coming from the Special Service Troops and the rest from the Allgemeine SS and the Death Head Troops. Concentration-camp guard duties came to be performed primarily by members of the Allgemeine-SS. The Waffen-SS fought in every campaign with the exception of those in Norway and Africa. By the end of the war it is estimated to have comprised about 580,000 men. Thus, it was numerically by far the larger branch of the SS, the Allgemeine-SS having declined in strength to less than 40,000.
>
> (Nuremberg Military Tribunal, 1946: Vol 5:214)

The SS rose to significance within the Nazi world by being utilised to spy on other members of the party and other party organisations (Muhlberger, 1991). Himmler and the SS were also used by Hitler to counter the growing power and threat from Ernst Rohm and the *SturmAbteilung* (SA) or Nazi Brown Shirts, who were the original foot soldiers of the Nazis. The political reliability of the SS was confirmed when members of the *Leibstandarte* and other SS units were used by Hitler to eradicate the leadership of the SA in 1934 during the Rohm purge, the so-called Night of the Long Knives. During this action the SA leadership was emasculated and its leaders executed. As a result the organisation was never again a serious political threat. At Nuremberg, SS General Paul Hausser denied any involvement of the Waffen-SS in this incident. Other Waffen-SS generals stated a different story. *SS-Obergruppenführer* Karl Wolff later related his role on this night after the war. He recounted how a "charming fellow", who was the personal adjutant for Rohm, the leader of the SA, and "... also a close personal friend, we often dined together" was executed (Messenger, 2002). Clearly friendship was not to stand in the way of the SS.

For murdering many of their former comrades the SS earnt Hitler's favour and gratitude. Waffen-SS General Von Eberstein had this to say when asked about killing their former comrades:

> MAJOR JONES: You are not answering my question, you know. You are wandering off into details that have no relevance to my question at all. I suggest to you that the killings by the SS on the 30th of June 1934 were a characteristic use of the SS as the fist of Nazism.
>
> VON EBERSTEIN: The events of the 30th of June 1934 were, according to my firm conviction and to that of my comrades, the result of a state of emergency and the orders which were given were adhered to because they were the orders of the head of the State.
>
> (The International Military Tribunal, 1946: Vol 20:312)

The *Leibstandarte SS Adolf Hitler* supplied troops that executed a number of high-ranking SA officials. The affirmation of their loyalty and that of other SS units to Hitler was signed in the blood of their former SA comrades. Waffen-SS General Otto Kumm noted: "That is then that the image of the SS really changed for the first time, after the Führer said 'SS men, your honour lies in loyalty'. You see for us that was naturally very uplifting" (Halliley, 2003). As a result of the Rohm purge the SS became the most powerful elite organisation within the Nazi state. The role of the SS in the Rohm purge effectively ensured that from now on the SS displayed a will to act in conformity with the will of the Führer.

There can be little doubt that the men of the Waffen-SS enjoyed a special relationship with Hitler. For instance on Hitler's birthday members of the Waffen-SS usually received a bottle of wine from their Nazi political officer as a gift (Verton, 2007). Nicolaus Von Below was Hitler's *Luftwaffe* adjutant from 1937 to 1945. He provides a glimpse of Hitler's special relationship with the Waffen-SS:

> Hitler sped by train to Metz, where the *Leibstandarte SS Adolf Hitler* were quartered. Among these men he was always in good spirits. In his speech he gave this feeling visible expression. The *SS-Leibstandarte* must always expect to be deployed to the hottest spots of the battle. He said, "It is for you who are honoured to carry my name to stand at the forefront of the struggle". (Von Below, 1980:80)

It was in this role that the Waffen-SS came to represent a sort of elite that placed heavy emphasis on loyalty to one's comrades, common values and practices and a sense of obedience to the Nazi cause and ideology (Gingerich, 1997; Ripley, 2004; Staub, 1989; Stein, 1966; Sydnor, 1990; Wolfson, 1965; Ziegler, 1989). This notion of the SS being a Nazi elite attached to the SS because of the fact that its duties were carried out on behalf of the Nazi regime. It was seen to be an elite from a social, racial and political aspect. In this respect limited research of some Waffen-SS officers has indicated that many joined to ensure that they could achieve "… a more satisfying self" through the apparently legitimate and socially acceptable means of joining this elite (J. Steiner, 1963:416).

The SS had proven its loyalty beyond doubt; it was for this reason that the Führer could place absolute faith in his SS legions. As such the SS were independent from both the Police and the *Wehrmacht,* and available for Hitler's exclusive use. To this purpose Hitler issued a secret Führer order on the 17th of August 1938, which outlined the role and uses of the Waffen-SS both in peacetime and in war. He clearly delineates that the Waffen-SS is indeed different from just ordinary soldiers.

> II. The Armed Units of the SS.
>
> The SS-Verfügungstruppe.
>
> 1. The *SS-Verfügungstruppe* is neither a part of the *Wehrmacht* nor a part of the police. It is a standing armed unit exclusively at my disposal. As such and as a unit of the NSDAP, its members are to be selected by the *Reichsführer-SS* according to the ideological and political standards which I have ordered for the NSDAP and for the *Schutzstaffeln*. Its members are to be trained and its ranks filled with volunteers…
>
> (The International Military Tribunal, 1946: Vol 4:170)

Soldiers of the *Leibstandarte SS Adolf Hitler* marching in Berlin.

Note that Hitler himself has described the Waffen-SS as an organisation of the Nazi Party. This statement by Hitler is strong evidence against those apologists of the Waffen-SS who claim that it was not an organisation with political affiliations to the Nazi Party. Himmler also stipulates the political roots of the SS in an indoctrination pamphlet where he states: "Now I come to the *Schutzstaffel* itself. It is a part of this National Socialist German Workers Party created and trained by Adolf Hitler. Within the movement of the Führer it has received its special task for the protection of the Reich internally" (Pruess Publishing, 2001:25). This task was being carried out by the SS as early as 1938 when Hitler's Army Adjutant, Major Gerhard Engel, recalled Himmler reporting to Hitler "about his cleansing measures" that were being undertaken in Vienna after Austria was absorbed into the German Reich (Engel, 1974:37). Hitler himself stipulated the role the Waffen-SS will play in times of conflict.

III. Orders in case of Mobilisation.

A. The employment of the *SS-Verfügungstruppe* in case of mobilisation is a double one.

1. By the Supreme Commander of the Army within the wartime army. In that case it comes completely under military laws and regulations, but remains a unit of the NSDAP politically.

2. In case of necessity in the interior according to my orders; in that case it is under the *Reichsführer-SS* and Chief of the German Police.

> In case of mobilisation I myself will make the decision about the time,
> strength and manner of the incorporation of the *SS-Verfügungstruppe* into
> the wartime army; these things will depend on the internal political situ-
> ation at that time.
> (The International Military Tribunal, 1946: Vol 4:170)

As can be seen from this order, the Waffen-SS was to undertake a policing role internally as well as take part in any conflict with external enemies.
This is clearly illustrated by comments made by Hitler during dinner on the
24th of July 1941 where he is referring to the losses suffered by the Waffen-
SS in the opening stages of the Russian campaign.

> For an elite force, like our SS, it's great luck to have suffered compara-
> tively heavy losses. In this way it is assured of the necessary prestige to
> intervene if need be, on the home front, which of course won't be neces-
> sary. But it's good to know that one disposes of a force that could show
> itself capable of doing so on occasion. (Trevor-Roper, 2000:13)

This is further proof that Hitler saw the Waffen-SS as a political force
to be used against their fellow Germans if need be, something that was not
expected of the other German armed forces. Hitler made the differentiation
of the Waffen-SS even more succinct when he commented on its role in
relation to the other armed forces after the war on the 4th of January 1942.

> As soon as peace has returned, the SS will have to be given its indepen-
> dence again, a complete independence *(from the Army)*.[11] There has
> always been a rivalry between troops of the line and guardsmen. That's
> why it's a good thing that the SS should constitute in relation to the oth-
> ers, an absolutely distinct world. In peacetime it's an elite police, capable
> of crushing any adversary. (Trevor-Roper, 2000:167)

During a conversation on the 19th of April 1938 Hitler expressed his
views on the Waffen-SS to his Army adjutant, Major Engel:

> He wants to keep this elite small or it will not be an elite for long. It has
> to be a political force blindly loyal to state and Führer. In the event of dis-
> turbances, this force would put them down brutally. He sees it as a real
> Praetorian Guard to snuff out all those, even within its own ranks, who
> swim against the current. (Engel, 1974:38)

Hitler's favouritism for the Waffen-SS was to display itself in other
forms as he insured that it remained independent of the German armed
forces.

The SS Courts

There was to be one important amendment to the order issued by Hitler regarding the role of the Waffen-SS. That was the removal of the SS from military justice and regulations by virtue of a Hitler decree on the 17th of October 1939 (Krausnick et al., 1965; Weingartner, 1983). All matters of military laws and regulations and enforcement were to be undertaken by the SS courts, not the military. Himmler saw this as being an important step in ensuring the independence of the SS from the *Wehrmacht*. It would ensure that the Waffen-SS was judged by their own under the supervision of Hitler and Himmler. Only Hitler could impose a death sentence on officers and commanders of the Waffen-SS, and Himmler reserved the right to make decisions in cases concerning SS men with membership numbers less then 15,000 (Krausnick et al., 1965).

The judges of the SS courts were almost entirely made up of Waffen-SS officers. An officer list of the SS courts in 1944 shows that some 599 belonged to the Waffen-SS with just six belonging the Allgemeine SS (Krausnick et al., 1965).

> The judges in the SS courts were SS commanders qualified for the office, they were nominated by Hitler himself, were necessarily members of the Waffen-SS, and for disciplinary matters were directly subordinate to the *Reichsführer-SS*. Membership of the Waffen-SS was obligatory since the privileged position of the SS in the possession of its own legal system was based upon the existence of the Waffen-SS... (Krausnick et al., 1965:253)

Himmler commented that "... we try to train our lawyers by putting them in the SS and infusing them with our own spirit" (J. Steiner, 1963:439). In the perverted view of the SS courts, justice would serve the ideological goals of the Nazi movement. The decisions of the SS judges were required to further the ideological aims of the regime and also serve as precepts supplementing the ideological indoctrination of SS members.

In an ominous premonition of what was to come, Hitler had removed the Waffen-SS from the accountability of normal military expectations; it was now to be judged by its own. This is of even more importance when one considers that initially only the SS units who were at the cutting edge of the SS operations were included under this protection. These units included the concentration-camp operatives, members of the SS bureau-cracy, the *SS-Verfügungstruppe*, members of police units on special actions and the *SS-Junkerschulen* (Weingartner, 1983). It would appear that the real intent of this move was to ensure that those SS units who could be called upon to commit crimes would be protected by the SS justice system. Himmler had in fact created a legal system in which the criminal orders that were to be issued had been legitimised.

Political and ideological roots

Even the German people held the Waffen-SS in some trepidation with secret reports indicating that the impression of some German citizens was that the Waffen-SS was "... the most ruthless force. It takes no prisioners, but totally annihilates its enemy" (Simpson, 1990:7). Himmler it seemed enjoyed his SS soldiers having this kind of reputation. In a pamphlet presented at the Nuremberg Trials titled, "The SS as an Anti-Bolshevist Fighting Organisation" (document 1851-PS), Himmler said this of his SS:

> I know that there are some people in Germany who become sick when they see these black coats. We understand the reason for this and do not expect that we shall be loved by too many. (The International Military Tribunal, 1946: Vol 4:182)

Many apologists argue that the Waffen-SS was just a military formation the same as the Army, Navy and Air Force. Former Waffen-SS adjutant to Hitler, Richard Schulze-Kossens argued that "The idea that with the Waffen-SS Himmler created a political troop after his own image is completely incompatible with historical reality" (Schulze-Kossens, 1982:33). Noted author Heinz Hohne attempts to paint senior Waffen-SS generals such as Hausser and Steiner as being non-political; as being soldiers "... who just wanted to devote themselves to an exclusively military job" (Hohne, 1969:449). Yet both Hausser and Steiner were members of the SA and also members of the Nazi Party (Yerger, 1997; , 1999). An order of the day issued by Steiner after heavy fighting dated the 30 July 1944 would seem to indicate that Steiner had political affiliations even up to the late stages of the war.

> Comrades, today you have gained a defensive victory ... With your excellent soldierly morale and performance you have proved your profound loyalty to our Führer Adolf Hitler. I deeply thank each of you for his unshakeable steadfastness and shake his hand in comradeship. Steiner. (Ertel & Schulze-Kossens, 2000:179)

In contrast to Hausser is SS Colonel, *SS-Standartenführer* Leon Degrelle, a Belgium national and favourite of Hitler who was the commander of the 28th SS *Wallonien* Division. He goes to great lengths to stress that the Waffen-SS was an "... organisation that was both political and military"

(Degrelle, 1983:11). The political nature of the SS is even more recognisable if one considers that "... from the very start the only personnel selected for the SS were those thought to have qualifications beneficial..." to the Nazi Party (J. Steiner, 1963:430). In the biography of *SS-Obergruppenführer* Karl Wolff it is noted when he filled out his application form to join the SS that it included the below statement under the heading of commitment:

> I commit myself to support Adolf Hitler's ideas, to observe the strictest party discipline, and to conscientiously carry out the orders of the Reich SS Leader. I am German, of Aryan descent, I do not belong to any Masonic Lodge or secret societies, and I promise to promote the movement with all my strength. (Von Lang, 2005:7)

This was the standard application form used for all SS men. As noted by at least one author the argument that the Waffen-SS was just another military formation may seem plausible on the face of it, however, an entirely different picture emerges when we consider its origins. SS General Hausser claimed that the Waffen-SS was part of the Army when questioned at Nuremberg.

> HERR PELCKMANN: Surely you felt yourself to be a part of the Army?
>
> HAUSSER: We were completely incorporated into the Army, and the designation "fourth branch of the Army," although it was not an official designation, was really much to the point.
>
> (The International Military Tribunal, 1946: Vol 20:367)

However, even the generals of the *Wehrmacht* made it clear that the Waffen-SS was not part of the regular army but rather a creature of Himmler's. Former chief of the *Wehrmacht* General Von Brauchitsch stated this at Nuremberg:

> DR. LATERNSER: Now, the subordination of the Waffen-SS will have to be cleared up as well. Just what was the subordination of a Waffen-SS division to the Army?
>
> VON BRAUCHITSCH: The Waffen-SS was subordinated to the Army only for tactical purposes. It was subordinated to the Army neither for discipline nor for judicial matters. The Army had no influence on promotions or demotions of people, and so forth.
>
> DR. LATERNSER: To whom was a Waffen-SS division subordinate, when it was not engaged in a tactical task? That is, when it was neither in battle nor in the operational area?
>
> VON BRAUCHITSCH: In any event, not the Army. It was subordinate to the *Reichsführer-SS* or to the High Command of the Armed Forces.

DR. LATERNSER: And to whom was it subordinate in the home area?

VON BRAUCHITSCH: To the *Reichsführer-SS.*

(The International Military Tribunal, 1946: Vol 20:580)

The Role of Himmler

The *Reichsführer-SS*; this was who the Waffen-SS answered to, except when in direct combat. In the years since the war many have painted Himmler as the meek and mild bureaucrat who committed atrocious acts of evil and yet was not the keeper of the Waffen-SS. Reality would paint a different picture. Himmler kept a tight control on the Waffen-SS by ensuring that administrative matters in relation to personnel of the Waffen-SS remained under his control. Himmler also remained the nominal Commander in Chief of the Waffen-SS through his field command post and all recruiting for the Waffen-SS was handled by the Main SS Office. As part of the rehabilitation process of the image of the Waffen-SS, Himmler in some respects has been portrayed as a leader "… held in contempt and frequently disobeyed" by the SS generals (Sydnor, 1973:340). SS General Paul Hausser had this to say when questioned as to Himmler's leadership capabilities:

> HAUSSER: Heinrich Himmler most assuredly tried in peacetime to exert his influence on the small *Verfügungstruppe*. During the war this was practically impossible. He did not address troops of the Waffen-SS. On occasion he did talk to some officers and commanders of some divisions in the field. It was generally known that Heinrich Himmler, who had done only one year's military service, had no conception of the military and underestimated the military tasks and the work involved. He liked to play the role of the strong man through exaggeration and through superlatives. If someone comes along with big words, the soldier on the front does not pay much attention. Therefore, the influence of Himmler was very insignificant during the war. He wore his uniform, of course, but the reputation of the Waffen-SS was established by its officers, by the example they set and by their daily work.
>
> (The International Military Tribunal, 1946 Vol 20:368)

While some Waffen-SS Generals and others have attempted to write Himmler off as somewhat of a nuisance, other authors state that Himmler was a powerful and effective leader, firmly in control of the entire SS organisation. At least one author raises the important point that the SS could never have reached its powerful position in the Nazi state without an effective leader in the form of Himmler (Noakes & Pridham, 1988). Respected author, Alexander Dallin (1981), makes the important point that if it had come to a showdown, no other leading Nazi would have been capable of matching Himmler in regards to power.

Those who deride Himmler's influence forget one important fact; he was successful in ordering the murder of millions of innocent people, a feat that someone, who is indeed a bumbling eccentric, would be unlikely to achieve. Indeed the SS was a conscious, preconceived and central concern of Himmler's social thinking. He controlled the Waffen-SS and directed it in accordance with the political and ideological will of the Führer. An order of the 4th SS *Polizei* Division provides evidence that Himmler remained in control of the political training of the troops even when they were serving with army formations:

> As of the day of integration into the *SS-Polizei* Division, the newly formed elements will be subordinated to the Commander in Chief of the army … the authority of the *Reichsführer-SS* and *Chef der Deutschen Polizei* in the area of political training … remains unaffected by this. (Husemann, 2003:10)

During the war the SS divisions, whose personnel owed their loyalty personally to Hitler rather than the German state, and whom he therefore trusted more were used time and time again for crucial operations that the Führer would rather entrust to his political soldiers than the regular army. As noted in the study of Krausnick et al (1965), to say that the Waffen-SS was a fourth branch of the armed services is totally untrue, it is politically and historically untrue; the Waffen-SS owed allegiance to the Führer.

A pamphlet on SS culture and titled Soldier had this to say about the Waffen-SS. "Today it may already seem incomprehensible that there were once non-political officers and non-political soldiers ... The great historical end of such ideological division came about through the Führer through the creation of the political soldier in his embodiment of the Waffen-SS!" (Pruess Publishing, 2004a:34). The apologists and others have often tried to maintain that the Waffen-SS was merely another military organisation. To this end they have at times enlisted the assistance of senior *Wehrmacht* generals such as Colonel-General Heinz Guderian, who stated:

> I can therefore assert that to my knowledge the SS divisions were always remarkable for a high standard of discipline, of esprit de corps, and of conduct in the face of the enemy. They fought shoulder to shoulder with the panzer divisions of the army and the longer the war went on the less distinguishable they became from the army. (Guderian, 1996:447)

The Waffen-SS was never meant to be a permanent part of the German military system. The Waffen-SS was part of the SS system; it was not part of the *Wehrmacht*. As such it is best to approach any study of the Waffen-SS by viewing it as an integral part of the SS rather than as an ordinary elite military force. It follows then that claims that the Waffen-SS was an organisation not controlled by Himmler or the SS are simply not true. This was to have chilling implications. With Himmler in control of the SS, legitimacy was lent to the criminal policies that would be issued and acted on by the Waffen-SS.

The Waffen-SS as political soldiers

The SS was a beast born of political necessity, and it was a political beast by nature. As has been noted, the Waffen-SS "... was one of the few military formations that owed its existence exclusively to the emergence of a particular political system, and whose nature reflected in microcosm the essence of the regime it served" (Lucas & Cooper, 1975:1). The initial members of the SS were made up of young political fighters who had been employed as bodyguards and bouncers by the Nazi Party. But it was not long before Himmler envisaged that their role would extend far beyond this. They were seen to be the revolutionary shock troops of the Reich. As such they were to hold a special place in the affections of the Führer. Units such as the *Totenkopf* Division could not deny their birthright; "... from the day of its creation until the end of the war, the *Totenkopf* Division remained bound by the general political, racial and administrative laws of the SS" (Sydnor, 1973:360).

Hitler's affection for the Waffen-SS is evidenced by the level and type of equipment they received. Certain Waffen-SS formations[12] received equipment in preference and far out of proportion to the size of it forces when considered against the *Wehrmacht* (Darman, 2004; Engel, 1974; Kren et al., 1976; Ripley, 2004; Weinberg, 1994). This was despite the fact that the *Wehrmacht* continually resisted the Waffen-SS receiving such equipment. One of Hitler's adjutants recalls that:

> During 1943 the importance of the Waffen-SS had increased. At the beginning of the war, and more so since the beginning of the Russian campaign, Hitler had built up these divisions systematically. They embodied all his ideas for a fighting force. Division

after division was formed; privileged as to its personnel and materiel ...
Hitler was extraordinarily proud of these SS divisions and trusted them
and their commanders utterly. (Von Below, 1980:189)

The preferential treatment the Waffen-SS received in relation to the
allocation of armour highlights this favouritism shown by the Führer to
them. An example of this is the *Schwere Panzerabteilung* (heavy tank battalions) that were formed by Hitler as a means to turn the tide of battle
through the use of superior technology to overcome the numerical superiority of the enemy. These units were heavily utilised on the Eastern Front.
SS General, *SS-Obergruppenführer* Arthur Phelps had begged that the Waffen-SS be given more tanks, "... get us tanks, without them this magnificent force will be ruined" (Hohne, 1969:471). Given the importance that
tanks had taken in combat, these units, which utilised the latest in Germany
technology and weaponry, were seen as elite. These units were normally
equipped with 40 to 50 tanks of either the Tiger 1 or later King Tiger variety. The Waffen-SS had three such *Schwere SS Panzerabteilung* assigned to
them, against some 10 for the *Wehrmacht*.

Overall, almost a third of all Germany's Panzer Divisions belonged to
the Waffen-SS. By the end of the war some of the SS Panzer Divisions had
tank battalions that were some 20 per cent stronger than equivalent army
units. Out of 38 Divisions the Waffen-SS had some seven Panzer Divisions
and seven Panzergrenadier Divisions[13]. This was a ratio that far exceeded
that of the *Wehrmacht*. The Waffen-SS in fact, while only being 10 per cent
of the strength of the *Wehrmacht*, made up a quarter of German Panzer
units.

The fact that many of Hitler's old party colleagues held commands in
the Waffen-SS also caused him to feel a special fondness for their units. He
had this to say about *SS-Oberstgruppenführer* Sepp Dietrich, commander
of the *Leibstandarte* Division:

> The role of Sepp Dietrich is unique. I've always given him opportunity to
> intervene at sore spots. He's a man who's simultaneously cunning, ener-
> getic and brutal. Under his swashbuckling appearance, Dietrich is a seri-
> ous, conscientious, scrupulous character. And what care he takes of his
> troops ... For the German people, Sepp Dietrich is a national institution.
> (Trevor-Roper, 2000:168)

SS-Oberstgruppenführer **Dietrich**

Hitler's regard for the Waffen-SS was so high that many of the divisions were permitted to wear the armbands that were the hallmark of German elite units. When the *Gotz Von Berlichingen* Division received their armbands a special ceremony was ordered by the division commander, and this was attended by Himmler. The divisional diary recorded the event as follows:

> The various preparations for the ceremony for the presenting of the armband to the division were completed on the 9.4.44. That same evening there also arrived the RF-SS (*Reichsführer-SS* Himmler), making the ceremony an extra special occasion. However, after his tiring journey the eminent guest retired early. (Perrigault & Meister, 2004:88)

This close relationship with Hitler is exemplified in the actions he took when the 6th SS Panzer Army[14] led by Dietrich failed in its offensive against the Russians near Vienna and Budapest in early 1945. Rather then remove or sack the SS generals as he had done to many of their Army colleagues, he ordered the Waffen-SS Divisions to remove the honorific armband titles[15] that he had allowed them to wear. This was the most demeaning punishment that he could think of for his SS soldiers. Former Deputy Chief Operations officer of the 6th SS Army, Georg Maier, wrote, "The decree was considered to be a moral punishment, and, in practice, meant the end of the Waffen-SS as an elite body in Hitler's eyes" (Maier, 2004:303).

It is of note that when formed the Waffen-SS was first and foremost a unit for use in internal policing tasks and only second was it to be used in an external role if a conflict arose. At all times, however, the use of the unit was at the personal discretion of Hitler. SS General Paul Hausser attempted to deny this policing role while giving evidence at Nuremberg:

> HERR PELCKMANN: Was the *Verfügungstruppe*, therefore, meant to be a political nucleus? The Prosecution accuses it of being a special instrument for the oppression and elimination of political opponents and of having aided realisation of the Nazi ideology by use of force.

> HAUSSER: That is not true. The *Verfügungstruppe* had neither political nor police tasks. It developed gradually into a test troop which incorporated all the old soldierly virtues with the requirements of our socialist age. It paid special attention to the relations between officers and men, encouraged advancement without special examinations, and did away with any and all exclusiveness. (The International Military Tribunal, 1946: Vol 20:358)

One will recall that the previous Führer order clearly outlined that the Waffen-SS was to be a political instrument. Himmler saw the Waffen-SS as political soldiery and to ensure this an indoctrination program was implemented that permeated all levels of the SS. As one Waffen-SS company commander wrote home, "This morning I have held an hour of ideological instruction, consequently the men have had the necessary political knowledge conveyed that they require for the battle against world Bolshevism" (Huffman, 2005:96). This program covered such issues as the threat posed to Germany by the Jews and Communism, and the importance of German Volk and the Nordic race. It needs to be remembered that the Waffen-SS in its initial stages at least, it was an all volunteer organisation, as such there can be little doubt that those volunteering were not aware of its close association with the Nazi Party and its ideology. However veterans still try to claim a lack of political affiliation with the Nazis as can be seen by the comments of *Wiking* Division veteran Hendrik Verton who stated "The field grey clad men of the SS did not want a political army and for that reason removed themselves from Himmler" (Verton, 2007:57).

Admission to the SS was ideologically anchored in the National Socialist doctrine of racial purity. The SS even had its own newspaper called the *Das Schwarze Korps,* which was approved in 1936 by Himmler and was published in an effort to widely distribute all of the SS messages of hate. It continued to be distributed up to the last month of the war.

> *Das Schwarze Korps* did mirror the ideas of the SS leadership, and in its pages basic elements of SS ideology are present. In this respect, it was indeed the voice of the SS and not just another Nazi newspaper. (Combs, 1986:35)

At Nuremberg, however, the defence witnesses for the Waffen-SS attempted to ignore this political affiliation. *Leibstandarte SS Adolf Hitler* officer Robert Brill gave the following evidence.

> HERR PELCKMANN: And now, to go back to the volunteers, can you tell us anything about the motives for volunteering?
>
> BRILL: Yes. In my office I read thousands upon thousands of applications for admission. I can say that up to 1939 the enthusiasm for the SS, for its decent and proper conduct, was the main reason for volunteering. Besides these, many volunteered for professional reasons.
>
> HERR PELCKMANN: Did that change after the beginning of the war?
>
> BRILL: After the beginning of the war, the main reason for volunteering was that the men wanted to do their military service in a clean, modern, elite formation. Professional reasons also played a part in volunteering. After the beginning of the war very few came to the Waffen-SS for political reasons...
>
> (The International Military Tribunal, 1946: Vol 20:341)

Brill's claims do not match the political reality of the Waffen-SS. For example, of the approximately 6000 Danes who volunteered for service in the Waffen-SS, some 75 per cent had some kind of affiliation with the Danish Nazi Party (DNSAP) (Smith, Poulsen, & Christensen, 1999). Of the 125,000 West European volunteers, about a third belonged to pro-Nazi organisations (Hohne, 1969). Some 30 per cent of the SS Flemish Legion were members of the Dutch National Socialist party (Buss & Mollo, 1978). Of the approximately 950 SS camp officers studied by MacLean about 80 per cent were members of the Nazi Party (MacLean, 1999a). A correct ideological attitude was necessary for entry into the SS; being a member of the Nazi Party made this all the easier. Himmler himself constantly reminded his soldiers of their underlying ideals and mission. Shortly after the Germans invaded Russia in 1941, Himmler made the following speech to Waffen-SS soldiers of Kampfgruppe *Nord.*

> For years, for over a decade now we old National Socialists have struggled in Germany with Bolshevism ... These animals, that torture and ill-treat every prisoner from our side, every wounded man that they come across and do not treat them the way decent soldiers would, you will see for yourself. These people have been welded by the Jews into one religion, one ideology, that is called Bolshevism... (Quarrie, 1991:64)

Speeches such as the above allowed the process of distancing to begin. The Waffen-SS was clearly being encouraged to distance itself from those elements of society viewed by the Nazis as dispensable. Despite the fact that the Waffen-SS was entwined with the roots of the Nazi Party former members still attempted to deny this association at Nuremberg. Brill goes on to explain why people joined the Waffen-SS for non-political motives.

> HERR PELCKMANN: Is it true that in Germany the Waffen-SS was considered as the fourth branch of the Armed Forces and not, as the Prosecution says, the picked troop of the Nazis?
>
> BRILL: Yes. I believe I can affirm this, at least for my field of duty. Only the selection was carried out according to SS directives, while acceptance for the Waffen-SS depended on the approval of the *Wehrbezirkskommando* ... We can also say that we had no connection whatever with the Party, for the Party gave us no orders. The few Party members who were in the Waffen-SS paid no Party dues for the period of their service...
>
> (The International Military Tribunal, 1946: Vol 20:344)

There were more than a few party members in the Waffen-SS; there can be little denial of the link between the Nazi Party and the Waffen-SS. Yerger (1997; , 1999) in his vast two-volume study examined the commanders of the Waffen-SS Divisions, corps and armies. He provides details for some 105 senior Waffen-SS commanders. An analysis of these commanders shows that some 97 per cent had joined the Nazi Party in 1933 or prior. Ninety per cent of these officers were members of the general SS prior to joining the Waffen-SS. A further 31 per cent had been members of the SA. In his study of the Waffen-SS, Wegner estimates that about two-thirds of the senior Waffen-SS officers had been members of the general SS prior to joining the Waffen-SS. An examination of the *Dienstaltersliste* or SS Officers list for January 1942 provides an interesting insight into the political affiliations of the senior officer corps of the Waffen-SS. Of the 30 Waffen-SS generals listed some 25, or 83 per cent, were members of the Nazi Party (Schiffer Publishing, 2000). The break-up is as follows.

Rank	Number of officers listed as members of the Waffen-SS	Members of the Nazi Party	% membership
SS-Obergruppenführer	3	3	100
SS-Gruppenführer	11	10	91
SS-Brigadeführer	16	12	75
Total	30	25	83

Note: Sourced from Schiffer Publishing 2000. The figures show those officers listed as having Waffen-SS rank in the SS-Officer list for January 1942.

By 1933 69 per cent of the future officers of the Waffen-SS were members of the Nazi Party. A further 20 per cent of these officers would join the Nazi Party at a later stage (Wegner, 1990). These figures can leave little doubt as to the consensus held among Waffen-SS officers as to their political views. Wegner makes the interesting observation that while the SS generals had about a 25 per cent membership of the Nazi Party prior to the Nazis taking power[16], this figure was as high as 50 per cent for lower ranks such as *SS-Obersturmbannführer* or Lieutenant-Colonel (Wegner, 1990). These were the officers who would be commanding the regiments and battalions of the Waffen-SS in the field. This political affiliation made obedience all the easier. The Organisation Book for the Nazi Party itself succinctly states the role of political obedience that the SS soldier was expected to show to the Nazi regime:

> Obedience is unconditionally demanded. It arises from the conviction that the National Socialist ideology must reign. He who possesses it and passionately supports it submits himself voluntarily to the compulsion of obedience. Therefore, the SS man is prepared to carry out blindly every order which comes from the Führer or is given by one of his superiors even if it demands the greatest sacrifice of himself.
>
> (The International Military Tribunal, 1946: Vol 4:179)

This clearly indicates the strong political affiliation that senior officers of the Waffen-SS had with the Nazi Party. As noted by Wegner:

> What matters is not so much the fact that there was a greater number of convinced Nazis in the Waffen-SS than in the army. What actually made the two officer corps so fundamentally different was the fact that within the Waffen-SS there was from the outset no place for officers whose political past could have been anything other than National Socialist. (Wegner, 1990:280)

But the SS was seen as more then just a political force driven by the Nazi ideology. Himmler saw that the SS man would have a two-fold role that would have the SS heavily involved in the political apparatus of the state and also the genetic foundation of the new Germanic nation as well. Himmler saw the SS as a kinship or tribal order that would bind Germanic men together with a view to strengthening Aryan blood.

The SS would essentially be the core of the new master race; they would be the biological agent with which he would achieve his Aryan dream. Himmler saw the SS being grounded in the terms of blood and bone; he held romantic visions of Nordic peasants forming a new elite in the Nazi Reich. These were not just the ramblings of a romantic Himmler, Hitler himself claimed to have seen the results of his SS propagating the species first-hand near his home at Berchtesgaden in April, 1942:

> At Berchtesgaden we owe a great deal to the infusion of SS blood, for the local population there was of specially poor and mixed stock. I noticed this particularly while the Berghof[17] was being built, and I was most anxious to do something to improve it. Today, thanks to the presence of a regiment of the *Leibstandarte*, the countryside is abounding with jolly and healthy young children. It is a practice which must be followed. To those districts in which a tendency towards degeneracy is apparent we must send a body of elite troops, and in 10 or 20 years the bloodstock will be improved out of all recognition. (Trevor-Roper, 2000:434)

This pure race was to be preserved by ensuring that only the purest of bloodlines were allowed to enter his SS (this would change later in the war as manpower needs took precedence). For this reason Aryan bloodlines had to be proved for generations as far back as 1750 for SS officers and 1800 for enlisted men. SS General Otto Kumm explained how the members of the SS were initially selected;

> I first took a look at them, how they were built, what impression they made on me and then we selected accordingly. There was such a lot of them that we couldn't take all those who applied. Big, blond, blue eyed, that was our first choice, we would only take the best. (Halliley, 2003)

It was for this reason that all recruit examinations for the Waffen-SS (at least in the early war years) consisted of a doctor and a racial examiner, who was to determine if the recruit was racially acceptable to the Nordic ideals. Recruits were required to possess a medical and racial fitness certificate before gaining entry to the Waffen-SS. The recruit, in the early days of the war at least, faced a five point racial check "… to evaluate the racial features of the applicant. This stretched from purely Nordic down to suspicion of extra-European blood mixtures" (Wegner, 1990:134). Clearly there can be no denying that the Waffen-SS was a racially based organisation.

Indeed as late as 1944 Himmler refused to reduce the racial standards for the Waffen-SS any further, arguing that the racial selection was an inseparable part of the SS Orden.

Waffen-SS veteran Jurgen Girgensohn related the importance of this concept of the master race in a post-war interview: "… the fact that we were genuine Aryans was a very important point. We as Aryans felt superior to other races, we believed that we really would rule Europe one day" (Halliley, 2003). This mixture of elitism in the traditional sense of a guard unit and the biological purity of the members would ensure that the SS would be capable of carrying out the revolutionary role it was envisaged to perform in the new order. Himmler explained the reasoning and importance behind his vision in a Nordic order in the following speech. This speech by Himmler was contained in a publication entitled, "Organisation and Obligations of the SS and the Police". It was published in 1937 in a booklet containing a series of speeches or essays by important officials of the Party and the State known as "National Political Course for the Armed Forces from 15 to 23 January 1937" (document 1992a-PS).

> Accordingly, only good blood, blood which history has proved to be leading and creative and the foundation of every state and of all military activities, only Nordic blood, can be considered. I said to myself that should I succeed in selecting from the German people for this organisation as many people as possible, a majority of whom possess this desired blood, in teaching them military discipline and, in time, the understanding of the value of blood and the entire ideology which results from it, then it will be possible actually to create such an elite organisation which would successfully hold its own in all cases of emergency … They are very thoroughly examined and checked. Of 100 men we can use on the average 10 or 15, no more. We ask for the political record of his parents, brothers and sisters, the record of his ancestry as far back as 1750, and naturally the physical examination and his record from the Hitler Youth. Further, we ask for a eugenic record showing that no hereditary disease exists in his parents and in his family.
>
> (The International Military Tribunal, 1946: Vol 4:176)

From the above it would be difficult to see how any recruit for the Waffen-SS could claim that they were unaware of the political or ideological basis of the SS. In the new world order envisaged by Himmler, seen from a neo-Darwinism viewpoint, only the strong would survive, the weak would be destroyed. As a veteran of the 4th SS *Polizei* Division recounted, "We are the race that must rule the world, that's what they said to us, and all other races must be subordinated to the Aryan race. They are no more then swine, we rule the whole world" (Halliley, 2003). Indeed a study conducted on members of the SS in 1933 showed that most were "... openly and viciously anti-Semitic...", and further, that those with the most intense anti-Semitism were in senior leadership positions (Staub, 2002:21).

The SS attempted to foster a tribal or family identity by involving itself in all aspects of its members' lives.

> Himmler's Germanisation policy, his proclamation of a tribal order instead of an exclusively male organisation, the marriage laws of the SS, the policy of Lebensborn, the promotion of births out of wedlock and Himmler's consideration of introducing polygamy, were all measures intended to infuse new blood into the German people. (Wegner, 1990:24)

This policy of Germanisation and promotion of Aryan blood was to be achieved not only by the culling of those of non-Aryan blood, but also by prolific reproduction of the Aryans. To facilitate this Himmler "... demanded total dedication, service and submission without contradiction to his own will, even in private matters" (Birn, 1991:356). Members of the SS were encouraged and even pressured to relinquish membership of the church. The level of church membership cancellations increased rapidly in the Waffen-SS as a result of an understanding. At every opportunity by the use of speeches, pamphlets and lectures the SS were exposed to an ideology that focused on the good of the Volk or race. Waffen-SS General Karl Wolff stated that "Himmler had set out to achieve a dream, he would inspire a new awakening of the Germanic race within the German people" (Bloomberg, 2000). This attempt to forge a family identity and involvement in all aspects of the members' lives led the SS to become a total institution; this being an institution where all life activities are undertaken uniformly by a single authority. For this reason the vast majority of the Waffen-SS officer corps "... were brought together under one and the same ideologi-cal roof" (Wegner, 1990:268). This would enable Himmler to call upon the SS to undertake a number of atrocities in the name of this shared idealism.

In many of his speeches Himmler referred to the extermination role that he and the SS had been called on to perform. He argued that this bur-den that they undertook was proof of their faith to the Germanic cause. Many of the Waffen-SS tried to distance themselves from Himmler after the war and stated that they did not take him seriously. It is not the case that the officers of the Waffen-SS were unaware of Himmler's intentions. Himmler clearly alluded to this ridding of undesirables in a speech to officers of the *Leibstandarte SS Adolf Hitler* Division in 1941 where he makes reference to the invasion of Russia and the tasks that will have to be undertaken there:

> Very often the member of the Waffen-SS thinks about the deportation of
> these people here. These thoughts came to me today when watching the
> very difficult work out there performed by the Security Police, supported
> by your men, who helped them a great deal. Exactly the same thing hap-
> pened in Poland in weather with 40 degrees of cold, where we had to haul
> away thousands, tens of thousands, hundreds of thousands; where we had
> to have the toughness, you should hear this but also forget it again imme-
> diately, where we had to have the toughness to shoot thousands of leading
> Poles, otherwise one might later sorely regret it.
>
> (The International Military Tribunal, 1946: Vol 20:348)

In a speech on the 16th of May 1944 to officers of the 14th SS *Galicia*
Division at Neuhammer Himmler stated that "Your homeland has become
so much more beautiful since you have lost – on our initiative I must say –
the residents who were so often a dirty blemish on Galicia's good name,
namely the Jews" (Littman, 2003:78). *SS-Obergruppenführer* Wolff
recounts how the men of the SS were:

> … subtly conditioned to see themselves as the sons of light, that they were
> engaged in a struggle against the powers of darkness, and it was their duty
> to feel that they were at all times on duty for the nation and in a wider
> sense for the new order in Europe. (Bloomberg, 2000)

Himmler, if ever the idealist, was also open to the practicalities of the
war. When addressing the 14th SS Division he made no mention of the subhuman Slav in his speech. This being because the division was constituted
by Ukrainians. Indeed, while most of the West European recruits received
the same ideological indoctrination as the German recruits, special
allowances were made for the recruits from Eastern Europe. The Ukrainians were not given lectures about the inferiority of the Slav race, and the
Bosnian Moslems were not exposed to the criticisms of organised religions.

These racial and ideological messages were well accepted by most of
the Waffen-SS. For instance, soldiers of the *Totenkopf* Division were
exposed to this depiction of the evil Jewish-Bolshevik enemy who would
destroy the German nation. As a result they fought the conflict on the Eastern front with indifference to hardship, contempt for death and genuine
hatred of the Jewish-Bolshevik enemy. The products of Eicke's tutelage
developed a lust for killing Russians and fought with a corresponding
tenacity that earned them the unqualified respect of their enemies. As a
former concentration-camp commandant and Waffen-SS officer in the 3rd
Totenkopf Division, *SS-Sturmbannführer* Johannes Hassebroek stated after
the war, "We were the best and the toughest" (MacLean, 1999a; Segev,

1987:63). Nor were the soldiers of the *Totenkopf* alone in this view of the world. This is reinforced by the comments of Waffen-SS *Hauptsturmführer* Mathieu Klein of the 1st Waffen-SS Panzer Division *Leibstandarte SS Adolf Hitler*:

> Why did I volunteer for the Waffen-SS and not the *Wehrmacht*? The Bol-sheviks were seen by me and by the Waffen-SS, as the principal enemy, against who I wanted to fight as a member of an elite force. (Williamson, 1995:22)

This view was reinforced by official ideological training manuals produced for the *Leibstandarte SS Adolf Hitler*, which included such subjects as German History, The Führer and the history of the National Socialist movement, Jewry and Bolshevism. Indeed, upon taking over the 5th SS Panzer Division *Wiking, SS-Obergruppenführer* Felix Steiner ordered the formation of an ideological training unit, which then gave the men a broad introduction to the racial and ideological themes of the Nazis (Smith et al., 1999). Waffen-SS veteran Oswald Van Ooteghem, a Flemish volunteer, outlined one of the main reasons for him joining the Waffen-SS was so that he could join the fight against Bolshevism (Halliley, 2003). In his post-war memoirs Swedish veteran Erik Wallin, a member of the 11th SS Panzer-grenadier Division *Nordland*, showed just how resilient this view of the enemy in the east was:

> After more then three years of struggle in the East, and two years of almost continuous retreat, our fighting spirit was still unbroken. We per-severed under the hardest conditions. Every day, comrades faced death and destruction. The last physical energy and mental force was almost drained out of the common soldier, but our fighting spirit was still there. Our faith lay firmly in the final victory of the superior power of our weapons. Our trust in our own combat skill, against the barbaric masses from the East, was as strong as ever. (Hillblad, 2002:11)

The above comment shows that even after years of defeat, members of the Waffen-SS still saw the Russians as barbarians, barbarians who could, however, consistently defeat an army of supposed Aryan supermen. As one Waffen-SS veteran commented;

> In retrospect I think that there was a very strong spirit of comradeship, which was based on the same beliefs so to speak. Based on the fact that we were convinced that we were conducting a just fight. That we were convinced that we were a master race. We were the best of this master race and that really does form a bond. (Halliley, 2003)

Other veterans have steadfastly maintained that the Waffen-SS was not a political or ideological beast, but rather just mere soldiers. Johann Voss, a member of the 6th SS Mountain Division *Nord,* argues this in his post-war memoirs:

> The notion of the Waffen-SS as politically or racially indoctrinated fanatics, driven by party ideology and hate, was in my experience far from reality. Our training was focused on preparation for victory in modern warfare, and all of us were volunteers who wanted just that kind of preparation. Yes, we did feel a bit different from the other parts of the armed forces... (Voss, 2002:57)

SS-Obersturmbannführer Richard Schulze-Kossens of the *SS Leibstandarte* division stated in a post-war interview that the Waffen-SS soldiers just laughed off the ideological ideas of Himmler. However, it is of note that later he stated, "... we would go into action if it ever became necessary – not for Hitler the man, but for Germany. As far as we were concerned, Hitler was the embodiment of the German State in those days" (Mollo, 1982:86). These comments from the veteran seem at odds, as on one hand he dismisses the influence of Hitler, but in the next sentence emphasises the importance of Hitler as a political leader and as such the political affiliation of the Waffen-SS to Hitler. The comments of Schulze-Kossens are undermined even further when one considers that the use of ideology in the Waffen-SS was "... therefore not solely a measure meant to impose mental uniformity on it own troops, but also to serve its ambition to assert itself vis-à-vis the *Wehrmacht*" (Wegner, 1990:213).

This ideological basis is what differentiated the Waffen-SS from the regular army. Certainly the account rendered by one veteran of the SS *Hitlerjugend*[18] Division, Herbert Walther, would seem to illustrate the loyalty to death shown by even the boy soldiers of this division of the Waffen-SS:

> A young lad who died in my arms, whose eyes I closed as I cried as a baby, said to me 'Leutnant, ask the leader of my company to write to my mother and tell her I died as a brave soldier, for my Führer and my fatherland". (Halliley, 2003)

Other veterans of the *Hitlerjugend* Division also confirm that "... to die for the Fatherland was an honourable act" (Luther, 1987:16). Veterans who try to paint the Waffen-SS as just simple soldiers are supported to some degree by authors who claim that the Waffen-SS units, for example the *Leibstandarte SS Adolf Hitler*, while not being ordinary soldiers, were not ideological fanatics. Rather they were an "... elite military unit which, infused with the freebooter spirit which recognised no moral limitations, acted as an immediate executor of the Führer's will..." (Weingartner, 1974:172). There is some difficulty with this statement. On the one hand the units are not ideological fanatics, yet on the other they are described as a military unit without moral conscience and acting at the will of an ideological and political demagogue. I fail to see much difference between the two concepts. Their actions on the Night of the Long Knives would seem to indicate the opposite to this claim.

When talking about the Waffen-SS as a whole I would agree with Sydnor who states that "... to conclude that all of these men were murderers or criminal lunatics who willingly indulged in atrocities would be just as ludicrous as the efforts by the apologists to prove that the Waffen-SS really was not part of the SS" (Sydnor, 1973:341). Certainly it is not the argument of this book that all the soldiers of the Waffen-SS were ideological warriors bent on destruction. But certainly the higher-command echelons and a large core group of the Waffen-SS were motivated by political and ideological concerns and carried out what could only be described as systematic or endemic atrocities. This raises the issue of group responsibility, which will be discussed later.

The Waffen-SS displayed anti-Slavic prejudices in its military activities. This type of attitude was contributed to by the ideological training of the Waffen-SS. As part of the preparation of his *Totenkopf* division, *SS-Obergruppenführer* Eicke had a special course of political indoctrination devised. This involved breaking the soldiers into small discussion groups with SS officers where they would discuss nationality and home, history, geography and biology (Sydnor, 1990). Eicke considered these topics to be of great importance as "... they represented most of the basic Nazi racial and political theories" (Sydnor, 1990:143). Of note is that;

> Many present-day apologists for the Waffen-SS, those who claim that its functions and conduct were strictly military and not political, maintain either that no such training programs existed, or that if they did the average SS man did not take them seriously. In the *Totenkopf* division such political and racial indoctrination definitely existed ...the reputation it subsequently earnt in Russia, moreover, leaves the distinct impression that Eicke's men took the lessons of their political training very seriously. (Sydnor, 1990:146)

The *Totenkopf* was not alone or peculiar among Waffen-SS units in this type of training and attitude towards certain groups of society. The *Leibstandarte SS Adolf Hitler* also had a course of weekly indoctrination lessons that were conducted by education officers. Sessions such as these were standardised for the entire SS in 1935 through the use of indoctrination journals, which carried the usual Nazi racial themes such as "... one had better not speak at all about a feeling of honour among Jews" (Weingartner, 1974:30). It has been argued that the Waffen-SS as a whole was not naive in relation to the aims and policies of the Nazi Party, "there is also no doubt that they were already aware of Hitler's racist policies, especially towards the Jews..." (Reynolds, 1999:3). When engaged in bitter fighting with Russian forces the Waffen-SS began to readily label the enemy as Jewish or other enemies of the Nazi state. It became standard practice that where there was desperate Russian resistance this would be attributed to:

> ... Jews, bandits, partisans or the sinister influence of commissars. The object was to intensify the SS men's hatred for the enemy by identifying the Russian soldier with the most pernicious and lethal enemies of the Third Reich, who would destroy Germany first unless annihilated. (Sydnor, 1990:165).

The above quote encapsulates the underlying ethos of the Waffen-SS that they were engaged in a battle of survival against ideological and political enemies, with which there could only be one outcome, destroy them or be destroyed. In conclusion it can be seen that the Waffen-SS was in fact part of the overall Nazi political apparatus. It was never a legitimate part of the armed forces, but rather an armed adjunct of the Nazi Party, available for utilisation at the will of the Führer. The arguments by veterans that they were just simple soldiers of no particular political persuasion do not hold up under examination. The Waffen-SS was an organisation that was heavily based on the racial, ideological and political beliefs of the Nazi Party.

2. The structure of the Waffen-SS

Understanding the ideology behind the Waffen-SS is but one part of understanding the organisation as a whole. To fully form a picture as to the organisation itself it is necessary to examine the structural, economic and sociological makeup of the organisation. This allows the spectator to appreciate the close relationship between the various arms of the SS Empire, and the Waffen-SS.

The Training Schools

In a post-war memoir Paul Hausser had this to say of the Waffen-SS: "For years the former soldiers of this troop, and also soldiers of the Heer, have been concerned to show and to prove that the Waffen-SS was trained according to the regulations and instructions of the Heer…" (Association of Soldiers of the Former Waffen-SS, 1973:9). In his plea for justice for the Waffen-SS Hausser is not accurate in describing how the Waffen-SS were trained. The SS trained their officers at separate officer candidate schools or *SS-Junkerschulen*. Each year the schools passed out some 300 militarily trained SS officers (Wegner, 1985). This number was in excess of that required by the Waffen-SS, so some of these officers served in other areas of the SS other then the Waffen-SS. It served two purposes, however, to have this excess, first, it meant that there was a ready reserve of militarily trained SS officers, and second it helped to strengthen the ties between the various SS components. As noted by *SS-Brigadeführer* Doerffler-Schuband: "The schools also trained young police officers for whom there was increased demand. Young SS officers who were slated for administrative assignments were also trained at the officer candidate schools of the SS" (Doerffler-Schuband, 1949:2). A number of *SS-Junkerschulen* operated between 1934 and 1945, with perhaps the *Junkerschulen* at Bad Tolz being the most well-known. The benefit of having separate training schools from the regular forces was that the SS could ensure that a political leadership corps was trained in the educational and ideological areas that Himmler saw as essential without interference. By 1944 some one-third of Waffen-SS regimental or battalion commanders were products of the *Junker-schulen*; they were, in fact, given preference for field commands (Wegner, 1990).

The *SS-Junkerschulen* provided a curriculum that dealt with "… military subjects and practical weapons and combat training, similar to the officer academies of the army" (Wegner, 1985:226). However, unlike the *Wehrmacht* the Waffen-SS under the auspices of ex-army officer *SS-Ober-gruppenführer* Felix Steiner adopted a more physical approach, with recruits training in athletics and sport rather than parade-ground drills (Gingerich, 1997; Hohne, 1969). It was this physical preparation that some Waffen-SS veterans' claim made them so combat effective in the harsh climates of Russia. The aims of the schools' training according to *SS-Brigade-führer* Doerffler-Schuband were to "… build character by emphasising integrity, fearlessness, chivalry, honour, obedience, helpfulness and good fellowship. Moreover, irreproachable conduct in public, and the development of a family spirit were further requirements" (Doerffler-Schuband, 1949:7).

Ideological training was also undertaken in an effort to produce a specifically National Socialist type of professional solider. Waffen-SS officer and commander of the Bad Tolz school, Richard Schulze-Kossens, attempted to deny any such indoctrination in his book on the *SS-Junker-schulen*: "A mental attitude developed in which common European interests ranked above official party doctrine … there was no sense in bothering European Junkers … in simplifying European history to a course of events in which the Nordic principle reigned supreme" (Schulze-Kossens, 1982:28). However, the purpose of the ideological indoctrination subject was:

> To support the cadet's inner acceptance of these military and specifically SS values by illustrating their ideological background … The basic themes of SS ideology constituted the contents of this subject: the eternal law of life, their realisation through National Socialism, but above all an extensive portrayal of German and European history since early Teutonic times from a racial and geopolitical perspective. (Wegner, 1990:171)

Other veterans would disagree with Schulze-Kossen's attempt to dismiss the ideological indoctrination undertaken at the *Junkerschulen*. As Leon Degrelle explains the Waffen-SS soldiers were "… taught why they were fighting, what kind of Germany was being resurrected before their very eyes ... they were taught that all Germans represented an ethnic unity" (Degrelle, 1983:16). As noted by Vuksic, "In addition to physical training, politics and ideology were an integral part of their training" (Vuksic, 2005:1). Instructors at the schools taught the students that the war was a continuation of the 2000-year-old conflict between the Aryan and the non-Aryan, the Jew and the Slav. This had the effect of creating distance between the Waffen-SS, the Aryans, and their potential victims.

Waffen-SS veteran, Zvonimir Bernwald, a racial German, recounted how they were trained at the officer cadet schools in military aspects, but above all in the principles of National Socialism (Halliley, 2003). As the veteran explained, this was seen as a crucial part of the soldier's craft for elite troops by the Waffen-SS (Halliley, 2003; Smith et al., 1999). This allowed indoctrination that stimulated the SS man's impetus to act according to a few basic rules of Nazi morality. A special training camp was set up at Ausbildungslager Sennheim for integrating Germanic volunteers into the Waffen-SS in 1940. As part of this training "... ideological education was considered the most important component of the program" (Gingerich, 1997:822). These training schools can be seen as the first step in momentum building on the path to genocide. The Waffen-SS officers were clearly being conditioned to move down the path of genocide against those elements that the Nazis saw as subhuman or politically dispensable.

Chief Waffen-SS recruiter, *SS-Obergruppenführer* Gottlob Berger, wanted to ensure the non-German recruits "... received the same ideological instruction as their German counterparts, learning about the great idea of Nazism, racial science and methods to recognise the enemy in all forms" (Gingerich, 1997:822). The enemy in all forms can be taken to include that enemies of the Reich were both external and internal. Of note, however, is that few officers in the Waffen-SS came from outside Germany. Wegner studied some 582 officers of the Waffen-SS and only 48 officers or eight per cent came from outside Germany (Wegner, 1990:235). As noted by Hatheway, the *SS-Junkerschulen* were inexorably linked to the Nazi Party and its ideological and political goals:

> From their inception in 1934 until their demise in 1945. The *Junker-schulen*, therefore, remained political institutions in service to the National Socialist revolution and to the various organisations of the party and state ... indeed it was precisely because the SS was so highly political and revolutionary that Himmler considered the development of a standardised, professional educational process essential. (Hatheway, 1999:9)

Ideological training took up some 10 per cent of a cadet's course work. Some may argue that this is a small component overall, however, ideological indoctrination was given special weighting in excess of its time allotment in the final evaluations of all officer candidates (Hatheway, 1999; Wegner, 1990). *SS-Brigadeführer* Doerffler-Schuband stated that political indoctrination was given the same weighting as tactics in the curriculum, with both subjects having the greatest time allocation compared to others (Doerffler-Schuband, 1949). He gives a breakdown of comparative weightings of subjects and it is reproduced below.

Subject	Weighting
Tactics	8
Political Indoctrination	8
Organisation of the German Army	5
Special Services Course	3
Terrain Orientation	3
Troop Duty	5
Signal Communication	3
Engineering	2
Aviation	1
Motor Transport	1
Gymnastics	5
Mounted Drill	1

Note: Sourced from Doerffler-Schuband 1949. The figures show the relative amount of time spent on each subject. For instance eight times as much time was spent on Tactics as compared to with the time spent on Motor Transport, etc.

It is interesting to read the post-war memoirs of some Waffen-SS members; despite trying to walk the politically correct line one can glimpse their deeper feelings coming to the fore. For instance, in his biography Hans Schmidt, a veteran of the *Leibstandarte SS Adolf Hitler* Division, comments on the training he received.

> Among other things we touched on such subjects as racial studies, culture, European history from a National Socialistic point of view, religion in general and social progress ... the many hours a week of our training was evenly split between practical field service and theoretical instruction ... During our instructions about race no attempt was made to imbue hate of other groups in us, although it was quite clearly pointed out that most of the accomplishments of the modern man, beginning with the ancient Greeks, came from white Aryans. Perhaps due to time limits we touched on the various characteristics of the major races i.e. white, yellow and black. Jews did not fall into either of these categories, and were, with one sentence, merely defined as a mixed race seemingly not worthy of greater consideration. (Schmidt, 2001:51)

Further on Schmidt comes to the following conclusion, which seems to suggest that he was instructed about the Jews with much more than just "one sentence".

> Leaders like Martin Luther and Frederick the Great had all been real Germans, and suddenly these giants and other like them had been supplanted by an ethnically and genetically different tribe that believed it could do everything better. In other words, no German solution of German problems was possible with the Jews still in power. (Schmidt, 2001:56)

This claim of training being conducted without any racial or ideological indoctrination was also put forward by *SS-Oberstgruppenführer* Hausser, who was initially in charge of the Waffen-SS training program.

> HERR PELCKMANN: The Prosecution is particularly accusing the *Verfügungstruppe* for inciting racial hatred and for the persecution of the Jews as one of its special tasks. Was the troop trained for these purposes?

> HAUSSER: The political and ideological training could only be achieved by schooling. I, personally, as director of the school and as an inspector, have closely watched this training, for I was a new man myself and had first to acquaint myself with these ways of thinking. I can testify that race hatred and the extermination of Jewry or of the Eastern peoples was never taught and was never demanded.

> (The International Military Tribunal, 1946: Vol 20:359)

SS-Oberstgruppenführer **Hausser**

This testimony from Hausser bears examination. This is the SS general who also claimed that he did not know about the concentration-camps, yet slave labour was employed at the *SS-Junkerschulen* that he was in charge of. In the *Junkerschulen* at Bad Tolz there were cells built underneath the school to house concentration-camp inmates whose job it was to maintain the facilities of the school. In fact, the cells in the basement of the school were used as a sub-camp for Dachau and could house up to 50 prisoners at any one time (Hatheway, 1999:83). As noted by Stein, to claim that the training of the Waffen-SS was not in ideological sync with the Nazis was just not true;

> … In view of the amount of time devoted to ideological indoctrination in the pre-war SS and the nature of the material presented, there can be little doubt that many of the men who made up the Waffen-SS of 1941 – particularly the officers and NCOs – subscribed to the basic view set forth in Himmler's statements on the racial struggle and similar matters. (Stein, 1966:125)

While the *SS-Junkerschulen* may have provided the training for the future leaders of the Waffen-SS, they and the future divisions of the Waffen-SS could not have operated without an economic and administrative apparatus to support them.

The Economic and Administrative Main Department (WVHA)

The Pohl Trial (or WVHA Trial) was the fourth of the 12 trials for war crimes the U.S. authorities held in their occupation zone in Germany in Nuremberg after the end of World War II. These 12 trials were all held before the NMT, not before the IMT. In this case, Oswald Pohl and 17 other SS officers employed by the *Wirtschafts- und Verwaltungshauptamt* (WVHA), the Economic and Administrative Department of the SS, were tried for war crimes and crimes against humanity committed during the time of the Nazi regime. The main charge levelled at them was their active participation in, and administration of, the genocide of the Jews and other target groups. They were also accused of slave labour, participation in the concentration-camp system, euthanasia programs, economic exploitation and various medical experiments carried out on camp inmates. The WVHA was the SS office that ran the concentration and extermination camps. It also handled the procurement for the Waffen-SS.

> As far as the Waffen SS was concerned, responsibility for supply was divided between the SS Operational Headquarters and the WVHA. Broadly speaking, the operational headquarters supplied arms, ammuni-

tion, and other technical equipment, while the WVHA was responsible for rations, clothing, fuel, and personal items of equipment. Among other things, *Amtsgruppe B* was responsible for the supply of food and clothing to concentration-camps.

(Nuremberg Military Tribunal, 1946: Vol 5:217)

Examples of the exploitation conducted by the WHVA for the benefit of the Waffen-SS are not hard to find. *SS-Obersturmbannführer* Bobermin reported how earthworks would be obtained for the Waffen-SS in a letter to WVHA Chief Oswald Pohl in 1944.

> ... considering that we have a technically well-equipped establishment, and that the men of the forced labour camp will be at our disposal at favourable conditions, we shall most likely show a profit. The main reason for the taking over is the sufficient supply of building material to the Waffen-SS.

(Nuremberg Military Tribunal, 1946: Vol 5:249)

The WVHA also played a role in the establishment of the Waffen-SS fighting divisions as is shown by this order concerning the setting up of the 17th SS Panzergrenadier Division *Gotz Von Berlichingen* in 1943.

> SS-FHA Amt IV will raise by 15.11.43 Section IVA of the division with the divisional treasury ... The personnel department of the SS-WVHA is requested to allocate the necessary administrative officers at once. (Perrigault et al., 2004:25)

The WVHA had the following organisational structure. Division A of the WVHA was responsible for the budget of the Waffen-SS as well as promotions and transfers of the Waffen-SS and the same such movements for the concentration-camps among other things. Division B was responsible for troop organisation including food supplies, military-camp stores, clothing factories and funds, maintenance of vehicles, etc. Division C was responsible for constructions and real estate, etc of the Waffen-SS. Division D was responsible for the command of the concentration-camps. Division W was responsible for economic enterprises. Pohl, when questioned before the NMT, confirmed that the WVHA was an integral part of the Waffen-SS.

> Q. What other agency of the German *Wehrmacht* could be compared with the WVHA as it was organised in February 1942? A. One could compare it with the army administrative office. What that office was for the army, the WVHA was for the Waffen-SS.

(Nuremberg Military Tribunal, 1946: Vol 5:327)

WVHA deputy, *SS-Gruppenführer* Georg Loerner, supported this when he was questioned about the role of the WVHA.

> Q. What, speaking quite generally, was the main field of task of the WVHA?
> A. The WVHA was the highest administrative authority of the Waffen-SS and to a lesser degree of the Allgemeine SS.
> (Nuremberg Military Tribunal, 1946: Vol 5:744)

A number of SS officers were brought to trial in relation to war crimes and crimes against humanity in relation to the actions of the WVHA. Of the 17 defendants brought to trial some 12 were officers of the Waffen-SS, some having served in various combat units. They included the below:

OSWALD POHL — *SS-Obergruppenführer* and General of the Waffen-SS; Chief of the SS Economic and Administrative Main Department *(SS Wirtschaftsund Verwaltungshauptamt*, commonly known as "WVHA") and chief of Division W of the WVHA.

AUGUST FRANK — *SS-Obergruppenführer* and General of the Waffen-SS. Deputy Chief of the WVHA and chief of Division A of the WVHA.

GEORG LOERNER — *SS-Gruppenführer* and Generalleutnant of the Waffen-SS. Deputy Chief of the WVHA, chief of Division B of the WVHA, and deputy chief of Division W of the WVHA.

HEINZ KARL FANSLAU — *SS-Brigadeführer* and Generalmajor of the Waffen-SS. Chief of Division A of the WVHA. Fanslau had also served in the 5th SS *Wiking* Division.

ERWIN TSCHENTSCHER — *SS-Standartenführer* and deputy chief of Division B and chief of Office I of Division B of the WVHA. Tschentscher had served in the 4th SS *Polizei* and the 5th SS *Wiking* Divisions.

RUDOLF SCHEIDE — *SS-Standartenführer* and chief of Office V of Division B of the WVHA. Scheide had served in the 1st *Leibstandarte SS Adolf Hitler* Division.

MAX KIEFER — *SS-Obersturmbannführer* and chief of Office II of Division C of the WVHA.

FRANZ EIRENSCHMALZ — *SS-Standartenführer* and chief of Office VI of Division C of the WVHA.

KARL SOMMER — *SS-Sturmbannführer* and deputy chief of Office II of Division D of the WVHA. Sommer saw combat with the Waffen-SS.

HERMANN POOK — *SS-Obersturmbannführer* of the Waffen-SS and chief dentist of the WVHA, of Office III, Division D. Pook saw combat with the Waffen-SS.

LEO VOLK — *SS-Hauptsturmführer*, personal adviser (Persoenlicher Referent) on Pohl's staff, and head of legal section (Leiter der Rechtsabteilung) in the executive office of Division W of the WVHA.

HANS BOBERMIN — *SS-Obersturmbannführer* and chief of Office II of Division W of the WVHA.

(Nuremberg Military Tribunal, 1946: Vol 5)

Of these officers Pohl, Eirenschmalz and Sommer were sentenced to death by hanging, the rest were sentenced to various terms of imprisonment. Scheide was acquitted. *SS-Brigadeführer* Glucks, responsible for the concentration-camps, was never tried as he committed suicide after being captured by the British.

Personnel Composition of the Waffen-SS

The Waffen-SS was severely limited by the *Wehrmacht* in the number of Germans it could recruit, so it was for this reason that it looked to sources of manpower outside Germany to expand. To address this manpower shortage the SS undertook three methods of combating it, first they attempted to negotiate higher conscript quotas with the *Wehrmacht*, second they attempted to encourage volunteers, and third they utilised sources of manpower outside of the German Reich.

To oversee this recruitment drive Himmler appointed chief of the SS Main office (SS-HA) and Waffen-SS General, *SS-Obergruppenführer* Gottlob Berger. Berger was to undertake his duties with relish and with his staff he "… developed the means and methods to provide the manpower which made the Waffen-SS a political and military force to be reckoned with" (Rempel, 1980:107). Of note is that when recruiting Berger had instructed his staff that they were to emphasise the following points when recruiting: "After a general discussion of compulsory military service and the role of the Waffen-SS as a branch of the armed services, recruiters were to sketch the history of the SS, stressing the concept of the political soldier." (Rempel, 1980:109). At the time of the invasion of Russia there were some 160,425 soldiers of the Waffen-SS with a combat strength of some 95,868 (Koehl, 1983:200). Some 90 per cent of these soldiers were Germans from within the German Reich, so even at this stage of the war the Waffen-SS was still very much a pure Nordic organisation (Koehl, 1983).

By 1938 the Waffen-SS officer corps contained some 90 per cent of officers who came from a peasant background as compared to only some two per cent for the army (Hohne, 1969; Simpson, 1990:18). This lack of military background is further illustrated when it is considered that only five per cent of Waffen-SS officers had a military background of this type as against some 49 per cent for army officers (Hohne, 1969; Simpson, 1990). Wegner argues, however, that at least for the generals of the SS they had the same percentage military backgrounds, some 25 per cent, as their army counterparts (Wegner, 1990).

The ever resourceful Berger identified the *Hitlerjugend* or Hitler Youth as an excellent recruiting ground for the Waffen-SS and even before the war Berger was recruiting heavily from this source of manpower. Himmler was always on the lookout for ideological suitable recruits. To this end he enticed leaders of the *Hitlerjugend* leaders to his *Junkerschulen* by offering them a shortened course for officer candidates, in this way many became officers and NCOs in the Waffen-SS (Rempel, 1980). The Waffen-SS relied heavily on the youthful idealism in Germany to provide this manpower. In 1941, for instance, of some 50,000 recruits over two-thirds of them were under the age of 20 (Rempel, 1980). Many of them came through the Hitler Youth movement to join the Waffen-SS; this had the benefit that both organisations were in ideological sync. Koehl gives a figure of some 40,000 Hitler Youth volunteering for the Waffen-SS in 1941/42, "... many with extensive political indoctrination" (Koehl, 1983:208). Hans-Joachim Lindow was a member of the Hitler Youth, who joined the Waffen-SS as a matter of course; it was seen as a natural progression (Halliley, 2003). He saw the Waffen-SS as a guards regiment with its associated attractions and benefits.

In addition to this there were a number of non-German volunteers who joined the Waffen-SS. In all it is estimated that some 125,000 West European volunteers served in the Waffen-SS. These included some 50,000 Dutch, 20,000 Walloons, 20,000 Flemings, 6,000 Danes and 6,000 Norwegians, etc (Hohne, 1969; Simpson, 1990; Stein, 1965). For example, in June 1941 within the ranks of the *Wiking* Division were some 1143 volunteers which included 631 Dutch, 294 Norwegians, 216 Danes, one Swede and one Swiss (Solarz, 2003:15). Other authors claim that up to 500,000 Waffen-SS soldiers came from foreign sources, with the result that almost half of the personnel of the Waffen-SS were from some non-German origin (Gingerich, 1997; Hatheway, 1999; Rempel, 1980). Some 375,000 of these came from countries in Eastern Europe, these being *racial* Germans (foreigners of German decent) (Hatheway, 1999; Lumans, 1993).

Whatever the exact figure of foreign nationals it highlights an important point, the myth of the Waffen-SS being a pure Germanic force of
Nordic warriors is not correct. Of note is that all foreign nationals who
undertook officer training "had to also prove Germanic (Aryan) origin, and
demonstrate to a board of examiners loyalty to Hitler, to the Reich, and to
National Socialism" (Hatheway, 1999:114). This ensured that the political
and racial loyalties of the Waffen-SS were still maintained to some degree.
At least in the initial stages of foreign recruitment it was still the intent of
the Waffen-SS to maintain their racial purity. For this reason recruitment
was limited to their fellow Nordic countries such as Sweden and Denmark,
etc.

> The recruitment of Germanic volunteers in fact developed as an expres-
> sion of SS racial and political thought and ambition. The decision to
> recruit non-Germans of "Germanic Blood" for the Waffen-SS was inex-
> tricably connected with the dream of radically transforming the face of
> Europe according to the Nazi concepts of race and ethnicity. (Gingerich,
> 1997:817)

Later years recruitment

By 1943 the Waffen-SS was suffering severe manpower shortages. As
a result Himmler and Berger were forced to look further afield and consider
sources that would never have passed inspection in the early years. Over
one-third of the original Waffen-SS Divisions had fallen in Russia by 1943
(Hohne, 1969). As a result, in 1943 some 25 per cent of Waffen-SS recruits
were racial Germans. Another change also took place in the recruitment of
the Waffen-SS. Whereas they had previously relied on an all-volunteer
force, now they were forced to resort to press-ganging conscripts into service (Hohne, 1969; Rempel, 1980; Stein, 1966). The judges of the IMT
noted:

> Until 1940 the SS was an entirely voluntary organisation. After the for-
> mation of the Waffen-SS in 1940 there was a gradually increasing num-
> ber of conscripts into the Waffen-SS. It appears that about a third of the
> total number of people joining the Waffen-SS were conscripts, that the
> proportion of conscripts was higher at the end of the war than at the
> beginning, but that there continued to be a high proportion of volunteers
> until the end of the war.
>
> (The International Military Tribunal, 1946: Vol 1:270)

They also received large drafts from the Air Force and Navy. This
affected the elite integrity of the Waffen-SS to some degree, as no longer

was it purely made up of ideologically aligned volunteers (Dallin, 1981; Hohne, 1969; Krausnick et al., 1965; Kren et al., 1976; Stein, 1966). SS General Karl Brenner noted the effect conscripts had on the 6th SS Mountain Division *Nord* in early 1945 after it had suffered some 50 per cent losses.

> Numerically, the losses had been more or less compensated by assignment of new replacements. These consisted for the greater part of young foreign nationals of German descent (*Volksdeutsche* – racial Germans) who had received only a brief training and had not volunteered, but been drafted to the Waffen-SS in the normal conscription procedure. Their fighting value was therefore correspondingly lower then had been the case with the former personnel and naturally lowered the combat efficiency of the entire division. (Brenner, 1947b:1)

Indeed Berger was forced to address issues that arose from the negative attitude towards the Waffen-SS that many of the recruits displayed. This negativity arose from the high casualty rates of the Waffen-SS, the fact it served in the military hot spots, hard training, little chance of promotion and forceful repudiation of religious beliefs. All of these Berger attempted to discount as only been rumours far removed from the truth (Rempel, 1980). It would appear, however, that the high casualty rates may have been more truth then fiction, as Hitler commented, "For an elite force like our SS, it's great luck to have suffered comparatively heavy losses. In this way it is assured of the necessary prestige..." (Trevor-Roper, 2000:13).

Even German Field Marshal Eric Von Manstein commented on high casualties in his post-war memoirs, where he claimed that the Waffen-SS "... paid a toll of blood incommensurate with its actual gains ... the blame for such unnecessary consumption of manpower must lie with the men who set up these special units for purely political motives..." (Von Manstein, 1982:188). He seemed to forget that he himself commanded the SS Divisions and in fact stated the following in an order of the day dated 12th July 1941: "The *SS-Totenkopf* Division attacked with great courage ... the division's regiments have suffered high casualties in this fighting. I express my gratitude to all the officers and men of this corps for their dedication; my recognition for your high achievement" (Ullrich, 2002:90).

So varied were the manpower sources of the Waffen-SS that it defies putting them into any specific group. In 1943 the 13th SS *Handschar* Division was formed by recruiting Bosnian Moslems. A second Moslem Division, the 23rd SS *Kama* Division, was planned but never reached divisional status, and its cadres were later transferred to the *Handschar* Division. Himmler was forced to some degree to lessen his racial standards and his abhorrence of religion. The *Handschar* Division was allowed Imams and the 14th SS *Galicia* Division made up of Eastern Catholics from the Ukraine was allowed chaplains (Bender & Taylor, 1975; Lepre, 1997). Two divisions were formed from policemen, these being the 4th and 35th SS Divisions. However, it is worth noting that even though Himmler was forced to reduce his racial standards in some respects, he still believed that they were essential to the nature of the Waffen-SS. To this end there was a

> Fundamental separation between the German and Germanic SS troops as part of the whole SS *Orden* on the one hand, and the numerous SS volunteer units without special racial qualifications – a sort of second-class Waffen-SS – on the other, which actually began the transformation of the SS from the Fuhrer's guard into a multinational army. (Wegner, 1990:139)

It was then the turn of the Baltic States to contribute to the SS war machine. Two further SS Divisions were raised by the Latvians, one by the Estonians. By late 1944 Germany was accepting any human material it could find and no source was left untapped. It is therefore not surprising that the Germans in their ingenuity turned to their own terror apparatus, the concentration-camps, to obtain more recruits for the Waffen-SS. SS Colonel Dr Oscar Dirlewanger, a PhD scholar and Waffen-SS *Oberführer*, proposed using camp inmates in his unit. He had already been using poachers and other criminals for some time. Now, however, he obtained permission to utilise political prisoners currently held in the camp system (Breitman, 1991; MacLean, 1998; Stein, 1966). Some 1910 men were recruited from camps such as Auschwitz, Buchenwald, Dachau, Ravensbruck and Mauthausen, etc in late 1944. This very reliance on such a variance of manpower sources provided a quandary for Himmler as they undermined his very vision of the Waffen-SS being ideologically and racially pure elite for the new German Reich. It was due to this expansion the Waffen-SS, while still remaining a tool of Nazi conquest and annihilation, lost some of its distinctive political and ideological makeup. While many of the West European volunteers fell into the ideological category, many of the East European members of the Waffen-SS were fighting for nationalistic reasons at best, or were reluctant to fight at all at worst.

There were still, however, some ideological reservoirs of manpower available to Himmler. In 1944 the Waffen-SS hierarchy decided to recruit a division from the young men and boys of the *Hitlerjugend*. As noted by *SS-Brigadeführer* Hugo Kraas, commander of the 12th SS Panzer Division

Hitlerjugend, as late as November 1944 the division could rely on the following replacements: "The young replacements consisted of volunteers, whose training had been very short" (Kraas, 1947:5). This reliance on the *Hitlerjugend* ensured that the soldiers were recruited from the "... racially, ideologically and physically fit youth of Nazi Germany" (Simpson, 1990:61). The other inherent benefit on drawing on such a resource was that the boys of the *Hitlerjugend* had been subjected to "... years of ideological indoctrination, coupled with the purposeful manipulation of youthful idealism within the Hitler Youth..."; in short they were the perfect ideological warriors for the Waffen-SS (Luther, 1987:12).

With this in mind some 17,000 were called up to form the *SS Hitlerjugend* Division, while another 25,000 were distributed to other Waffen-SS formations (Rempel, 1980). These boy soldiers would be as effective as any of the premier Waffen-SS divisions. In fact they were seen as almost a pseudo *Leibstandarte*, given their idealism and the fact that a large percentage of the officer and NCO cadre for the *Hitlerjugend* was transferred from the *Leibstandarte* Division. The fact that they were young boys however, could not be overlooked. As one veteran of the *SS Hitlerjugend* Division, Bernhard Heisig, recalled, "The youngest among us didn't get any cigarettes, well they didn't smoke anyway. They actually got sweets, confectionery" (Halliley, 2003).

Country of Origin	Approximate number of men	SS Formations
Netherlands	50,000	22nd and 34th divisions
Belgium	40,000	27th and 28th divisions
France	20,000	33rd division
Italy	15,000	29th division
Denmark	10,000	5th and 11th divisions
Norway	6000	5th division
Finland	3000	SS Regiment Nordland
Spain	1000	28th division
Sweden	300	5th and 11th divisions
Switzerland	300	5th division
Soviet Union	60,000	29th and 30th divisions
Latvia	80,000	15th and 19th divisions
Romania	50,000	7th and 8th divisions
Estonia	25,000	20th division
Hungary	20,000	25th and 26th divisions
Croatia	20,000	13th and 23rd divisions
Albania	7000	21st division
Bulgaria	600	Various
Serbia	10,000	Various

Note: Sourced from Bishop 2005. Some of the smaller nationalities that contributed to the SS are not mentioned here. The total figure of volunteers may differ from that of other authors but nonetheless gives an account of the varied sources of manpower.

The table above illustrates the numbers of various nationalities that served in the Waffen-SS and, main units that they served in. By the end of the war the Waffen-SS contained soldiers of foreign origin that included Danes, Norwegians, Finns, Swiss, Swedes, Flemings, Walloons, Frenchmen, Italians, Latvians, Estonians, Russians, Ukrainians, Croats, Bosnian Serbs, Hungarians, Albanians, Romanians, Netherlanders, Spaniards, and even some Britons and Indians. With this influx of foreigners the Waffen-SS had grown from a small Germanic elite body to a large multinational force. It had, in fact, gone from some 0.7 per cent of *Wehrmacht* strength in 1939 to 5.4 per cent in 1944 (Scherzer, 2006). According to one source by the end of 1944 the Waffen-SS contained some 400,000 German citizens, 310,000 *Volksdeutsche* (foreigners of Germanic origin) and 200,000 foreign volunteers (Ploetz, Schramm, & Hillgruber, 1960). This illustrates that even with the influx of foreigners the Waffen-SS was still, however, primarily Germanic. Some of these nationalities were only present in small numbers, but nonetheless they were part of the Waffen-SS at one point or another.

The apologists for the Waffen-SS have raised the argument that they were merely the replication of the post-war NATO military formations; they were, in fact, a European army (Mackenzie, 1997). The argument being that they were a multinational force formed to oppose communism. Indeed, former Waffen-SS officers have argued that the European volunteers were not pro-Nazi, but rather should be seen as "anti-Bolshevists" (Ertel et al., 2000:6). *SS-Obergruppenführer* Steiner argued in his post-war account of the Waffen-SS that "... the foreign volunteers were men of spirit who, like their German comrades, saw the diabolical threat to Western civilisation posed by Bolshevism and fought like lions against it under the banner of the Waffen-SS" (Mackenzie, 1997:138).

This stands some credence until one considers that the recruitment of Germanic volunteers was done "... with the Nazi goal of creating a Germanic Reich by drawing upon the Germanic blood in the entire world" (Gingerich, 1997). There were no plans for autonomy of the countries that the volunteers came from, they would continue after the war under the German yoke. Indeed, unlike NATO, which is a standing force among equal partners, the foreigners who served in the Waffen-SS were for expediency only and were certainly not equals in the relationship.

> Nor were the German-raised legions intended as a permanent force, since they were formed for one purpose and one purpose only – the defeat of the Soviet Union. Had the war ended with German victory, the legions were to have been disbanded, their purpose having been served. (Buss et al., 1978:10)

As well as this many of the foreign groups who joined the Waffen-SS later in the war "… were motivated to fight for different reasons than their Reich German counterparts" (Wegner, 1990:311). Many fought for nationalist reasons, however they still displayed and shared the German dislike for Jews and Bolshevism. The inclusion of racially inferior groups later in the war was done for the sake of military expediency as great holes were torn in the manpower of the Waffen-SS on the Eastern Front. The Waffen-SS remained a Germanic order. As Stein notes: "The Waffen-SS had indeed become an army of Europeans; it never was a European army" (Stein, 1965:22).

In summary it can be seen that the Waffen-SS was given special treatment in relation to its relationship with Hitler, in its training schools and the SS court system used to regulate it. These were benefits that were never given to the regular army units. The training of the Waffen-SS was deliberately aimed at producing effective military leaders who would also be politically and ideologically reliable. There can be little doubt that in the early days at least, the Waffen-SS was seen as the genetic base of the new Germanic Reich, and for this reason Himmler and Hitler held it in special regard. While in the later years of the war the racial and political elite was diluted to some extent due to manpower shortages, there did, however, remain a large hard core of Waffen-SS officers and men who were aligned with the racial, political and ideological views of the Nazis. This consensus on a world view would allow the Waffen-SS to undertake massive atrocities in a systematic way as the revolutionary shock troops of the Third Reich during their war of destruction in Russia.

It can be seen that the Waffen-SS organisation was a mixture of situational and dispositional factors that were conducive to the conduct of evil acts. It was an organisation created to undertake whatever was necessary to further the Nazi state and it attracted and accepted (in the early years at least) only those who were in ideological sync with its aims. It can also be seen that the Waffen-SS was setting the foundations for the genocide that was to follow.

3. Combat operations of the Waffen-SS

> I can imagine the need to dig an antitank dike and about 10,000 Russian women dying of exhaustion during the course of the work. This is of no interest to me. The only question is whether the dike is completed or not.

This speech given by Himmler to officers of the Waffen-SS in Posen in 1943 succinctly outlines the brutal practicality of the SS psyche. In fact it gives clear representation of what I would term instrumental evil. The logic was let 10,000 Russians die, their loss will prevent the loss of German lives and for this result the cost is acceptable. Indeed according to *SS-Obergruppenführer* Bach-Zelewski, as early as the beginning of 1941 Himmler had a meeting with twelve *SS-Gruppenführers*; where he stated that the purpose of the Russian campaign was to reduce the indigenous population by some 30 million people (Breitman, 1991:147).

In dealing with the actions of the Waffen-SS on the Eastern Front it is necessary to clearly outline the aspects that this book will address. The previous chapters have already set the scene and tone of the conflict, what this discussion shall attempt to do is outline *what* actions the Waffen-SS undertook on the Eastern Front. Indeed the conflict on the Russian front has an unenviable association with the SS due to "… their part in policing the country, in the massacres of Jews, in the hunt for political commissars and partisans, in the reprisals on villages, and in the round-up of slave labour" (Reitlinger, 1957:166).

It is not my intent to discuss the military exploits of the Waffen-SS to any large degree, that is not my purpose. I do intend, however, to examine various acts of the Waffen-SS in an attempt to show that this military force did commit some of the most heinous acts to occur during World War II. To this purpose I intend to examine the following areas in the following

chapters in an effort to provide examples of what may later be called evil
actions. These areas will include:
    General combat duties;
    Anti-partisan operations;
    Einsatzgruppen operations;
    The concentration-camps and;
    Other miscellaneous actions.

It is important to outline to some degree the actions of the Waffen-SS
as it will provide support for my conclusions in the final chapter when I
conduct an analysis of the Waffen-SS.

The use of the Waffen-SS on the Eastern Front saw the instigation of a
war of ideology and racism.

> The invasion of Russia saw the Waffen-SS build a formidable reputation
> as a fighting force, but it also confirmed that they were warriors for a
> truly evil cause. (Ripley, 2004:73).

It has been noted that the Waffen-SS in general earnt a reputation for
brutality in the way it conducted itself in armed conflicts. During the conflict on the Eastern Front the shooting of prisoners, the massacre of civilians and the destruction of villages became signature behaviour of the
Waffen-SS. The Waffen-SS were accused of violations of the Geneva Convention and the generally accepted rules of war during the conflict in Russia and also to a lesser extent in the Western conflict. It is acknowledged
that the conflict on the Eastern Front was fought with barbarity on both
sides, however, the "… brutal reprisals for Soviet crimes taken by Waffen-
SS soldiers were out of all proportion, and repugnant to many of their fellow country men" (Hohne, 1969:469).

The SS went to great lengths to portray the Russian soldier as a different opponent to those encountered in the West. The SS newspaper showed
"… Russian prisoners who look especially non-Aryan, and they are
described as being in rags and lice-infested" (Combs, 1986:138). All this
was designed to ensure that the Waffen-SS soldier did not see the Russian
as a fellow soldier, but rather as a subhuman. *SS-Gruppenführer* Max
Simon clearly espoused the view held of the Russian soldier in a post-war
manuscript, "… the primitive way of thinking and the mental sluggishness
of the Russian peasant did not permit the employment of complicated
weapons" (Simon, 1949:12). The Eastern Front was not a place of com-
radely pity for a vanquished foe. An example of this thinking is given by a

German Army officer, Bern Freytag Von Loringhoven, who recounted how he saw a row of Russian prisoners lined up and a group of SS soldiers getting ready to shoot the prisoners. When queried an SS corporal turned to Von Loringhoven and said, "Ah Lieutenant, they are just brutes" prior to killing them (Halliley, 2003). He is not alone in recounting incidents like this. At Nuremberg, evidence was given about the execution of prisoners by the Waffen-SS in 1941 by a captured Russian soldier, Mojzesz Goldberg:

> On 23 June 1941 I was called up into the Soviet Army in Lemberg. In the middle of July I was taken prisoner by the Germans. At a locality five kilometres from Podwoloczysk the SS companies sought the Jews out of the whole mass of prisoners and shot them on the spot. I remained alive as they did not recognise me as a Jew. I stress the fact that it was the Waffen-SS who did this.
>
> (The International Military Tribunal, 1946: Vol 20:388)

SS-Gruppenführer **Max Simon**

The high command of the *Wehrmacht* issued guidelines for the "Conduct of Troops in Russia" in which it was stated that Bolshevism was the mortal enemy of the German people and the fight against this enemy demanded "... ruthless measures against Bolshevists agitators, irregulars, saboteurs and Jews" (Heer, 1999:126). This allowed individuals to commit acts that, could then be ideologically and morally justified (note that this would be *subjective* moral justification) in that context. An example of this was the shooting of Russian Army political commissars[19] on sight when captured. The Waffen-SS soldiers of the *Totenkopf* division readily executed Commissars and the records of the division indicate that the "...men zealously carried out Hitler's Commissar order" (Sydnor, 1990:314).

An example of these criminal orders being carried out was Waffen-SS lieutenant, *SS-Untersturmführer* Taubner, who was attached to the Waffen-SS 1st Brigade[20] in Russia in 1941. Taubner was not part of the killing units or involved in cleansing operations against the Jews or so-called partisans, he was part of a workshop detail repairing equipment (Klee, Dressen, & Riess, 1988; Rhodes, 2002). Taubner and a number of other Waffen-SS men took it upon themselves to commence killing Jews that they came across, often with incredible brutality. Taubner organised and participated in the killing of children, women and men, often pausing between the killings to play his accordion. Of note is the fact that Taubner was eventually brought up on charges before an SS court, which delivered the following verdict:

> The Jews have to be exterminated and none of the Jews that were killed is any great loss ... the accused should have recognised the fact that the extermination of the Jews was the duty of commandos which have been set up especially for this purpose ... It is not the German way to apply Bolshevik methods during the necessary extermination of the enemy of our people. In doing so the conduct of the accused gives rise to considerable concern. The accused allowed his men to act with such vicious brutality that they conducted themselves under his command like a savage horde. (Klee et al., 1988:201).

The actions of Taubner did not fit in with Hitler's ideas of "A new anti-Semitism based on reason". This type of thinking resisted killings that were based on emotions such as pleasure or revenge. Indeed Himmler had indicated that SS men who carried out unauthorised shootings for political purposes should not be subject to punishment, but those who carried it out for sadistic or sexual reasons should be tried for murder. As early as 1935 Himmler had laid down strict instructions regarding actions against the Jews. In an order dated the 16th of August 1935, SS men were prohibited from independent individual action as "... the solution of the Jewish question, as of all other questions, is the business of the Führer, and not of individuals. And even the most minor contravention of this order will by punished by dismissal from the SS" (Krausnick et al., 1965:351).

Clearly Taubner was acting out his need to satisfy his personal sadistic disposition, he was not required by the organisation to undertake such actions. An important factor in the behaviour of Taubner was that he was an initiator of independent actions, not just a soldier following orders of the authorities. The most poignant fact is that he was punished for his actions by the very organisation that was undertaking the extermination of the Jews. His role in the system was not meant to be that of a killer. He was meant to repair equipment. But by undertaking the killings he had allowed his personal disposition to interfere with the running of the organisation and as such was punished by the organisation.

Indeed Taubner's case is an example of one flaw that has been seen in applying situational models such as Milgram's[21] to events such as the Holocaust. This perceived flaw is that Milgram's experiment was highly centralised. The students were under the direct control of the authority figure (Blass, 1993; Hilberg, 1980; Milgram, 1974). Clearly Taubner was not under the direct control of Hitler or Himmler. He was in fact thousands of miles away from Berlin, the centre of authority in relation to the extermination policies. Further, his unit was not part of the killing system that had been put in place. He was the producer of his own actions in relation to the killings of Jews. It would appear that his disposition drove him to commit acts of evil. Indeed the killings were not only propelled by the bureaucracy, but also by "… individual initiative and a shared set of beliefs, values and goals" (Kressel, 2002:163).

Examples of this type of behaviour can be found from other sources. A soldier of the 16th SS Panzergrenadier *Reichsführer SS* Division wrote in a letter that,

> In the vicinity of our camp there is situated a Russian prisoner-of-war camp. In there they did not want to correctly obey orders. Now we have shot 800 men. Now they are quiet. Yes, they must be happy that they still live, since we know no mercy. Now they have the first warning, the confounded dogs. (Huffman, 2005:153)

Waffen-SS veteran Hans Schmidt recounts in his autobiography an incident with a sergeant on the Russian Front in 1944:

> The sergeant and I had been talking about rather mundane things when we came upon the wounded enemy soldier. When we came closer and saw the horrible shape the fellow was in the sergeant quietly lifted his machine gun, aimed at the wounded man, shot him dead with a short burst of fire, and then walked on as nothing had happened. (Schmidt, 2001:231)

Schmidt later attempts to justify this act as a mercy killing and did not consider it a war crime. Two Swedish volunteers in the Waffen-SS had this to say during a visit to the Swedish embassy in Berlin in 1941:

> Prisoners were seldom taken by the Waffen-SS. Unless they surrendered in greater numbers than company size they would be shot on the spot. The prisoners were harshly treated and were then moved forward by kicks and beatings. Female soldiers were killed instantly... (Christensen et al., 2003:21)

Even as the war ended in 1945 soldiers of the Waffen-SS acted with cruelty towards Russian soldiers. For example, two escaped Russian POWs were executed by a solider of the *Leibstandarte SS Adolf Hitler* in March 1945[22] (Ruter & de Mildt, 2004: Vol 16). This dismissal of the value of life is clear in the comments of Hans Hossfelder, an officer of the *Das Reich* Division:

> It was one thing to enter Russia and combat the Red Army, kill partisans and the like. We had been indoctrinated to believe that they were a sub-human culture, slightly above the status of animals, and this was not too hard for many of us to believe. However, for the men who entered Greece before June 1941 (the invasion of Russia), as I was one of them, it would have been difficult to carry out or issue an order to kill people simply because they had to die. This was not the case in Russia. Now when these people returned from Russia and the brutal anti-partisan war in Yugoslavia, it was just a different matter. Men had seen and done so much killing, it almost seemed to be just a part of the job. I do not say that it is right now, or even that it was right back then. It was only right according to the times we found ourselves in, given the particulars of the circum-stances. It was very sad. (Heaton, 2001:85)

This type of attitude was exhibited by a host of Waffen-SS units. So commonplace and widespread were these acts of brutality that I would con-tend these types of actions were endemic to the Waffen-SS units as a whole.

Foremost among them was the *Totenkopf* division, which conducted such actions as "... the burning of villages, the murder of prisoners and the summary execution of captured commissars and politruks" and earnt its reputation as one of the most brutal SS units on the Eastern Front (Sydnor, 1990:316). It is with little surprise then that at the end of the war the Rus-sians asked for and succeeded in getting all *Totenkopf* personnel who had surrendered to the Western Allies handed over to them for punishment. The *Totenkopf* was not alone in the destruction of villages and the killing of civilians. On the 2nd of July 1941 men from the *Westland* Regiment (part of the 5th Waffen-SS *Wiking* Panzer Division) exacted revenge with the destruction of a village and reprisals against the inhabitants in return for a sniper killing their commander, *SS-Standartenführer* Wackerle (Smith et al., 1999). The *Leibstandarte SS Adolf Hitler* conducted the murder of 200 Russian civilians near the town of Slucz for the murder of German soldiers. The civilians were herded into a petrol-soaked cottage; "The windows and doors were then barricaded and a hand grenade dropped down the chimney. The explosion and holocaust were spectacular..." (Wykes, 1974:125).

Some Waffen-SS veterans claimed that no atrocities were ever committed. As one veteran of the 6th SS Mountain Division *Nord* stated "... as I recall my time with the battalion on Russian territory, I can't think of any actions which could have tarnished our battalion's honour. It is also my firm belief that this notion is true of the other units." (Voss, 2002:147). It is of interest that later in the memoirs of this particular veteran he describes his first combat with American forces where the Americans were allowed to tend to their wounded on the field. He states, "I couldn't believe my eyes. What kind of war was this? Nothing like that would have happened at the Eastern Front, but here some of the rules of war seemed still to be in force, valid for both sides" (Voss, 2002:183). This statement would seem to contradict his earlier claim regarding a lack of atrocities or knowledge of such on the Eastern Front.

During June 1941 the soldiers of the Waffen-SS began to fight their way into Russia against disorganised Russian resistance. Huge losses were being inflicted upon the Russians, the result being large groups or pockets of Russian soldiers that were bypassed and cut off from their main forces. The 1st *Totenkopf* Infantry Regiment (part of the 3rd Waffen-SS *Totenkopf* Division) was subjected to attacks by these groups of straggling Russian soldiers with the result that the regimental commander, *SS-Standartenführer* Max Simon, ordered that these Russian soldiers be seen as partisans and be "... dealt with most ruthlessly" (Mann, 2001; Sydnor, 1990:160). This, Sydnor (1990:160) argues, resulted in the likely consequence that the SS soldiers "... shot the majority of the Russian stragglers they encountered, especially those who offered resistance rather then immediate surrender".

This claim is supported by several reports from Waffen-SS officers of this unit to higher commands describing the Russian soldiers in panic-stricken terms as "... fanatical, inhuman creatures who employed the vilest tricks to kill German soldiers" (Sydnor, 1990:160). To support these claims the officers gave examples such as some 200 Russian soldiers coming forward to surrender with hands raised, who then suddenly began firing on the SS soldiers. The result being that the SS killed all of the Russians, including those who later attempted to surrender (Sydnor, 1990). At Zhitomir the SS *Wiking* Division carried out the following orders in the town.

> Its men were given the instructions to search every home and building for, in addition to People's Commissars, all of the town's officials, whether civilian or military. When these officials were rounded up, they were shot. (Butler, 1978:106).

The attitude of the Waffen-SS to the Russian civilians is reflected in the comments of Waffen-SS General Karl Herrmann. He recalls:

> During the entire advance we encountered scattered snipers, saboteurs and partisan groups. Usually dressed as civilians, these partisans carried on insidious guerrilla warfare behind our lines; they engaged in raids, demolition and all other forms of sabotage ... the employment of these partisan groups as combat units constituted a flagrant violation of the rules of warfare ... as a rule captured partisans were hungry and filthy. Among them were half-starved underworld characters. Some were adolescents, 15 to 17 years old, whose faces betrayed their lust for murder ... women were also among the partisans. Almost all of them claimed to be doctors or nurses, but to judge by their hard and brutal faces, there was many an active partisan among them. (Herrmann, 1947:2)

When the Dutch SS volunteers of the *Nederland* division found that their communications were being sabotaged the commander of the division, *SS-Brigadeführer* Jurgen Wagner, decided that an example needed to be made. As a result certain areas were declared off limits. The SS soldiers then conducted a sweep of the area.

> Every Latvian who could be found was rounded up. In a short space of time, more than 150 civilians were captured ... Wagner decided to have a number of them executed in front of everyone so as to warn the people of the gravity of the consequences of partisan activity. (Pierik, 2001:240)

Eyewitness Andrej Wachranov recalled how upon entering the newly conquered Russian town of Borisovo in 1941, SS soldiers of the *Das Reich* Division collected all the village activists, the head of the collective farms, etc and took them to a trench and executed them, claiming that they were partisans (Halliley, 2003). *SS-Obersturmbannführer* Otto Weidinger, the last commander of the 4th SS Panzer Grenadier Regiment *Der Führer*, wrote an extensive history of the *Das Reich* Division. It is of note that he

refers to the battle for Borisovo between the 21-23 of October 1941, however, no mention is made of the above shootings (Weidinger, 1998, , 2002).
He recalls how after entering the town the Waffen-SS soldiers engaged in
"... bitter house-to-house fighting" to root out the Russian defenders (Weidinger, 2002:145). An order of the day was issued on the 23rd of October
1941 by the divisional commander, *SS-Brigadeführer* Wilhelm Bittrich,
which stated:

> SS-Division Reich has attacked from the 6-21 October 1941 with hardly
> a break ... strong enemy forces were defeated or eliminated ... bottomless
> roads, storms and biting frost presented just as little hindrance to the divi-
> sion as the determined counterattacks of the numerically far superior
> enemy ... We will help destroy Bolshevism so that Germany can live. Hail
> to the Führer. (Weidinger, 2002:148)

No mention is made of the massacre of civilians. In November 1942 the
8th SS *Florian Geyer* Division was involved in the encirclement of several
Russian units, which was called the Beliye pocket (Trang, 2000). At the
conclusion of the battle the pocket "... was finally closed after five days
fighting, with the Soviet unit completely wiped out. Only a few elements
managed to escape in an isolated breakout at Zizina" (Trang, 2000:89).
Danish volunteers in the Waffen-SS recounted the killing of Russian POWs
for minor infractions and also in retaliation for deaths of their comrades
(Smith et al., 1999). They executed a number of Russian prisoners in retaliation for the death of their commander, with one officer writing home that
no prisoners were taken that day (Christensen et al., 2003). As one Danish
volunteer wrote in his diary:

> 6/9/1942 A Jew in a greasy kaftan walks up to beg some bread, a couple
> of comrades get a hold of him and drag him behind a building and a
> moment later he comes to an end. There isn't any room for Jews in the
> new Europe, they've brought too much misery to the European people.
> (Smith et al., 1999:92)

During fighting in February 1943 the *Leibstandarte SS Adolf Hitler*
reported killing some 500 Russian soldiers while taking only five prisoners
(Weingartner, 1974). These high enemy death rates and low prisoner counts
were not unusual for other units of the Waffen-SS. During the 6th of July
1941 the SS soldiers of the *Totenkopf* division engaged in such fierce fighting that no prisoners were taken for the day (Sydnor, 1990). The 49th SS
Panzergrenadier Regiment *De Ruyter*, part of the 23rd SS Panzergrenadier
Division *Nederland*, reported during fighting in the Kurland pocket in 1944
that in a few days fighting 520 Russian soldiers were killed with only some
14 being taken prisoner (Pierik, 2001:239).

This viciousness of the fighting between the Waffen-SS and Russian army units is highlighted by the fate of the 9th Waffen-SS Mountain Corps during its defence of Budapest in early 1945. Among other units the Corps contained the 8th SS Calvary Division *Florian Geyer* and the 22nd SS Calvary Division *Maria Theresa*. Some 24,000 German soldiers (the majority of which were Waffen-SS) attempted to break out of the city through Russian lines on the 11th of February 1945. For many of the Waffen-SS soldiers this attempt to escape was to result in their slaughter. Members of the 22nd Division were ambushed by Russian troops as they tried to break out of the encirclement, the Russians "… slaughtered the Germans but spared the Hungarians" (Ungvary, 2005:235). Of 24,000 who attempted to break out only some 170 Waffen-SS soldiers were successful in reaching the German lines[23]. For those Waffen-SS soldiers who were captured an ominous end awaited them. "The Waffen-SS and wounded were most at risk. The former were killed for political reasons … in the sports ground in Budakezi, SS soldiers were forced to dig their own graves before being shot." (Ungvary, 2005:333).

The pinnacle of the Waffen-SS, the battle of Kharkov

In 1943 the Waffen-SS gained a great victory in the battle of Kharkov where they destroyed substantial Russian forces and recaptured the city. It was to be the last major victory by German troops on the Eastern Front. But more than this, it was solely a Waffen-SS victory, the feat being achieved by the 1st SS Panzer Corps containing the *Leibstandarte SS Adolf Hitler, Das Reich* and *Totenkopf* Panzer Divisions. Hitler's special relationship with the Waffen-SS is evident by the fact that he lavished a large number of Knight's Crosses on his political soldiers for their actions in retaking the city. Fourteen went to the *Leibstandarte*, 10 to the *Das Reich* and five to the *Totenkopf* (Butler, 1978; Schneider, 1993). The battle turned into a massacre by its end. During the fighting soldiers of the *Totenkopf* division:

> Drew alongside the retreating Russians at distances of 20 to 30 yards, machine gunning at will the trucks crammed with infantry … the Russians had abandoned most of their vehicles and equipment and were trying to escape on foot … the SSTK First Panzergrenadier Regiment … methodically cut down the panicked herds of stampeding Russians fleeing… (Sydnor, 1990:269)

SS-Sturmbannführer Ralf Tiemann of the *SS Leibstandarte* Division described the action as follows:

> Panzers of the 7.*Panzerkompany* drove through Bulachi to the position of the breakthrough and were able to effectively support the grenadiers of the II battalion during the annihilation of the enemy forces ... At a distance of 3000 to 4000 metres we could observe the Soviet horse-drawn sleds and tanks. During the attack I successfully positioned my panzer III in a small depression and was able to kill 48 Russians with machine-gun fire. (Tiemann, 1998:35)

This type of action is graphically illustrated in Nipe's (2002) photo essay on the Kharkov campaign. It shows a series of pictures depicting some Russian soldiers with horse-drawn carts on the empty steppe trying to flee from Waffen-SS soldiers of the *SS Leibstandarte* division. The SS soldiers, heavily armed and mounted in halftracks and assault guns, rapidly overtake the Russian soldiers, who with no hope of flight attempt to surrender. The SS soldiers then machine gun the soldiers attempting to surrender. One author describes the action as follows, "... for the soldiers of the SS Panzer Corps it was like a field day with live ammunition and moving targets" (Simpson, 1990:58). Clearly the above actions are in contravention of Article 23 of the Hague Conventions, which states it is forbidden "... to kill or wound an enemy who, having laid down his arms, or having no longer means of defence, has surrendered at discretion...". Plainly here the actions of the Waffen-SS are outside of such. Gunter Oehmke, a soldier in the *Leibstandarte SS Adolf Hitler*, admitted that "... especially in offensive combat units such as the Panzer and fast-moving Panzergrenadier elements, prisoners were at times shot or simply not even taken basically because of military necessity" (Huffman, 2005:151).

During the battle for Kharkov in 1943 the *Leibstandarte SS Adolf Hitler* Division was accused of setting fire to a building containing 300 wounded Soviet soldiers in one incident and shooting some 400 wounded officers in their hospital beds in another (Darman, 2004; Reynolds, 1999; Ripley, 2004; Stein, 1966). When the Russians recaptured Kharkov evidence was uncovered of atrocities committed by the Waffen-SS. This included some 10,000[24] civilians who were killed by *Einsatzgruppen* and other units following behind the Waffen-SS (Darman, 2004; Halliley, 2003; Stein, 1966). One doctor recounted how SS soldiers "... threw incendiary grenades through the windows, the buildings began to burn and the wounded tried to save themselves", few survived (Halliley, 2003). This matter was investigated after the war and one author had the following to say.

In response the judicial authorities in Nuremberg carried out a lengthy inquiry, examining no less than 688 witnesses, all but 13 of whom were former members of the *Leibstandarte*. Only four of them professed to having ever heard of Soviet prisoners having been shot and the general view was that the *Leibstandarte* would never have been permitted to shoot defenceless prisoners. What could be established was that the hospital itself was within the area of the attack made by the 1st SS Panzergrenadier Regiment and that the main Soviet defensive belt was just north of the hospital. It is thus very likely that it became embroiled in the battle, and given that street fighting is often confused and merciless, it is quite possible that the *Leibstandarte* soldiers may have believed that they were being fired upon from the hospital and decided to eradicate all possible opposition inside it. (Messenger, 1988:211)

The above explanation hardly stands scrutiny when examined in the light of the background and other actions of the Waffen-SS in general, and the *Leibstandarte* in particular. Himmler arrived in the city shortly afterwards and a recording was made of the following speech to the Waffen-SS soldiers of the 1st SS Panzer Corps. At this point in time *SS-Oberstgruppenführer* Paul Hausser commanded the corps. Footage of the time shows an eager Hausser greeting Himmler with the Nazi salute as he arrives in Kharkov. Himmler's speech contained the following exhortation to his soldiers:

> We have but one task. To fight this racial battle without mercy. This great weapon of fear and terror which has guided us since the victory of Kharkov must never be allowed to weaken; instead we must strengthen it further. Heil Hitler. (Halliley, 2003)

Hausser attempted to play down this speech later when it was introduced into evidence before the IMT. However, the comments of *Das Reich* veteran Hans-Joachim Lindow serve to illustrate the motivations of the Waffen-SS at this point in time; "... at one point there was this silly saying, that the *Leibstandarte* saw it as their mission to lay Kharkov at Hitler's feet, and that motivation was certainly there, lets not fool ourselves" (Halliley, 2003). The city changed hands on a number of occasions and the Waffen-SS were responsible for its defence. In preparing the defences of the Kharkov the *SS Leibstandarte* used slave labour in the form of 25,000 Russians, presumably both prisoners of war and conscripted civilians to carry out the work required (Weingartner, 1974). The involvement of the Waffen-SS in committing atrocities was to continue in a variety of conflicts.

The Warsaw Uprisings

Two actions stand out in the history of the Waffen-SS and these both concern the city of Warsaw in Poland. Two uprisings took place in this city. The first being the uprising of the Jews in the ghetto in 1943; and the second being the offensive of the Polish Home Army in 1944.

The uprising of the Warsaw Ghetto

On the 19th of April 1943 the Jews in the Warsaw Ghetto rose up against their Nazi oppressors and engaged in combat against them for some 28 days. This was as a result of some 300,000 Jews being transported from the ghetto to the death camp at Treblinka since July 1942. Time was running out for the remaining 60,000 or so Jews. The Waffen-SS was to have a major role in suppressing this uprising both from a command point of view and also in relation to the combat units utilised.

The command of suppressing the uprising was put in the hands of Waffen-SS General, *SS-Brigadeführer* Jurgen Stroop, who was later to take on the position of SS and Police Leader (SSPF) Warsaw. Stroop had served in the *Totenkopf* Division on the Eastern Front in 1941. He then became the Higher SS and Police Leader (HSSPF) for Russia South and was then made SSPF for Lvov in the Ukraine before being sent to Warsaw to deal with the Jews. After the war he was extradited to Poland and tried for the crimes committed during the Ghetto uprising. He was convicted and executed on the 8th of September 1951 (MacLean, 2001). While Stroop had direct control of the operations in Warsaw, he was overseen by *SS-Obergruppenführer* Friedrich Wilhelm Kruger. Kruger was the HSSPF for the Polish area. He gained extensive experience in the Waffen-SS battle formations by serving command positions in the 6th SS *Nord* Division, the 7th SS *Prinz Eugen* Division and he then commanded the 5th SS Mountain Corps. He committed suicide on the 9th of May 1945 to avoid capture (MacLean, 2001; Yerger, 1999).

Stroop had the following SS units available to him to combat the uprising: The 1st and 2nd battalions of the 22nd SS Police Regiment, the 3rd battalion of the 23rd SS Police Regiment, the 3rd SS Panzergrenadier Training and Replacement battalion (this was the replacement battalion for the *Totenkopf* Division) and the SS Calvary Field Replacement Detachment (this was the replacement unit for the SS Calvary Division) (MacLean, 2001).

As with many German actions Stroop kept detailed reports as to the actions undertaken by the units under his control. These were then sent to Himmler to keep him informed of events. Stroop compiled a final report dated the 16th of May 1943 to catalogue his destruction of the ghetto and it is titled; "The Warsaw Ghetto is no more". It was tendered as an exhibit (document number 1061-PS) at Nuremberg and provides proof of Waffen-SS involvement and actions undertaken during the combat operations (Office of the United States Counsel for Prosecution of Axis Criminality, 1946: Vol 3:718). On page one of the report Stroop lists the daily average of troops in action during the conduct of the conflict (number of soldiers involved indicated as *officers/men*). Of interest is the involvement of the Waffen-SS.

> Waffen SS:
>
> SS Panzer Grenadier Training and Reserve Battalion 3, Warsaw   4/440 .
>
> SS Cav. Training and Res Bat. Warsaw   5/381
>
> (Office of the United States Counsel for Prosecution of Axis Criminality, 1946: Vol 3:718)

The Germans were better armed and better trained. The Jews could never hope to win such a one-sided fight, and they did not. From the start of the conflict Stroop makes it clear in his report that the hardest measures were used against the Jews:

> The resistance put up by the Jews and bandits could be broken only by relentlessly using all our force and energy by day and night. On 23 April 1943 the *Reichsführer-SS* issued through the Higher SS and Police Führer East at Cracow his order to complete the combing out of the Warsaw Ghetto with the greatest severity and relentless tenacity.
>
> (Office of the United States Counsel for Prosecution of Axis Criminality, 1946: Vol 3:725)

The fighting proved tough and hard, even for the soldiers of the Waffen-SS as Stroop recounts:

> Then the men of the Waffen SS, the Police or the *Wehrmacht* Engineers courageously climbed down the shafts to bring out the Jews and not infrequently they then stumbled over Jews already dead, or were shot at. It was always necessary to use smoke candles to drive out the Jews. Thus one day we opened 183 sewer entrance holes and at a fixed time lowered smoke candles into them, with the result that the bandits fled from what they believed to be gas to the centre of the former Ghetto, where they

could then be pulled out of the sewer holes there. A great number of Jews, who could not be counted, were exterminated by blowing up sewers and dug-outs.

(Office of the United States Counsel for Prosecution of Axis Criminality, 1946: Vol 3:725)

Eventually all the Jews were killed or evacuated from the Ghetto to the death camps. Stroop paid special homage to the troops of the Waffen-SS units and their resilience:

The longer the resistance lasted, the tougher the men of the Waffen SS, Police and *Wehrmacht* became; they fulfilled their duty indefatigably in faithful comradeship and stood together as models and examples of soldiers. Their duty hours often lasted from early morning until late at night. At night, search patrols with rags wound round their feet remained at the heels of the Jews and gave them no respite. Not infrequently they caught and killed Jews who used the night hours for supplementing their stores from abandoned dugouts and for contacting neighbouring groups or exchanging news with them.

(Office of the United States Counsel for Prosecution of Axis Criminality, 1946: Vol 3:726)

Stroop continues on and praises the dedication with which the Waffen-SS applied themselves to the destruction of the Jews of Warsaw;

Considering that the greater part of the men of the Waffen-SS had only been trained for three to four weeks before being assigned to this action, high credit should be given for the pluck, courage and devotion to duty which they showed ... Only through the continuous and untiring work of all involved did we succeed in catching a total of 56,065 Jews whose extermination can be proved. To this should be added the number of Jews who lost their lives in explosions or fires but whose numbers could not be ascertained.

(Office of the United States Counsel for Prosecution of Axis Criminality, 1946: Vol 3:726)

This report contains an interesting fact, that many of the SS soldiers had only been members of the Waffen-SS for some weeks. These were not the SS stormtroopers of the 1930s. Yet they were still prepared to undertake the massacre of unarmed civilians and fight with the most brutal of tactics. I believe that this provides strong evidence of the effect of the situation on individuals. When called upon these new recruits showed no hesitation in committing atrocities. Stroop went on to go into detail as to the killing wrought on the Jews:

Of the total of 56,065 Jews caught, about 7,000 were exterminated within the former Ghetto in the course of the large-scale action, and 6,929 by transporting them to T.II, which means 14,000 Jews were exterminated altogether. Beyond the number of 56,065 Jews an estimated number of 5,000 to 6,000 were killed by explosions or in fires.

(Office of the United States Counsel for Prosecution of Axis Criminality, 1946: Vol 3:727)

Despite the high numbers of killed only minimal weapons were located by the Germans. Stroop listed the *booty*, as he called it, that he recovered from the Jews.

7 Polish rifles, 1 Russian rifle, 1 German rifle, 59 pistols of various calibres

Several hundred hand grenades, including Polish and home-made ones

Several hundred incendiary bottles

Home-made explosives

Infernal machines with fuses

A large amount of explosives, ammunition for weapons of all calibres, including some machine-gun ammunition.

(Office of the United States Counsel for Prosecution of Axis Criminality, 1946: Vol 3:728)

It can be seen without doubt that obviously most of those killed were unarmed civilians. Some of the Waffen-SS soldiers such as Hugo Mielke of the 8th *Florian Geyer* Calvary Division were brought to trial for their crimes after the war.[25] Mielke was convicted and sentenced to life imprisonment for leading a destruction unit that set fire to houses and shot Jews as they tried to escape from being burnt alive (Ruter et al., 2004: Vol 3). SS General Paul Hausser was questioned in relation to the use of the Waffen-SS for combat duties behind the front lines, with reference to the Ghetto uprising:

HERR PELCKMANN: Apart from the accusation concerning the concentration-camps, the Prosecution further asserts that the Waffen-SS, on the basis of its training, was a particularly cruel military tool; and that is to be shown, allegedly, by the participation of the Waffen-SS men in the evacuation of the Warsaw Ghetto and, so says the Prosecution, in the violations of international law such as the murder of prisoners of war. Is that correct?

HAUSSER: I already testified, yesterday, that our training was not organised to that end, that our method of fighting was supervised and ordered by the Army, and that we did not gain prestige through cruel methods. The commanders who had personal pride in leading a clean fighting unit against the enemy saw to that. I learned only here of the participation of small units of the Waffen-SS in the evacuation of the Warsaw Ghetto or in the executions which took place in Bohemia and Moravia. This can only be a question of small details of replacement units, which were temporarily subordinated for a brief period of time.

(The International Military Tribunal, 1946: Vol 20:367)

Hausser raises an important point here that training and replacement battalions of the Waffen-SS formations were used for combat operations behind the lines when necessary. This was a result of Himmler gaining an agreement with the *Wehrmacht* in 1941 that these types of unit would remain under SS control. The result was that:

Himmler lost no time in scattering the SS replacement units all over German-occupied Europe, thus men who had been recruited for front-line service found themselves at times during their training period called upon to engage in 'police activities'. (Stein, 1966:47)

This ensured that Himmler would have a ready source of politically reliable troops available to deal ruthlessly with situations just such as the Ghetto uprising. The city of Warsaw would feature again in yet another terror campaign undertaken by the Waffen-SS.

The uprising of the Polish Home Army

On the 1st of August 1944 the Polish Home Army General Bor-Komorovski, with a force of between 35,000 and 50,000 partisans, attacked the Germans in Warsaw. The uprising was instigated as the Red Army was on the outskirts of Warsaw, however, the Russian offensive came to a stop outside the city and the Germans were able to direct all their attention to the insurgents. The conflict was to last for some 63 days before it was defeated. A number of Waffen-SS units took part in the combat against the Polish Home Army.

One such unit was the Waffen-SS *Sturm Brigade Rona* (also known as the Kaminski Brigade after its commander), which was formed in July 1944 from elements of the Russian People Freedom Army (RONA) (A. J. Munoz, 1997; Nafziger, 2001; Stein, 1966; Westwood, 2001). This unit would later form the 29th SS Grenadier Division, but would only exist for a short period of time. In June 1944 this unit came under the control of the *Reichsführer-SS* after being transferred from army control. The unit was sent to Warsaw to combat the uprising. Units of the *Totenkopf* and *Wiking* divisions were also used to suppress the uprising (Davies, 2003; Quarrie, 1981).

> A huge sweep through the forest was launched on the 27 September by three battalions of the Hermann Goering Panzer Division and the SS Panzer Divisions *Totenkopf* and *Wiking*, who acted like beaters in a grouse shoot. All the villages, which had given the insurgents shelter, were burned, all the male villagers shot. It was typical Nazi anti-partisan warfare. (Davies, 2003:397)

These Waffen-SS units came under the overall command of Waffen-SS General Bach-Zelewski. Here they engaged upon an orgy of slaughter and rape. The Kaminski Brigade entered a hospital for cancer patients and raped and killed most of the staff and patients. The actions of this brigade extended to shooting of innocent civilians in a carte-blanche fashion. So excessive were the tactics of the brigade that several sources claim that the SS lured the Brigade's commander Kaminski to a meeting and then executed him for his actions (Clark, 1965; MacLean, 1998; A. J. Munoz, 1997; Stein, 1966).

This, however, was not the only Waffen-SS unit present at the battle; nor was it the only one to commit atrocities. The Dirlewanger *SS-Sonderkommando* was also sent to the city and there it fought with its usual brutality and ruthlessness.

> During the defeat of the uprising, the Dirlewanger brigade burned prisoners alive with gasoline, impaled babies on bayonets and stuck them out of windows and hung women upside down from balconies... (MacLean, 1998:177)

Dirlewanger had a history of evil actions and would be amply suited to putting down the uprising with terror. It needs to be remembered that in war there will always be some form of harm inflicted to achieve the goals of the conflict. But generally the international laws regulating war seek to ensure that minimum or reasonable force is used to achieve these aims. Clearly the conduct of Dirlewanger would go outside these limits and could be claimed to be evil. As Himmler explained to Goebbels the purpose of this was to create such terror and sheer violence that the uprising would be stopped "... in a very few days" (Clark, 1965:391). To ensure this aim was achieved Hitler and Himmler issued an order to the commander of the SS forces in Warsaw, *SS-Obergruppenführer* Bach-Zelewski to undertake the following:

> Captured insurgents ought to be killed regardless of whether they are fighting in accordance of the Hague Convention or not. The part of the population not fighting, women and children, should likewise be killed. The whole town must be levelled to the ground... (MacLean, 1998:177).

During the conflict Dirlewanger's unit operated as part of a *Kampfgruppe* under the direct control of *SS-Gruppenführer* Heinz Reinefarth, who was later to command the 18th SS Corps. While under his command the Dirlewanger unit "...used crowds of women and children as human shields while advancing on rebel strong points" (MacLean, 1998:188). For his command during the Warsaw conflict Reinefarth was awarded the Oak leaves to his Knight's Cross. Dirlewanger was also rewarded for his actions during the conflict by being awarded Germany's highest military honour, the Knight's Cross, on the 30th of September 1944 (MacLean, 1998; Schneider, 1993).

Yet despite men from this unit being awarded Germany's highest military awards, many Waffen-SS veterans simply ignored the unit's existence when writing their memoirs. Dirlewanger's recommendation for the award referred to him as belonging to the "... bravest of the brave" and was warmly supported by *SS-Obergruppenführer* Bach-Zelewski (MacLean, 1998:195). One would wonder how the killing of innocent civilians could be deemed brave. Bach-Zelewski offered a different version, however, while giving evidence before the IMT.

> DR. THOMA: If I understood you correctly, you disapproved of the manner in which the fighting against partisans was carried on, involving many innocent people; and you disapproved also of the existence of the Dirlewanger Regiment...
>
> BACH-ZELEWSKI: Yes.
>
> (The International Military Tribunal, 1946: Vol 4:493)

SS-Obergruppenführer **Bach-Zelewski.**

A German officer offered a different view when he recounted how he had told Bach-Zelewski that the executions were a waste of resources, "Bach-Zelewski voiced his opposition to this notion and stated he was fulfilling a duty to the fatherland" (Klee et al., 1988:122). Bach-Zelewski's inaccurate memory did not end there. He was awarded the Knight's Cross also on 30th of September 1944 for his leadership during the crushing of the rebellion. However, when asked about this before the tribunal he claimed the following.

> BACH-ZELEWSKI: No. I received no decoration for the war against the partisans. I received all my decorations, beginning with the clusters to the Iron Cross II, at the front and from the Wehrmacht...
>
> (The International Military Tribunal, 1946: Vol 4:493)

Dirlewanger and his unit were a military abnormality by any standards. During the defence of Hungary in 1944, Colonel-General Friessner noted the following when he visited Dirlewanger's unit:

> When I reached Dirlewanger's staff I was met by a strange sight. The *Brigadeführer*, a not very appealing adventurer type, was sitting at his desk with a live monkey perched on his shoulder. The monkey was said to have accompanied him everywhere, including Poland. When I discovered that the staff was packing up I ordered them to stay on the spot. The unit was, as suggested before, a wild bunch. One company, communists who were expected to prove themselves on the front, had just deserted to the enemy. (Ungvary, 2005:30)

The uprising was subsequently defeated, but surprisingly given the ferocity with which the Waffen-SS had treated the general population the remnants of the Polish Home Army were treated as POWs when they surrendered. When queried by the prosecution at Nuremberg in relation to the role of the Waffen-SS in this conflict, *SS-Oberstgruppenführer* Paul Hausser attempted to deny that the Waffen-SS had any involvement:

> MAJOR JONES: ...Those were crimes of the SS, were they not, Witness?
>
> HAUSSER: That was not the Waffen-SS. They are always only a group of men who belonged to Himmler and who had nothing whatsoever to do with the fighting troops. We never fought at Warsaw.
>
> MAJOR JONES: Are you denying that the Waffen-SS took part in the destruction of Warsaw?
>
> HAUSSER: I have not been there and therefore I cannot make any comments. But to my knowledge, there was no fighting there; it was a riot, which was quelled, as several witnesses have testified.
>
> MAJOR JONES: It was a revolt and then the mass extermination by the SS troops; that's what happened in Warsaw, wasn't it?

HAUSSER: The Waffen-SS participated only to a very small extent because the Waffen-SS was in combat.

(The International Military Tribunal, 1946: Vol 20:382)

The evidence of this discussion would suggest otherwise.

Other examples of the Waffen-SS ethos in combat

In this section I intend to provide some general examples of the actions of the Waffen-SS in combat. I do not intend to account every atrocity committed, but rather provide the reader with an appreciation of the ethos of the Waffen-SS as indicated by the actions of the soldiers themselves. During the battle of Taganrog soldiers of the *SS Leibstandarte* located six of their fellows who had been mutilated and tortured. The discovery of the men's bodies was made on the 28th of March 1942, when the remains were located in the former GPU[26] building in Taganrog. The following are the results of the autopsies performed on the men:

> ... *Sturmann* Gehrken had four fingers of his right hand missing. His skull was shattered, but there were no gunshot wounds to the body. *Sturmann* Lippke had been shot in the right temple. *Sturmann* Schwillinsky had a shattered skull and no gunshot wounds were found. *Sturmann* Steiner had a shattered skull and broken spine, no gunshot wounds. *SS-Mann* Plotz had a broken spine and shattered left rid cage. No gunshot wounds. (Mooney, 2004:87)

As a result the commander of the Division, *SS-Oberstgruppenführer* Sepp Dietrich, ordered that no Russian prisoners be taken for the next three days (Quarrie, 1991; Reitlinger, 1957; Stein, 1966; Weingartner, 1974; Wykes, 1974). This resulted in some 4000 Russian soldiers being executed (Quarrie, 1991; Reitlinger, 1957; Stein, 1966; Weingartner, 1974; Wykes, 1974). Of note is that Article 23 of the Hague Conventions forbids the declaration that no quarter will be given. By an objective assessment the actions of the Waffen-SS would seem to indicate that they are outside the norm of acceptable behaviour.

The Waffen-SS was to feature far more prominently in war crime reports than their small numbers would suggest. A report by the General Office of the *Wehrmacht* in 1943 into the commission of war crimes concluded that; "... in the period covered by this report 151 cases of this nature came to notice. In 19 cases the culprits' belonged to the army, in 53 cases to the Waffen-SS, while in 79 cases the culprits units could not be established" (Hohne, 1969:470). Clearly the ethos of hardness and no pity for the enemy stood the Waffen-SS out and above the *Wehrmacht* when it came to the commission of war crimes.

During the trials of the IMT evidence was offered as to Waffen-SS complicity in the shooting of civilians. This evidence came in the form of a letter from the Chief of the Command Office of the Waffen-SS to the *Reichsführer-SS*, dated 14 October 1941; subject: "Intermediate Report on Civilian State of Emergency". The letter clearly outlined the types of actions that were being undertaken on the Eastern Front:

> I deliver the following interim report regarding the commitment of the Waffen-SS in the Protectorate Bohemia and Moravia during the civilian state of emergency. In turn all battalions of the Waffen-SS in the Protectorate Bohemia and Moravia were assigned to shootings and hangings. Up till now there occurred in Prague 99 shootings and 21 hangings, in Brünn 54 shootings and 17 hangings; total: 191 executions (including 16 Jews). A complete report regarding other measures and on the conduct of the officers, non-commissioned officers and men will be made following the termination of the civilian state of emergency. (The International Military Tribunal, 1946 Vol 4:221)

This would not be the first nor the last time the Waffen-SS would be used to put down uprisings in conquered territories. In August 1944 a rebellion rose up in Slovakia against the puppet government of President Joseph Tiso. To quell this uprising units of the 14th SS *Galicia* Division, the 18th SS *Horst Wessel* Division and *Einsatzgruppen* H were utilised by the HSSPF for the area, Waffen-SS General *SS-Obergruppenführer* Hermann Höfle (Bender et al., 1975). It was put down with the usual Nazi efficiency and harshness. The units of the 14th Division came under the direct command of *SS-Obersturmbannführer* Friedrich Beyersdorff; he was to lead his units in the commission of a number of atrocities that will be discussed shortly.

As the war came to an end many soldiers of the Waffen-SS committed what are termed final-phase crimes. For instance in early 1945 a soldier from the 12th SS Panzer Division *Hitlerjugend* shot two Russian labourers for allegedly threatening a German woman[27] (Ruter et al., 2004: Vol 13). Waffen-SS soldiers executed some 151 Russian labourers on the basis of danger to the German people due to German troops having to withdraw in 1945 from the advancing Russian army[28] (Ruter et al., 2004: Vol 16).

The actions of the Waffen-SS were not solely directed at the enemy, other Germans also fell foul of the brutal tactics of these soldiers. An exam-

ple of this occurred in April 1945 at Baden in Austria, where members of
the Waffen-SS *Jagdverband Süd* shot two German soldiers and a priest for
making derogatory remarks about the crumbling German military situation[29] (Ruter et al., 2004:Vol 2). These cases highlight that even up to the
end of the war Waffen-SS units were prepared to commit atrocities. Fried-
helm Busse, a veteran of the SS *Hitlerjugend* Panzer Division, offers the
following insight into why the Waffen-SS were so prepared to kill their own
country-men in the final days. He recounts an execution he witnessed of
Germans.

> We stood there in the square and the sentence was read out. And all of a
> sudden the barrels were kicked away and they dangled there. And I must
> say that my feelings at the time were that the pigs deserved to hang
> because they stabbed us in the back. You don't give up in war, you don't
> sabotage, you have to do your duty until the end. (Halliley, 2003)

This attitude was reflected by SS soldiers of the SS *Hitlerjugend* who
shot a civilian for calling them war prolongers[30] (Ruter et al., 2004: Vol 13).
Another example of Waffen-SS atrocities can be found in the actions of *SS-
Oberführer* Dirlewanger who commanded an *SS-Sonderkommando* on the
Eastern Front that was responsible for the hunting down of Jews and Russ-
ian partisans:

> Then he made so-called scientific experiments, which involved stripping
> the victims of their clothes. Then they (the victims) were given an injec-
> tion of strychnine. Dirlewanger looked on, smoked a cigarette, as did his
> friends, and they saw how these girls were dying. Immediately after that
> the corpses were cut into small pieces, mixed with horsemeat and boiled
> into soap. (MacLean, 1998:61)

As the IMT surmised, it was not surprising that units of the Waffen-SS
and the branches that had thus been employed in extermination actions and
in the execution of civilians were also to be found violating the laws of warfare when carrying on ordinary combat operations. For the Waffen-SS the
law of war did not hold sway on the Eastern Front. Rather this was an ideological crusade that had to be won at any cost. It was for this reason that
the Waffen-SS were feared opponents and highly respected for their combat value on the Eastern Front. But it was in the anti-partisan role that the
Waffen-SS would reveal its true brutality. It is behind the front lines that a
more menacing picture of the Waffen-SS appears.

4. Anti-partisan and Einsatzgruppen operations

If the reputation of the Waffen-SS was sullied in the maelstrom of front line combat on the Eastern front, it was to be destroyed in the conflict that went on behind the front lines. For it was here that the soldiers of the Waffen-SS could give full vent to their political and ideological fanaticism. Under the auspices of the anti-partisan operations, and by contributing to the *Einsatzgruppen,* the Waffen-SS would irretrievably link itself to the crime of genocide.

The Partisan problem and the German response

The conflict with the partisans on the Eastern Front served to unleash a barbaric conflict in areas behind the front lines. Orders such at the one issued by General Von Reichenau (regarding conduct of the troops on the Eastern Front) accused the Jews of being behind the ever-increasing partisan attacks that the German forces were experiencing in rear areas. This was a common accusation made by the German authorities and served as an excuse under which to conduct their extermination program. There is little evidence to support such accusations and in fact much to the contrary. A member of the German Military Economics Department in the Ukraine prepared a report on the Jews and commented that "… there was no evidence that they were widely engaged in sabotage and similar acts, nor that they could be considered to represent a threat to the German *Wehrmacht*" (Krausnick et al., 1965:65).

In his directive 33A dated the 22nd July 1941 Hitler had given the go ahead for German forces to act outside the law of war in the conduct of partisan warfare. This was confirmed during by the evidence of Waffen-SS General Bach-Zelewski:

> COL. TAYLOR: Was an order ever issued by the highest authorities, that German soldiers who committed offences against the civilian population were not to be punished in the military courts?

BACH-ZELEWSKI: Yes, this order was issued.

COL. TAYLOR: Was this order an obstacle to correcting the excesses of the troops?

BACH-ZELEWSKI: Yes, in my opinion this order prevented the orderly conduct of operations, since one can train troops only if one has adequate disciplinary powers and jurisdiction over them and is able to check excesses.

(The International Military Tribunal, 1946 Vol 4:479)

Hitler already recognised that having sufficient manpower to manage the captured territory was going to be a problem. To circumnavigate this he authorised an order outlining the action to be taken:

> The troops available for securing the conquered Eastern Territories will, in view of the size of this area, be sufficient for their duties only if the occupying power meets resistance, not by legal punishment of the guilty, but by striking such terror into the population that it loses all will to resist … The Commanders concerned are to be held responsible … they will contrive to contain order, not by requesting reinforcements, but by employing suitably draconian methods. (Trevor-Roper, 1964:144)

This order was given only a month after the invasion of Russia commenced and it is clear evidence that Hitler sought to fight the war outside the normal bounds of conflict and that he expected his soldiers to do likewise. Examples of the Waffen-SS carrying out such draconian measures are found in reprisal shootings they conducted in retaliation for casualties they suffered. The following is an extract from a report by SS-*Sturmbannführer* Breimeier,[31] who was the commander of a battalion in the *Prinz Eugen* Division:

> On 3 November 1943, around 2000 hours, a German soldier on the Velika Street in Sinj was ambushed and killed. Since, despite all efforts, the culprit has not been found and the population has not supported us in this matter, 24 civilians will be shot and one hanged. The sentence will be carried out on 5 November 1943 at 0530 hours. —Signed— Breimeier, *SS Sturmbannführer* and Battalion Commander

(The International Military Tribunal, 1946: Vol 20:402)

SS-Brigadeführer Otto Kumm had this to say about reprisals in his history of the 7th SS *Prinz Eugen* Division.

> Their activities (the partisans) were made possible by sympathetic elements of the local population. It was, therefore, necessary for the troops to take measures against these through local reprisals, in order to ensure

that the partisans did not maintain the initiative. However, the soldiers disdained actions against the local population. So such operations were only carried out when necessary. (Kumm, 1995:268)

Exactly what *necessary* situations entailed is open to conjecture, but there can be little doubt that the Waffen-SS utilised reprisals as terror tactics in the fight against the partisans on a widespread scale. In response to the assassination of *SS-Obergruppenführer* Reinhard Heydrich in Prague in 1942 Waffen-SS general, *SS-Obergruppenführer* Karl-Hermann Frank, ordered SS forces to destroy the villages of Lidice and Lezaky with over 1,300 people being killed. Frank issued the following specific instructions:

> All adult inhabitants are to be shot. All females are to be evacuated to a concentration camp. The children are to be collected together, if capable of Germanisation, they are to be delivered to SS families in the Reich, and the rest are to undergo a different education. The place is to be burnt and razed to the ground. (Miller, Schulz, & McCanliss, 2006:359)

The euphemism of different education can only intone the murder of innocent children. In 1943 Waffen-SS soldiers from the *Nordland* Division came under fire while performing anti-partisan duties in Yugoslavia, with the result that they attacked a village "... and finding no adult men there they apparently killed the inhabitants" (Christensen et al., 2003:13). Such reprisal actions were considered in the *Einsatzgruppen* trial where the relevant law of war was applied by the NMT. They found that the actions of the SS in reprisals were unjustified in that there was a lack of nexus between the acts and the victims of the reprisals:

> While generally the persons who become victims of the reprisals are admittedly innocent of the acts against which the reprisal is to retaliate, there must at least be such close connection between these persons and these acts as to constitute a joint responsibility.
>
> Article 50 of the Hague Regulations states unequivocally —
>
> "No general penalty, pecuniary or otherwise, shall be inflicted upon the population on account of the acts of individuals for which they cannot be regarded as *jointly and severally* responsible."
>
> (Nuremberg Military Tribunal, 1946: Vol 4:493)

That many of the reprisals conducted by the SS were disproportionate to the original act was also noted by the NMT. Waffen-SS General, *SS-Obergruppenführer* Erich Bach-Zelewski gave evidence at the IMT as to the severity in which the anti-partisan operations were conducted. At the end of 1942 Bach-Zelewski was appointed Chief of Anti-partisan Combat Units on the Eastern Front and he reported directly to Himmler.

COL. TAYLOR: Did the highest military leaders issue instructions that anti-partisan operations were to be conducted with severity?

BACH-ZELEWSKI: Yes.

COL. TAYLOR: Did the highest military authorities issue any detailed instructions as to the methods to be used in anti-partisan operations?

BACH-ZELEWSKI: No.

COL. TAYLOR: What was the result, in the occupied territories, of this lack of detailed directives from above?

BACH-ZELEWSKI: This lack of detailed directives resulted in a wild state of anarchy in all anti-partisan operations.

COL. TAYLOR: In your opinion, were the measures taken in anti-partisan operations far more severe than the circumstances warranted, or were they not?

BACH-ZELEWSKI: Since there were no definite orders and the lower commanders were forced to act independently, the operations varied according to the character of the officer in command and the quality of the troops. I am of the opinion that the operations often not only failed in their purpose but even overshot their mark.

COL. TAYLOR: Did these measures result in the unnecessary killing of large numbers of the civilian population?

BACH-ZELEWSKI: Yes

(The International Military Tribunal, 1946 Vol 4:479)

The above testimony highlights two important facets of the conflict on the Eastern Front. First unlawful actions by German soldiers were approved by higher authorities; and second as previously mentioned the removal of such actions from judicial review or punishment. As such the conduct of anti-partisan warfare by the Germans was an integral part of the war of annihilation and exploitation that was the campaign against the Soviet Union. The Waffen-SS also had the benefit that even though its units might be serving with the Armed Forces, they were not subject to its military justice. The Waffen-SS came under the control of the SS in relation to personnel, training, replacements and military justice. The obvious point being here that given the ideology of the SS this was tacit approval for atrocities as long as they fell within the goals and aims of the SS.

This is evidenced by a statement of Hitler where he responded to Stalin's call for Red Army soldiers to become partisans if trapped behind enemy lines. Hitler argued that "… this partisan warfare gives us an advantage by enabling us to destroy everything in our path … in this vast area, peace must be imposed as quickly as possible and to achieve this it is necessary to execute even anyone who doesn't give us a straight look" (Buchler, 1986:14). A further example of this is an order, which was issued to the SS *Wiking* Division just prior to the invasion that stated civilians could be shot without trial as partisans (Smith et al., 1999).

To be fair it was not the case that brutality was only used on one side. The partisans in fact used various tactics in an effort to incite the German forces to greater crimes. One standard tactic of the partisans was to attack German forces then withdraw into a nearby village, with the expectation that the Germans would attend the village and carry out reprisal killings that would "...create even more partisans" (Heaton, 2001:111; Lucas, 1991). This annihilation was made all the easier by the tactics used by the partisans and the Germans in reprisal. As *SS-Brigadeführer* Otto Kumm commented, this type of action had predictable results.

> Naturally the destruction of villages, killing people even if proven to be partisans, rapidly destroyed our credibility, and increased the resistance against us ... What was perhaps the worst thing for us was the narrow-minded approach we as a collective military body used in handling these problems. The lessons should have been learned much sooner, but unfortunately they were not. (Heaton, 2001:128)

A Waffen-SS officer gives a further example of the provocative action by the partisans. He recovered the bodies of a number of German soldiers after a partisan attack on a *Wehrmacht* convoy. "The partisans had first shot them, and immediately afterwards mutilated or stripped them. As we found the murdered soldiers belongings in one of the isbas, it was a clear-cut affair..." (Trang, 2000:89). The SS then identified and executed the suspected partisans; of interest is that upon returning to the train a *Wehrmacht* officer asked why the whole village was not shot, after all guilt was not a prerequisite for punishment on the Eastern Front. The partisans were not averse to dealing ruthlessly with SS men who fell into their grasp. The Bielski Partisan group was mainly made of Jews. In his account of the group Tec (1993) outlines the fate of three captured SS men. One witness recalled that the following:

> I will never forget it, how on their knees the SS men were begging for their lives. They pleaded for mercy because they had children and wives at home. They swore that they're not to blame for anything that had happened to the Jews ... Then two partisans came out leading a tall, blond German, hands tied behind his back ... The first to reach the SS man was Pupko, the oldest man in the otriad ... With knife in hand, Pupko screamed: "God, my grandfather was not a murderer, my father was not a

murderer, but I will be a murderer"...As if in a trance this main actor began the job of cutting up the SS man ... In a few intense, highly charged moments the SS man was unrecognisable and dead. The other two were shot. (Tec, 1993:197)

To counter the activities of the partisans the Germans, in particular the Waffen-SS, resorted to a brutal doctrine of counterinsurgency activity. These brutal tactics extended to the taking of hostages and shooting of innocent civilians in reprisal for acts of terrorism and sabotage. For example, on the 23rd of August 1941 the SS Calvary Brigade entered the town of Starobin in Russia and took the following action:

> The tension by now was extreme: the new mayor was killed by three Jews and during the night the partisans tried to burn down many houses. Waldemar Fegelein[32] ordered all male Jews in the area to be shot in reprisal. Altogether 21 persons were executed. (Trang, 2000:35)

The use of this doctrine, while helping to ensure survival of the Waffen-SS units, also contributed to the Russian civilians joining the partisans in response to the actions of the Germans. The doctrine utilised by the Germans also had the result of "... enhancing the legendary brutality that would be attributed..." to various Waffen-SS units (Heaton, 2001:117). The majority of Waffen-SS divisions had some involvement in fighting partisans and the associated atrocities committed during such.

By late 1942 partisan activity had reached such significant levels that Hitler felt obliged to issue a directive detailing how this menace was to be combated. He issued directive 46 on the 18th of August 1942 and in it he outlined the action to be taken and the command role the SS was to play in the fight against the partisans:

> In recent months banditry in the East has assumed intolerable proportions, and threatens to become a serious danger to supplies for the front and to the economic exploitation of the country ... The following measures are necessary. 1. Rapid, drastic and active operations against the bandits by the co-ordination of all available forces of the Armed Forces, the SS and Police which are suitable for the purpose... (Trevor-Roper, 1964:198)

Hitler went on to outline the type of principles that he expected his armed forces to use in the fight against the partisans.

> The fight against banditry is as much a matter of strategy as the fight against the enemy at the front. It will therefore be organised and carried

out by the same staffs. The destruction of the bandits calls for active operations and the most rigorous measures against all members of the gangs
or those guilty of supporting them ... In this struggle against the bandits
the co-operation of the local population is indispensable. Deserving persons should not be parsimoniously treated; rewards should be really
attractive. On the other hand, reprisals for action in support of the bandits
must be all the more severe. (Trevor-Roper, 1964:198)

To carry this fight to the partisans Hitler entrusted it to his loyal fol-
lower Himmler, and his Higher SS and Police Leaders (HSSPF).

The *Reichsführer-SS* and the Chief of the German Police is the central
authority for the collection and evaluation of all information concerning
action against the bandits. In addition, the *Reichsführer-SS* has the sole
responsibility for combating banditry in the Reich Commissioners territories ... Higher SS and Police Leaders will if necessary assume temporary command of forces of the Armed Forces for use in their operations.
(Trevor-Roper, 1964:199)

Just how seriously Hitler and Himmler took the fight against the partisans is shown by the creation in 1944 of the Anti-partisan War Badge for all
soldiers who took part in such activities for a certain number of days. This
shows that the military campaign against the partisans was seen an important contribution to the overall military effort. It is of interest that numerous Waffen-SS officers involved in the fight against the partisans were
awarded the highest German Military honours. *SS-Obergruppenführer*
Bach-Zelewski was awarded the Knight's Cross for the suppression of the
Warsaw Rising in 1944. Prior to this he had been awarded the Iron Cross 1st
and 2nd Class and the German Cross in Gold for his actions against the partisans (Schneider, 1993; Yerger, 1997). *SS-Oberführer* Oskar Dirlewanger
was awarded the Knight's Cross in 1944 and had also been awarded the Iron
Cross 1st and 2nd Class and the German Cross in Gold for his actions
(Schneider, 1993; Yerger, 1997). *SS-Gruppenführer* Hermann Fegelein was
awarded the Knight's Cross in 1942 with the later addition of Oak leaves in
1942, and swords in 1944. As well as this he had been awarded the Iron
Cross 1st and 2nd Class and the German Cross in Gold (Schneider, 1993).
SS-Obergruppenführer Friedrich Jeckeln received the Knight's Cross in
1944 with that later addition of Oak leaves in 1945. As well as this he was
awarded the Iron Cross 1st and 2nd Class and the German Cross in Gold
(Schneider, 1993; Yerger, 1997). The majority of the awards were issued at
the time of these officers performing anti-partisan duties.

The 8th *Florian Geyer* Division, an anti-partisan unit, had more Knight's Crosses awarded than front-line Panzer divisions such as the 12th *Hitlerjugend*, the 9th *Hohenstaufen*, the 10th *Frundsberg* and the 23rd *Nederland*. A number of anti-partisan units had substantial numbers of the Knight's Crosses awarded. These included the *Florian Geyer* Division with 23,[33] *Prinz Eugen* Division with six, *Handschar* Division with four and the *Maria Theresa* Division with six (Simpson, 1990; Williamson, 1994). These were the highest military accolades that Germany could confer; they were also the same accolades that the recipients from the front line units received.

For the purpose of this discussion I will adopt the definition used by Heaton and define a partisan as being "... an irregular force politically motivated into paramilitary action against an armed external aggressor, imbued with limited military or paramilitary capabilities and dedicated to waging unconventional warfare through small localised units on an individual level as well as collective basis" (Heaton, 2001:18). *SS-Gruppenführer* Hermann Fegelein, the commander of the units that would become the 8th SS Calvary Division *Florian Geyer*, offers the following insight into combat operations against partisans in Russia:

> The enemy forces were always wiped out when they were made up of regular Russian Army troops. The greatest difficulties were posed by the partisans. Militarily they were the biggest threat to be found behind a fighting army. Ruthless, brave up to the moment of annihilation, with Asian cruelty. (Trang, 2000:35)

It was for this reason that Fegelein could report the following divisional results in 1943. In May and June 1943 Operation *Vistula* was conducted, Fegelein reported some 4,018 persons killed, the deportation of 18,860 labourers, the confiscation of 21,000 head of cattle and the destruction of 61 villages in the area southwest of Gomel. During Operation *Zeithen* conducted in June 1943 Fegelein destroyed some 63 villages and was in personal contact with Hitler who instructed him to neutralise all partisans found. During Operation *Seydlitz* Fegelein reported some 96 villages destroyed, 5,106 persons killed, 9,166 persons deported and the confiscation of 19,941 head of cattle (Miller et al., 2006:313).

It was in the combat against the partisan groups that the Waffen-SS began to fight with extreme brutality.

> For the first time during the Russian campaign the *Totenkopf* division's records mention the shooting of civilians and indicate that when SSTK units encountered groups of partisans or suspects no prisoners were taken. (Sydnor, 1990:201).

Indeed it was clear that the conflict with the partisans was used as an excuse for the annihilation of Jewry and Slavism. A number of SS Death's Head regiments (*Totenkopf* Standarten) came under the personal command of Himmler where they were used for the fight against partisans which was a convenient cloak under which the SS could cleanse the occupied Eastern Territories of all political, intellectual and racial enemies. The brutality extended to murder of innocent civilians and destruction of villages. Substantial operations were carried out where the populations of suspect areas were simply rounded up and shipped out as slave labour. In January 1943 *SS-Sonderkommando* Dirlewanger conducted an anti-partisan operation in the Minsk area where "*SS-Sturmbannführer* Magill ordered the battalion to round up all persons in the area between the ages of 16 and 50 who were fit for work- they would be shipped off to Germany as slave labour" (MacLean, 1998:107).

The 2nd SS Panzer Division *Das Reich* developed an infamous reputation for dealing out of hand with suspected partisans or guerrillas. *SS-Hauptsturmführer* Hans Hossfelder, an officer of the *Das Reich* Division, related in a post-war interview the situation faced by Waffen-SS soldiers as they saw it:

> Many people have often wondered if we actually had standing orders to shoot women and children, and I know that there have been many denials regarding this by former SS members. However, it was unfortunately true. I can state that the types of orders were not as commonplace in my unit as in others, obviously. When we speak about partisans, it must be understood that these were of course criminals even according to the Geneva and Hague Conventions, since they forfeited their non-combatant status upon taking up arms against us. Our handling of these people was considered within our right, although there were many excesses and outright war crimes committed against innocent people. This cannot be completely overlooked. (Heaton, 2001:127)

This opinion would not seem to be supported by Articles 1 and 2 of the Hague Conference of 1907, Laws and Customs of War on Land (Hague IV); October 18, 1907, which outline the duties and regulations respecting the laws and customs of war on land regarding belligerents:

> Article 1.
>
> The laws, rights, and duties of war apply not only to armies, but also to militia and volunteer corps fulfilling the following conditions:
>
> To be commanded by a person responsible for his subordinates;
>
> To have a fixed distinctive emblem recognisable at a distance;

To carry arms openly; and

To conduct their operations in accordance with the laws and customs of war.

In countries where militia or volunteer corps constitute the army, or form part of it, they are included under the denomination "army".

Art. 2.

The inhabitants of a territory, which has not been occupied, who, on the approach of the enemy, spontaneously take up arms to resist the invading troops without having had time to organise themselves in accordance with Article 1, shall be regarded as belligerents if they carry arms openly and if they respect the laws and customs of war.

I see the Hague Conventions useful in that they can be used to form the basis of an objective assessment of actions. Heaton contends that it was the failure of some irregular forces to comply with the identification requirements that caused them to be exposed to the full extent of German retaliation. While this may be legally acceptable it certainly does not extend to the shooting of hostages, killing of civilians, the destruction of property and the shooting of suspected partisans without trial, which was the norm on the Eastern Front. Furthermore, the assumption here is that people had actually carried out the crimes for which they had been executed; direct evidence indicates that such accusations of criminality were simply manufactured by the Germans. The judges of the NMT considered the question of partisans in the *Einsatzgruppen* case and they arrived at the following conclusion when considering the relevant sections of The Hague Conventions and the actions of the SS:

> It is unnecessary to point out that, under these provisions, an armed civilian found in a treetop sniping at uniformed soldiers is not such a lawful combatant and can be punished even with the death penalty if he is proved guilty of the offence. But this is far different from saying that resistance fighters in the war against an invading army, if they fully comply with the conditions just mentioned, can be put outside the law by the adversary. As The Hague Regulations state expressly, if they fulfil the four conditions, "the laws, rights, and duties of war" apply to them in the same manner as they apply to regular armies. Many of the defendants seem to assume that by merely characterising a person a partisan, he may be shot out of hand. But it is not so simple as that. If the partisans are organised and are engaged in what international law regards as legitimate warfare for the defence of their own country, they are entitled to be protected as combatants. The record shows that in many of the areas where the *Einsatzgruppen* operated, the so-called partisans had wrested considerable territory from the German occupant, and that military combat action of some

dimensions was required to reoccupy those areas. In belligerent occupation the occupying power does not hold enemy territory by virtue of any
legal right. On the contrary, it merely exercises a precarious and temporary actual control. This can be seen from Article 42 of the Hague Regulations which grants certain well-limited rights to a military occupant only
in enemy territory which is "actually placed" under his control. The lan-
guage used in the official German reports, received in evidence in this
case, show, however, that combatants were indiscriminately punished only
for having fought against the enemy. This is contrary to the law of war.
(Nuremberg Military Tribunal, 1946: Vol 4:492)

Another Waffen-SS veteran, *SS-Sturmbannführer* Rudolf von Falken-
hahn claimed "I rarely met soldiers regardless of rank who actively pursued
non-combatants. I did see it happen and it was wrong..." (Heaton,
2001:135). The above comment seems confusing to say the least. On one
hand the officer is saying he knew no-one who committed atrocities, but he
then says that he saw them being committed. Otto Kumm, while an officer
of the *Das Reich* Division, related how in one fight with partisans near
Kharkov in February 1943 soldiers of the *Der Führer* Regiment stormed a
barn containing partisans and killed or captured the entire force. Those captured were summarily shot, a decision, which Kumm claimed, he disagreed
with (Heaton, 2001:142). It is of note that Kumm would later go on to command one of the most brutal anti-partisan formations, the SS *Prinz Eugen*
Division (Bender & Taylor, 1972; Heaton, 2001; Kumm, 1995; Westwood,
2001). Clearly there was a role played by the Waffen-SS in combating the
partisan threat. Let us now examine this role.

The role of the Waffen-SS

Leading Waffen-SS General, Paul Hausser, when asked about the role
of the Waffen-SS in anti-partisan operations, denied that they were
involved:

> HERR PELCKMANN: Witness, was the Waffen-SS a special fighting
> unit for the combating of partisans, and was the fight against the partisans
> considered to be a war of extermination?

> HAUSSER: The fight against partisans is a general military and political
> police measure, which can be assigned to any troop; front-line troops of
> the Army and of the Waffen-SS were used only in exceptional cases, for
> instance when they were in the rear areas. There were usually no partisan
> fights in the operational areas; they mostly took place in the rear areas
> only. This fighting was mainly the task of the Security Division of the

Army and special defence battalions, and besides these of police troops. Units of the Waffen-SS at the front were not especially trained for this kind of fighting and were assigned this duty just as little as Panzer divisions of the Army, for instance. In the East, units of my divisions were never used in the fight against partisans at any time. Therefore it was not a special task for SS units, and they were not especially trained or instructed for this purpose.

(The International Military Tribunal, 1946: Vol 20:365)

The Führer seemed to have other ideas. At a military conference on the 1ˢᵗ of December 1942 he was talking about the partisan problem with his generals. The conversation lead to the use of the Waffen-SS and the appointment of Waffen-SS General Bach-Zelewski to head anti-partisan operations. Hitler had the following to say:

It *(the SS)³⁴* has more experience. Listen to what is being said about the SS, because it has this experience. They are always saying that the SS acts brutally ... Bach-Zelewski is one of the cleverest people. Even in the party, I used to always use him for the most difficult things. If the Communist resistance couldn't be broken somewhere, I took him there and he smashed it. (Heiber et al., 2003)

By the end of 1944 the Germans had been driven out of Russia and the need for a higher anti-partisan command was made redundant. Bach-Zelewski later commented that the corps staff from the 14ᵗʰ SS Corps "consisted mainly of the personnel of the former operational staff of the Chief of the anti-partisan formations" (Bach-Zelewski, 1946:2). This would not be the only transfer of Waffen-SS soldiers to and from anti-partisan duties.

The use of the Waffen-SS as both the conductor and orchestra for anti-partisan operations led to a series of campaigns in 1942-43 that were conducted so brutally and ruthlessly that nothing living was left in vital communications zones. The claim that the fighting units of the Waffen-SS were not involved with extermination actions can be rejected. *SS-Obergruppenführer* Kurt Knoblauch was appointed to the staff of the *Reichsführer-SS* as the chief of the Waffen-SS Command branch in July 1942. Knoblauch had previously served in the *Totenkopf* Division in 1940 (Westwood, 2001). Himmler gave him the role of co-ordinating support for the army "... with the SS and to provide all Higher SS and Police Leaders in the East with SS units as needed" (MacLean, 1998:77). These units were available to the HSSPF who were responsible for extermination measures being carried out in occupied areas (Littman, 2003; Padfield, 1990; Reitlinger, 1957). As noted by Stein "... there were many other occasions when field units of the Waffen-SS were employed against partisans, suspected partisans, or ordinary civilians who had the misfortune of being proscribed under Nazi racial policies" (Stein, 1966:275).

For example one rear area company of the *Das Reich* division helped "to massacre 920 Jews at Lachoisk, near Minsk" as part of an extermination operation (Reitlinger, 1957:169). In July 1941 the 4th SS *Polizei* Division as part of Army Group North was confronted by an alleged serious partisan problem, which resulted in a "decisive and ruthless response" (Heaton, 2001:123). In May 1944 the *Germania* Regiment, which was part of the *Wiking* Division, took part in operation *Maigewitter*, "… the goal of which was the liquidation of the Peoples Army (AL) partisan divisions in the Parczew forest" (Solarz, 2003:55). *SS-Obergruppenführer* Lothar Debes recalled how units of the 6th SS Mountain Division *Nord* were "… committed against the partisan troops who were threatening the supply from the north" (Debes, 1947:16). *SS-Brigadeführer* Otto Kumm confirmed in his post-war interrogation by the US Army that the 7th SS Division *Prinz Eugen* was used extensively in 1944/45 to combat partisans in Yugoslavia (Kumm, 1947).

Waffen-SS units were heavily involved in combating the partisan problem on the Eastern Front and its occupied territories. Due to the vast expanses of Russia there were insufficient German security forces to deal with the partisan threat, in response front line units were called upon to assist with security operations and these units were primarily Waffen-SS. In fact some units such as the 8th SS Calvary Division *Florian Geyer* were specifically created and designed for the anti-partisan role. The 14th Waffen-Grenadier Division, also know as the *Galicia* Division, was constituted mainly of Ukrainian volunteers. It was formed primarily to be a police formation (Bender et al., 1975; Dmytryshyn, 1956; Littman, 2003). The German Order Police were asked by *SS-Obergruppenführer* Gottlob Berger, of the Main SS office, to supply training officers so that the division would be "… effective in fighting bandits before being moved to the front line" (Dmytryshyn, 1956; Littman, 2003:62).

The statement of Hausser regarding the Waffen-SS not being involved in anti-partisan operations is inaccurate to say the least. The Waffen-SS was to play a major role in the combat of partisans on the Eastern Front and its occupied territories. It was necessary to call upon any Waffen-SS units which might happen to be in the vicinity when combating the partisan problem. To this end at the start of the invasion *SS Totenkopf* infantry regiments remained under the control of Himmler for use in operations against the partisans, which served as a cloak for the mass execution of civilians.

The SS Calvary Brigade,[35] consisting of the 1st and 2nd SS Calvary Regiments, was under the control of the HSSPF for Central Russia. These units were used by the Commander of the Army Group Centre rear area in Russia in July 1941 who commented, "... the strangers in the area, Red Army soldiers and Jewish Commissars, were taken prisoner by the SS, and the majority of them were shot" (Birn, 1997). Indeed the regiments were able to report to the HSSPF leader the "... execution of some 14,000 marauders, who were actually Soviet soldiers that had been cut off from their units, partisans and racially undesirable civilians (Jews and Gypsies)" (Trang, 2000:33). Some have argued that as these units were under the direct control of Himmler they should not be considered Waffen-SS units. SS General Fegelein obviously held a different view when on the 27th of November 1940 he had this to say about the activation of the cavalry units: "The Führer has authorised our regiments for deployment. We are now beginning the cavalry tradition in the Waffen-SS" (Landwehr, 1998:67). Members of this Brigade were brought to trial for these operations in the 1960s and they admitted that such operations were nothing less then the wholesale execution of Jews in the area (Birn, 1997). In 1941 the partisan threat was not great and there was little partisan activity, in fact the operations were nothing less then a subterfuge for racial cleansing. In his post-war interview *Wehrmacht* Colonel-General Erhard Rauss confirmed the above by stating that "... generally speaking, Russian partisan groups on the Eastern Front were formed in early 1942" (Tsouras, 1995:138).

In June 1940 Himmler authorised the transfer of *SS-Obersturmführer* Oskar Dirlewanger to the Waffen-SS. At the instigation of Hitler and Himmler he was to form an anti-partisan unit of Waffen-SS soldiers consisting of convicted poachers, concentration-camp inmates and other criminals (MacLean, 1998). This unit would be known as the *SS-Sonderkommando Dirlewanger*, before later becoming the 36th SS Grenadier Division. It is often argued by apologists for the Waffen-SS that this and other units like it were not part of the Waffen-SS. *SS-Obergruppenführer* Bach-Zelewski was asked about the Dirlewanger unit at the International Military Tribunal while he was giving evidence.

> DR. EXNER: Was it a formation of the Army or the SS?
>
> BACH-ZELEWSKI: No, it was not a formation of the Waffen-SS; it was supplied by the Allgemeine SS[36], that is, by the Berger office.
>
> (The International Military Tribunal, 1946: Vol 4:487)

Paul Hausser also attempted to distance the Waffen-SS from the Dirlewanger unit when asked about it:

> HAUSSER: Dirlewanger was the commander of a picked troop of men from the concentration-camps. He had no connection with the Waffen-SS. I did not meet him personally, nor his troops, so I can give no further testimony from my own knowledge.
>
> (The International Military Tribunal, 1946: Vol 20:383)

This is simply not true. The unit was commanded by Waffen-SS officers, it received commands from the headquarters of the Waffen-SS, and also received replacements from the main fighting units such as the *Das Reich* Division, which on the 28th of August 1940 was asked to arrange for the "… transfer of four junior non-commissioned officers" to assist with the formation of the unit (MacLean, 1998:57). On the 29th of January 1942 the unit received orders from the Waffen-SS command to undertake duties under the command staff of the *Reichsführer-SS* and his HSSPF in Russia: "It is clear that the *Sonderkommando*, at this point in time, was clearly considered a unit of the Waffen-SS proper…" (Krausnick et al., 1965; MacLean, 1998:65).

The *SS-Sonderkommando Dirlewanger* would burn a path of death and destruction through Russia. Tactics employed by the unit included rounding up innocent civilians and marching them through minefields, as well as this Dirlewanger would fly on reconnaissance over suspect areas, and if he received fire from a village he would later return and burn the village and kill the inhabitants (MacLean, 1998). HSSPF Von Gottberg conducted Operation *Hornung* in February 1943 in the Mogil'ov area, the *SS-Sonderkommando Dirlewanger* was among the units involved in the operation. At the conclusion of the operation Von Gottberg claimed to have killed some 9662 partisans; in a message to another SS leader Von Gottberg admitted that some 3300 Jews were killed in the operation (MacLean, 1998:113). In April 1943 the *Sonderkommando* took part in operations *Draufganger* one and two. Records indicate that during these operations the unit collected slave labourers, confiscated agricultural products and killed a number of partisans as well as executing some 65 women and children (MacLean, 1998:119).

Other frontline Waffen-SS units were used in the fight against the partisans. The 1st and 2nd SS divisions were just two of the premier Waffen-SS divisions who at some point in time conducted anti-partisan operations. Soldiers of the 1st SS Panzer Division *Leibstandarte SS Adolf Hitler* engaged in anti-partisan combat duties in Croatia during 1943 (Mooney, 2004). Parts of the division were ordered to combat partisans in the Kiev sector of the Eastern Front in late 1943 (Tiemann, 1998). The first act of the newly formed 3rd SS Panzer Corps under the command of *SS-Obergruppenführer* Felix Steiner in 1943 was to undertake anti-partisan duties in Croatia (Tieke, 2001). The Corps consisted of the 11th SS Panzergrenadier Division *Nordland* and the 14th SS Police regiment in September 1943. In the brutal fighting that ensued members of the 24th SS Panzergrenadier Regiment burnt down villages and exterminated the occupants (Smith et al., 1999). The 18th SS *Horst Wessel* Division undertook anti-partisan operations in Moravia in 1945 (Bender et al., 1975). The 13th SS *Handschar*, 21st SS *Skanderbeg* and 23rd SS *Nederland* Divisions all undertook anti-partisan duties (Ertel et al., 2000).

As the partisan problem grew the Waffen-SS began the creation of Waffen-SS units for special use in partisan-filled areas. The 7th SS Mountain Division *Prinz Eugen* was one of these units. It was to earn itself a reputation for brutality and featured prominently in the Nuremberg trials. As one author noted the actions of the *Prinz Eugen* Division in Yugoslavia "... blazed a notably ruthless path throughout the country" (Heaton, 2001:100). The division was mainly made up of ethnic Germans from Serbian Banat, these having to be supplemented by others from Rumania (Bender et al., 1972; Kaltenegger, 1995; Windrow & Burn, 1982).

At Nuremberg a report was entered into the record from the Yugoslav State Commission into war crimes committed by the Nazis. It outlines the activities of the *Prinz Eugen* Division in an anti-partisan operation called Operation Black, which was conducted in May 1943 in the Niksic area:

> Immediately after its invasion, this formation, opening fire with all its arms, commenced to commit outrageous crimes on the peaceful villages for no reason at all. Everything they came across they burned down, murdered and pillaged. The officers and men of the SS Division Prinz Eugen committed crimes of an outrageous cruelty on this occasion. The victims were shot, slaughtered and tortured, or burned to death in burning houses. Where a victim was found not in his house but on the road or in the fields some distance away, he was murdered and burned there. Infants with their mothers, pregnant women and frail old people were also murdered. In short, every civilian met with by these troops in these villages was murdered. In many cases whole families who, not expecting such treatment or lacking the time for escape, had remained quietly in their homes, were annihilated and murdered. Whole families were thrown into burning houses in many cases and thus burned. It has been established from the

investigations entered upon that 121 persons, mostly women, and including 30 persons aged 60-92 years and 29 children of ages ranging from six months to 14 years, were executed on this occasion in the horrible manner narrated above.

(The International Military Tribunal, 1946: Vol 20:375)

SS-Gruppenführer Arthur Phelps, commander of the division, considered it a waste of time to be precise with reprisal methods against partisans, it was much easier just to choose the closest village to where the attack took place and destroy it (Gumz, 1998). Indeed the atrocities being committed by the division under its second commander, *SS-Brigadeführer* Carl Reichritter Von Oberkamp, reached such a level that in correspondence to Phelps, Himmler asked him to intercede with his old division and restore some order as it was affecting relations in Croatia.

In July 1943, a company from *Prinz Eugen* machine-gunned the residents of the Muslim town of Kosutica, women and children included, after the company found the body of a dead SS man in the town. Concluding that partisans were endangering the unit, the commander ordered his men to open fire on a crowd of residents, who were then listed as enemy dead. (Gumz, 1998:42)

SS-Obergruppenführer **Phelps**

Despite the efforts of Phelps, Himmler was soon informed that the division had in the spring of 1944 killed some 3000 civilians in Dalmatia.[37] As a result Phelps, who was now commander of the 5th SS Mountain Corps "... attempted to submerge the civilians killed as enemy dead, an indication of the wide latitude German combat commanders had assumed" (Gumz, 1998:42). After the conclusion of the war the Yugoslav War Crimes Commission found that the division had committed:

> Some of the worst atrocities attributable to any soldiers during the Second World War ... it committed various excesses such as the murder of unarmed prisoners, looting and burning of villages and the torture and massacre of helpless civilians. (Bender et al., 1972:16)

Phelps was not alone in his ambivalent attitude towards actually identifying who the partisans were and who the civilians were. At Nuremberg a report from the *Wehrmacht* 1st Mountain Brigade commanding officer, Colonel Pericic, outlined how SS troops had been attacked by partisans in a village in Bosnia and forced to retreat. During the retreat the SS commander reported that "... when he had to retreat, he had killed all persons who were in the open because he had no chance to distinguish between the loyal population and the partisans." (The International Military Tribunal, 1946: Vol 20:373).

The 14th SS *Galicia* Grenadier Division, consisting mainly of Ukrainian volunteers, was involved in anti-partisan operations in 1944 in Poland in the Chelm area where units under the control of *SS-Obersturmbann-führer* Friedrich Beyersdorff and *SS-Hauptsturmführer* Bristot committed a number of atrocities. Beyersdorff was commander of the 14th SS Artillery Regiment of the Division, Bristot was later to command the Fusilier Battalion of the Division (Bender et al., 1975; Westwood, 2001). Over the next few months these units would be involved in numerous atrocities against "bandits" and civilians that would result in the hanging, torture, beating, burning and shooting of civilians as well as executions in gas vans. At the conclusion of these operations it was estimated that the units led by Beyersdorff had "... shot, hanged, gassed and burned more than 1500 men, women and children between February 1943 and March 1944" (Littman, 2003:74). German Field Marshal Walter Model noted that the troops had fought *gallantly* during this period.

In June 1944 the 14th SS *Galicia* Division had conducted a long battle against partisans in Yugoslavia and claimed the following losses among the partisans. 4526 counted dead, 3766 additional dead, 1246 prisoners.

However they only located 19 machine guns and 825 rifles (Lepre, 1997:222). Less then one weapon for each 10 partisans. The only conclusion can be that the majority of dead were in fact innocent civilians. On the 27th of February 1945 men from the 14th SS Division along with other troops surrounded the village of Huta Pieniacka in Poland and attacked it after two SS soldiers had been killed in a small firefight near the village the previous day. As a result of the SS attack more than 1200 villagers were killed and executed and the village destroyed (Littman, 2003:77). These examples show that front-line fighting units of the Waffen-SS did commit numerous atrocities while engaged in anti-partisan activities. The majority of these actions were done under the auspices of the HSSPF, Himmler's representatives in the occupied areas.

The Higher SS and Police Leaders

It is worth exploring the role of the SS Police Leaders or HSSPF and their relationship with the Waffen-SS. The HSSPF were responsible for the conduct of anti-partisan and extermination operations behind the front lines. The aim of Himmler in creating these positions was to bring all the components of the SS and police, including the Waffen-SS, under one command in the occupied territories and areas of command of the HSSPF. Not only was it an attempt at integration of these units, but it was also intended that the HSSPF would provide political direction to these units. For example, *SS-Obergruppenführer* Otto Winkelmann was the HSSPF for Hungary, and was responsible for the concentration and deportation of Jews in 1944. He was also in charge of the Waffen-SS units in Budapest until shortly before the city was besieged by the Russians in late 1944 (Lozowick, 2000; Ungvary, 2005).

In an order issued on the 21st of May 1941 Himmler ordered that "The Higher SS and Police Leader is placed in charge of SS and Police troops and also of the operational personnel in the Security Police in order to carry out the tasks allocated to him by me personally" (Headland, 1992:138). During the Pohl case, HSSPF for Italy *SS-Obergruppenführer* Karl Wolff confirmed the close link between the HSSPF and Himmler:

> Q. As a Highest SS and Police Leader, who was your immediate superior?
> A. The Reich Leader SS.
>
> (Nuremberg Military Tribunal, 1946: Vol 5:771)

It was in this role that the HSSPF became the agents for implementing the whole range of occupation policy insofar as Himmler was – or could be argued to be – responsible for it. Indeed the role of the HSSPF in Russia would flourish in its attempt to put into action the ideological ideas of the SS. The ability to command units of the Waffen-SS meant that the HSSPF could use this authority to carry out "… ruthless directives to conduct anti-partisan warfare and reprisals" (Sydnor, 1989:253). As well as having these units under their control most HSSPF also had the SS courts attached to their headquarters (Weingartner, 1983). This relationship would prove useful should there be any problems with special directives carried out at Himmler's behest.

The Waffen-SS units were at the disposal of the HSSPF. An example of this is a letter from Himmler to Waffen-SS General, *SS-Obergruppenführer* Wilhelm Koppe, the HSSPF for Poland. In this letter Himmler told Koppe to use the 14th Waffen-SS Grenadier Division "… in any way necessary to hold down resistance" in the Polish area in 1944 (Littman, 2003:73). *SS-Oberstgruppenführer* Paul Hausser attempted to distance the Waffen-SS from the HSSPF and their activities. When asked by the defence counsel for the SS about the HSSPF he had the following to say.

> HERR PELCKMANN: Did the Higher SS and Police Leaders belong to the officer corps of the Waffen-SS?
>
> HAUSSER: The Higher SS and Police Leaders did not belong to the Waffen-SS. They had no authority to command and they had nothing to do with us.
>
> (The International Military Tribunal, 1946: Vol 20:366)

The link between the HSSPF and command of the Waffen-SS was strong. Many of the HSSPF had served in the Waffen-SS. Of approximately 58 HSSPF leaders,[38] at least six HSSPF leaders, or 10 per cent, held commands at divisional level or higher within the Waffen-SS at some point in time. In fact, Himmler sent several SS Officers marked as HSSPF to units of the Waffen-SS for a period of military training. The link between the HSSPF and the Waffen-SS was cemented even further when Himmler ordered that all HSSPF were to become part of the Waffen-SS in 1944. SS General and HSSPF Friedrich Von Eberstein gave the following evidence to the IMT when questioned by the defence counsel for the SS:

> HERR PELCKMANN: You just said that you were a general of the Waffen-SS. So far you have told the Tribunal only that you were a member of the General SS. When and for what reason did you become a general of the Waffen-SS, although up to then you had had nothing whatever to do with the Waffen-SS?

VON EBERSTEIN: In the fall of 1944 Himmler became commander-in-chief of the reserve army. When he took over this office, the Prisoners of War Organisation also came under his jurisdiction. In the fall of 1944 Himmler transferred to the Higher SS and Police Leaders the responsibility for safeguarding prisoner-of-war camps against mass escapes and against attempts from the outside to liberate prisoners. For this purpose, the Higher SS and Police Leaders were made senior commanders of the prisoners of war in their defence areas. According to international regulations regarding prisoners of war, police could not be used to guard prisoners of war, so the Higher SS and Police Leaders were taken over into the Waffen-SS and appointed generals of the Waffen-SS.

(The International Military Tribunal, 1946: Vol 20:306)

Eberstein fails to mention how he authorised the removal of 400 Russian prisoners of war from Regensburg to Buchenwald where they were executed on the orders of Gestapo chief Heinrich Muller (Miller et al., 2006:277).

As has been noted, the contributions to genocide by the Waffen-SS units under the command of the HSSPF was "… no less significant in quantity or brutality as those of the *Einsatzgruppen*" (Buchler, 1986:14). The following discussion gives some insight into this relationship between the HSSPF and the Waffen-SS. Under each HSSPF were a number of subordinate SS and Police Leaders (SS und *Polizeiführer* - SSPF) who controlled smaller areas within the overall area of control of the HSSPF. Erich Bach-Zelewski *SS-Obergruppenführer* and General of the Waffen-SS and Police, was also the HSSPF for central Russia. He was provided the SS Brigades by Himmler to undertake the mass murder of the Jews in occupied Russia. These units were assisted in 1942 by the Danish SS *Freikorps*[39], a unit made up of Danish volunteers, in anti-partisan duties (Smith et al., 1999). He was hospitalised in 1942 as a result of suffering "the psychological effects of carrying out orders involving the extermination policies in the East within his HSSPF command" (Yerger, 1997:37). He was appointed by Himmler as his special deputy for anti-partisan warfare in October 1942 and eventually took command of all anti-partisan operations on the Eastern Front until 1944. This position gave him the responsibilities of issuing reports, proposing courses of action and acting as a liaison between the High Command, the Army and SS on anti-partisan matters. He went on to command the 10th SS Corps in late 1944. An example of the complicity of Bach-Zelewski is that he ordered the SS Calvary Brigade to refer to murdered Jews as looters and partisans in their reports to hide the true nature of their actions. He survived the war, and to escape death gave evidence at the Nuremberg trials.

A further example of this close link between the Waffen-SS and the anti-partisan command structure is *SS-Gruppenführer* Heinz Lammerding, who was the chief of staff to Bach-Zelewski in 1943 and was responsible for the clearing of the Pripet Marshes and its associated killing operations, which resulted in the deaths of 15,000 Russians (Mann, 2001; Yerger, 1999). He served in the 3rd SS Division and later went on to command the 2nd SS and 38th SS Divisions.

SS-Obergruppenführer and General of the Waffen-SS and Police Kurt Von Gottberg took over from Bach-Zelewski and served as the HSSPF in Central and White Russia. He initially served in the indoctrination office of the SS and gave up his Waffen-SS rank in 1942, but was promoted to the above rank in the Waffen-SS on June 30th 1944 after serving for some time in his HSSPF role fighting the partisans in Russia (Yerger, 1997). Gottberg carried out a number of operations against supposed partisans in the occupied areas for which he received various awards. Of interest are a number of operations that were run in 1943, which earnt him the German Cross in Gold.

The following information was drawn from extracts of reports submitted for these operations. Operation *Erntefest* resulted in 3721 enemy casualties, however, the arms tally was only 433 rifles, nine heavy machine guns, 19 light machine guns, eight machine pistols, etc (Yerger, 1997). The *SS-Sonderkommando* Dirlewanger served in this operation in January 1943. During the course of the operation the *Sonderkommando* reported killing 48 partisans, while it captured 26 partisans, executed 34 suspicious persons for the loss of three killed and four wounded (MacLean, 1998:110). Operation *Cottbus* resulted in 6042 enemy casualties in battle. Some 3709 men suspected of being partisans were executed, 599 men were taken prisoner for the loss of only 127 German soldiers killed (Miller et al., 2006; Yerger, 1997). The weapons captured consisted of some 19 cannons, 30 heavy machine guns, 45 machine pistols, 903 rifles, etc. Von Gottberg tacitly admitted that prisoners were being killed when he issued an instruction on the 11th of August 1943 to units under his control that "Henceforth no captured partisans or partisans who had deserted to the Germans would be shot" (MacLean, 1998:132).

SS-Oberführer **Dirlewanger**

When one looks at the figures there is a great disparity between the number of supposed partisans killed and actual weapons captured. For example in Operation *Cottbus* less then one partisan in nine had a gun if the figures in Gottberg's reports are accurate. For Operation *Erntefest* the ratio was eight partisans to each rifle. Clearly what was termed *partisans* could only have been a euphemism for outright slaughter of civilians. The low casualty rate for German forces also supports this proposition. This and other terms such as *pacification* and *purification* could only serve as code words for the wanton murder of innocent people. Other operations such as Operation *Turov*, which was conducted by the elements of the SS Calvary Brigade, had similar disproportionate results. In this operation the SS soldiers reported that 600-700 partisans were killed with just 10 taken prisoner. The 2nd SS Calvary Regiment reported the death of some 400 partisans for the loss of just four Germans dead and 12 wounded (Trang, 2000:35).

Even the German authorities themselves admitted this disparity, as was shown at Nuremberg. The results of Operation *Cottbus* was subject of a report from the General Commissar for White Ruthenia to the Reich Minister for Occupied Eastern Territories that was critical of the slaughter of civilians:

SS-Brigadeführer, Major General of Police Von Gottberg reports that the operation "Cottbus" had the following result during the period mentioned ... the figures mentioned above indicate that again a heavy destruction of the population must be expected. If only 492 rifles are taken from 4500 enemy dead, this discrepancy shows that among these enemy dead were numerous peasants from the country. The Battalion Dirlewanger especially has a reputation for destroying many human lives. Among the 5000 people suspected of belonging to bands, there were numerous women and children.

(The International Military Tribunal, 1946:Vol 4:220) [40]

In a letter dated the 19th of July 1943 a Police general stationed in the Ukraine complained to *SS-Obergruppenführer* Von Herff, head of the SS Personnel office that:

Yesterday a *Gauleiter* and *General-Kommissar* unintentionally and unwittingly broadcast certain secret reports intended for the Führer, showing that some 480 rifles were found on 6000 dead partisans. Put bluntly, all the men had been shot to swell the figures of enemy losses and highlight our own heroic deeds. (Krausnick et al., 1965:346)

Indeed it has been noted that "... the massive anti-partisan operations he conducted in the first half of 1943 in the Lake Pelik area were especially brutal" (Yerger, 1997:204). At the conclusion of operation *Cottbus* a German propaganda officer toured the area and noted that "... some of the partisans had been burnt alive and their half-roasted bodies had been eaten by pigs" (MacLean, 1998:141). Von Gottberg went on to command the 12th SS Corps in 1944. He committed suicide in May 1945.

Friedrich Jeckeln, *SS-Obergruppenführer* and General in the Waffen-SS and Police, served as the HSSPF leader for the Baltic States and North and South Russia. He saw combat service in the Western campaign with the *Totenkopf* Division before taking on the role of various HSSPF appointments in Russia in 1941 (Birn, 1991; Simpson, 1990). He personally oversaw the first killing action of *Einsatzkommando* 4 in the Ukraine where some 90 Jews were killed (Lozowick, 1987). His reign in Russia was punctuated by various massacres where:

Mass executions took place on numerous occasions ... at Kamenets-Podolsky, Jeckeln's units killed 23,600 people in August 1941. In a ravine outside of Kiev on September 29/30, 1941, another 33,000 people were executed ... In Dnepropetrovsk, 15,000 were killed during October 1941, and a further 15,000 were executed in Rovno on November 7/8... (Yerger, 1997:274)

In the month of August 1941 it is estimated the Jeckeln was responsible for the murder of some 44,000 Jews in the area of the Ukraine (Buchler, 1986; Lower, 2002). Jeckeln is mentioned in various Operational Situation Reports of the *Einsatzgruppen,* which outline the above atrocities. In Operational Situation Report 80 dated 11th of September 1941 it outlines the assistance provided by Jeckeln in supplying a commando to assist with the liquidation of Jews at Kamenets-Podolsky (Arad, Krakowski, & Spector, 1989). Operational Situation Report 101 dated the 2nd of October 1941 outlines how police units under the control of Jeckeln assisted the *Einsatzgruppen* with the slaughter of Jews in Kiev. This was the infamous slaughter of Babi Yar. The report states that a number of Jews and communists were killed. With typical thoroughness the *Einsatzgruppen* nominated the numbers involved.

> ... In the period covered by the report, the towns of Nikolayev and Kherson in particular were freed of Jews. Remaining officials there were appropriately treated. From September 16 to 30. 22,467 Jews and communists were executed. Total number 35 782... (Arad et al., 1989:168)

At least one source lists units of the Waffen-SS assisting with the slaughter at Babi Yar (Lozowick, 1987). Operational Situation Report 136 dated the 19th of November 1941 outlines how:

> Of approximately 100,000 Jews originally living in Dnepropetrovsk, about 70,000 escaped before the German troops entered the town. Of the remaining 30,000 approximately 10,000 were shot on October 13, 1941 by a detachment of the Higher SS and Police Chiefs. (Arad et al., 1989:242)

Jeckeln performed various anti-partisan combat duties in 1942 and 1943 where he had control of the SS Volunteer Legion *Norwegen,*[41] units of the 4th SS *Polizei* Division and various army units. In *Aktion Sumpffieber* (Operation Malaria), carried out in early 1942, the anti-partisan units under his command in Belorussia liquidated many ghettos and slaughtered tens of thousands of Jews (Gutman, 1990). He was promoted to General of the Waffen-SS in 1944 while he continued to fill the post of HSSPF leader (Yerger, 1997). At the end of the war Jeckeln was captured by the Russians and tried. He was hung in Riga, Latvia on the 3rd of February 1946.

Friedrich-Wilhelm Kruger was an *SS-Obergruppenführer,* a General in the Waffen-SS and the Police. He was also the HSSPF leader for East Poland, a position to which he was appointed in October 1939 (Yerger, 1999). So brutal were his actions against the Poles that a failed assassination attempt was made on the 20th of April 1943. He was responsible for the liquidation of various ghettos and the operation of the Belzec, Sobibor and Treblinka extermination camps, where 1,720,000 Jews were murdered (Gutman, 1990). He received divisional-level training with the *Prinz Eugen* Division from November 1943 to April 1944 and was given the rank of General of the Waffen-SS in 1944. He was made commander of the 6th SS Mountain Division *Nord* in 1944 and later went on to command the 5th SS Mountain Corps (Bender & Taylor, 1971; Westwood, 2001; Yerger, 1999). He committed suicide at the end of the war.

SS-Gruppenführer and General of the Waffen-SS Carl Graf Von Pückler-Burghaus served as deputy HSSPF for Central Russia to Bach-Zelewski from January 1942 until taking the latter's place in late 1942 when Bach-Zelewski was sick until early 1943 (Yerger, 1999). He transferred to the Waffen-SS on the 1st of August 1942 and took command of the 15th SS Latvian Grenadier Division in 1943. He surrendered to the Americans, but was handed over to the Russians. To avoid a trial he committed suicide on the 12th of May 1945.

SS-Gruppenführer Odilo Globocnik served in an SS division in Poland as an enlisted man. He was later responsible for the supervision of the extermination camps of Belzec, Sobibor, Treblinka and Majdanek (Arad, 1987; Birn, 1991; Krausnick et al., 1965; MacLean, 1998; Poprzeczny, 2004; Reitlinger, 1957). Majdanek received the official title Waffen-SS Prisoner of War Camp Lublin. The camp was constructed by the Lublin Central Construction Board of the Waffen-SS and Police (White, 1990). Himmler had instructed that "In operations against guerrilla troops, men, women and children suspected of guerrilla activities will be rounded up and shipped to the camps in Lublin or Auschwitz" (Nuremberg Military Tribunal, 1946: Vol 5:234). This resulted in thousands of children being consigned to the Majdanek camp. Globocnik had seen his role in the East as being the "… biological crushing of the Polish people from the East and West" (Scheffler, 1985:32). As the SSPF for the Lublin district in Poland Globocnik:

> Had the power of life and death over everyone in or passing through this recently acquired distinct; Pole, Jew and Ukrainians. By the time he left he had, in various ways murdered no fewer then 1.5 million Jews … Two of his large killing compounds were situated within this district, Belzec and Sobibor, while the third, Treblinka, was outside the district. (Poprzeczny, 2004:93)

The work of Globocnik was noted by the NMT in the Pohl Trial.

> The extermination camps in the vicinity of Lublin, such as Treblinka and
> Majdanek, gave rise to special problems because of the magnitude of their
> operations. These camps were, until the latter part of 1943, under the
> jurisdiction of one Odilo Globocnik, the Higher SS and Police Leader,
> Lublin. In order to coordinate the undertaking, a special staff "G" was
> created within the framework of the WVHA. The head of this staff was
> Globocnik, while the administrative and accounting personnel was sup-
> plied by the WVHA. It was the task of special staff "G" to seize and
> account for all property in the Government General of occupied Poland
> derived from the extermination and enslavement of Jews.
> (Nuremberg Military Tribunal, 1946: Vol 5:254)

So inspirational were the actions of Globocnik to the Nazis that they
were deemed worthy of a major story in the SS newspaper *Das Schwarze
Korps*, titled Picks and Spades for the work that the Jews were doing. The
article praises:

> ...SS-Brigadeführer Odilo Globocnik, the police commander in Lublin,
> for having provided so many tasks for the Jews there that they scarcely
> have time to catch their breath. It says that getting things done in Poland
> requires "guys" who understand how to get to the root of the Jewish prob-
> lem. Only special personalities and character suffice. (Combs, 1986:131)

Other members of the HSSPF had close ties with the Waffen-SS. Josef
Fitzthum had served in the Flemish Volunteer Legion in 1942 (Birn, 1991;
Miller et al., 2006; Westwood, 2001). As an *SS-Gruppenführer* he later went
on to command the 18th SS Panzergrenadier Division *Horst Wessel* and the
21st SS Mountain Division *Skanderberg* for short periods in 1945.[42] Konstantin Kammerhofer served in the 5th SS Panzer Division *Wiking* in
1941(Westwood, 2001). Walter Schimana was responsible for the formation
of the 14th SS Grenadier Division *Galicia* before being transferred to
Greece as the HSSPF (Birn, 1991).

In her study of five HSSPF leaders in the Balkans, Birn (1991) found
that they were deeply involved in the persecution of the Jews. To achieve
this the HSSPF leaders relied on the contribution of all parts of the SS
apparatus, including the Waffen-SS:

> The whole machinery was involved on a routine basis. The Waffen-SS
> divisions, for instance, set up under the supervision of the HSSPF, were
> very active in anti-Jewish measures, contrary to the popular belief that
> they were fighting units uninfluenced by Nazi ideology. (Birn, 1991:358).

In 1943 Himmler ordered the Jews of Lublin, Poland to be dealt with. To this end he had an order passed on to *SS-Obergruppenführer* Friedrich Kruger to undertake this action and to assist in this he was to "... form a special cordon of 2000 soldiers from units of a Waffen-SS Brigade" to deal with the Jewish problem (Poprzeczny, 2004:105) This involvement in operations against the Jews is supported by the fact that the HSSPF were made fully aware of the nature of the cleansing operations to be undertaken by troops under their control. The HSSPF were informed in a telegram from *SS-Obergruppenführer* Heydrich dated the 2nd of July 1941 of the activities to be undertaken by the *Einsatzgruppen* (Headland, 1989; Krausnick et al., 1965; Longerich, 1997). This order contained a list of those who were to be eliminated:

> Comintern functionaries and communist professional politicians generally, lower functionaries of Party central, higher, middle and (radical lower) functionaries of Party central, regional and local committees, Peoples Commissars, Jews in party and state positions, other radical elements... (Longerich, 1997:262)

Certainly the above order was taken to extend to all Jews by the commanders of the killing units. Indeed some of the commanders of the *Einsatzgruppen* testified in later trials that the order to kill all Jews was given to them prior to entering Russia. In any event the *Einsatzgruppen* certainly undertook the systematic liquidation of certain ethnic groups with great gusto.

In the area of Serbia, *SS-Gruppenführer* August Meyszner undertook the daily routine of killing Jews. Further to this as a result of his actions Meyszner received several million marks from confiscated Jewish property for the newly formed *Prinz Eugen* SS Division (Birn, 1991). This was not an unusual arrangement; often Waffen-SS units would receive benefits from the actions against the Jews in the form of goods or money. In the district of Lublin, SSPF *SS-Gruppenführer* Globocnik had various SS men and Jews assigned to his staff who were "... involved in sorting and storing the high value possessions removed from hundreds of thousands of Jewish families" who had been killed or transported to the camps (Poprzeczny, 2004:115). This collection of material was reported to Waffen-SS General, *SS-Obergruppenführer* Oswald Pohl, who was in charge of the SS Economic and Administrative Main Department (*SS Wirtschafts und Verwaltungshauptamt*, commonly known as "WVHA") and chief of Division W of the WVHA (Nuremberg Military Tribunal, 1946: Vol 5:200).

On 4 July 1944, Pohl, in a communication to the Main Office chiefs, announced the names of officers responsible for the property seized in several areas, and stated: "As a matter of principle, it has to be kept in mind that the entire Jewish property is to be incorporated into the Reich property." Property from the Action Reinhardt which had been delivered to the Reich Main Treasury was kept in a separate account, appropriately called, "Department Booty." Moved by the Christian spirit of Christmas, Pohl, on 6 November 1943, wrote to Himmler, stating that he intended to make gifts of watches and fountain pens to SS units.

(Nuremberg Military Tribunal, 1946: Vol 5:988)

SS-Gruppenführer Frank of the WVHA gave evidence as to where the money that Globocnik obtained went, "… the money, the cash, went into the treasuries of the Waffen-SS…" (Nuremberg Military Tribunal, 1946: Vol 5:759).

Witnesses for the Waffen-SS before the IMT denied knowing about this type of activity during the war. *SS-Obergruppenführer* Von Eberstein gave the following evidence.

MAJOR JONES: Did you ever hear of Oswald Pohl?

VON EBERSTEIN: Yes.

MAJOR JONES: He was the head of the Economic and Administrative Main Office of the SS, was he not, the WVHA?

VON EBERSTEIN: Yes.

MAJOR JONES: Did you know that this organisation, using SS personnel, was employing murder as a means to establish loot on a colossal scale for the benefit of the Waffen-SS and other SS organisations?

VON EBERSTEIN: Yes; I heard that from the reports on this trial while I was in the camp. I had never heard before that gold teeth, etcetera, were collected.

MAJOR JONES: Did you know of the great business in death that was bringing millions of marks to the coffers of the Reich bank? And it was involving numerous departments of the Third Reich.

VON EBERSTEIN: No, I did not know that.

(The International Military Tribunal, 1946: Vol 20:315)

The following letter from Waffen-SS General, *SS-Obergruppenführer* August Frank to the Auschwitz concentration-camp and Lublin District SS administrations (document No–724) leaves little doubt as to the utilisation by the Waffen-SS of the property of the camp inmates. The letter has not been produced in full, however, the salient parts are below:

To the Chief of the SS Garrison Administration Lublin

To the Chief of Administration Concentration-camp Auschwitz

Subject: Utilisation of property on the occasion of settlement and evacuation of Jews.

Without taking into account the overall regulations which are expected to be issued during October, pertaining to the utilisation of mobile and immobile property of the evacuated Jews, the following procedure has to be followed with regard to the property carried by them — property, which will in all orders in the future be called goods originating from thefts, receiving of stolen goods, and hoarded goods ... Watches and clocks of all kinds, alarm clocks, fountain pens, mechanical pencils, hand and electrical razors, pocket knives, scissors, flashlights, wallets and purses are to be repaired by the Economic and Administrative Main Office in special repair shops, cleaned, and evaluated; and have to be delivered quickly to front-line troops. Delivery to the troops is on a cash basis through the post exchanges. Three-fourth price grades are to be set and it has to be made sure that each officer and man cannot buy more than one watch ... Ordinary furs (lamb, hare, and rabbit skins) are to be reported to the SS WVHA, Amt B II, and are to be delivered to the clothing plant of the Waffen-SS, Ravensbruck near Fuerstenbern (Mecklenburg) ... It has to be strictly observed that the Jewish Star is removed from all garments and outer garments which are to be delivered. Furthermore, items which are to be delivered have to be searched for hidden and sewed-in values. This should be carried out with the greatest possible care.

ACTING FOR

[Signed] FRANK

SS-Brigadeführer and Brigadier General of the Waffen-SS.

(Nuremberg Military Tribunal, 1946: Vol 5:695)

Not only were the Waffen-SS directly involved in the atrocities, but they also benefited materially from the persecution of the Jews and other racially undesirable elements.

The involvement of the HSSPF and Waffen-SS units in atrocities continued with members of the 31st SS Grenadier Division killing Jews who up to 1944 had been used as slave labourers in mines (Birn, 1991).

In the village of Czervenka, the Hungarian guards were relieved by units from the 31st SS Division ... During the night the SS men shot several hundred Jews, who were buried in a mass grave. The next day, on the march, the SS men amused themselves by shooting at the Jews for target practice, and the roadside was littered with corpses well into Hungarian territory. (Birn, 1991:359)

In Croatia similar actions were conducted by the Waffen-SS under the guidance of *SS-Gruppenführer* Konstantin Kammerhofer. Soldiers of the 13th SS Mountain Division *Handschar* and the 23rd SS Mountain Division *Kama* committed regular atrocities in the persecution of the Jews (Birn, 1991; Heaton, 2001).

> The Handschar killed 22 Jews in Tuzia, where it was stationed during the summer of 1944 ... a building unit consisting of members of both divisions ... were guarding Hungarian Jewish forced labourers building fortifications at the Austrian village of Jennersdorf. They treated the Jews with such cruelty that local villagers were infuriated. Many of the inmates who were incapable of working were ultimately taken from the group and shot. (Birn, 1991:360)

The 7th SS Mountain Division *Prinz Eugen* also had a hand in the killing of Jews in late 1943. In the Town of Split on the Adriatic coast of Croatia, members of the division used Jews to exhume the mass graves of previous victims, "... after which they themselves were shot" (Birn, 1991:361). The divisional commander recalled that in early 1944 a German supply column was ambushed near the town of Otok in the Split area, as a result "... all the residents of the town were killed. The battalion from the Division *Prinz Eugen* participated" (Kumm, 1995:269).

In Albania it was the role of HSSPF Josef Fitzthum, *SS-Gruppenführer* and general in the Waffen-SS and Police, to ensure action was taken against the Jews. He utilised the 21st SS Mountain Division *Skanderbeg* to take action against the Jews as he held the view that they were to blame for "... all political agitation and economic shortages" (Birn, 1991:363). This division, under the control of *SS-Brigadeführer* August Schmidhuber, rounded up Jews and executed any who resisted. Many of those rounded up were later transported to Belsen concentration-camp where they perished. Schmidhuber served in the *Germania* Regiment in Poland. He was then a regimental commander in the *Prinz Eugen* Division before serving as a divisional commander for both the *Prinz Eugen* and *Skanderbeg* Divisions. Schmidhuber had also been in command of the *Prinz Eugen* Division when it had committed its earlier atrocities in the towns of Split and Dubrovnik (Birn, 1991; Kaltenegger, 1995; Westwood, 2001; Yerger, 1999). Of interest is that Schmidhuber never joined the Nazi Party and was, in fact, opposed to their political views. By his actions it is clear however that he was ideologically aligned with them. He was captured by the Russians in May 1945, tried in Belgrade and executed for war crimes on the 19th of February 1947.

The SS Calvary Brigade also participated heavily in anti-partisan oper-ations, first as this Brigade and later as the 8th SS Calvary Division *Florian Geyer* (Trang, 2000). One veteran of the division recalls how a partisan group was neutralised in operations during 1943 when it was placed at the disposal of Bach-Zelewski:

> In one intensive operation several bands were neutralised. A partisan was taken prisoner. The man was sentenced to be hanged. The entire company had strict orders to watch the execution. The time came and a whistle was blown as I was sitting comfortably with a few comrades. Everyone set off at a run. Some were even quite merry. (Trang, 2000:97)

During one of these operations the division managed to encircle and wipe out a large group of partisan: there were 1256 killed (including many during summary executions) and 206 prisoners. The SS had casualties of 22 killed and 56 wounded (Trang, 2000:95).

The fact that the Waffen-SS command not only participated in the actions but also had extensive knowledge of such is shown in the comments of *SS-Obergruppenführer* Karl Wolff, who recounted that Himmler had asked senior Waffen-SS officers on how to address the partisan problem. These officers included at least two divisional commanders of the Waffen-SS, *SS-Obergruppenführer* Felix Steiner and *SS-Brigadeführer* Otto Kumm. Wolff recalls that at Himmler's behest he spoke to these two offi-cers about the partisan problem:

> I spoke to Felix Steiner and Otto Kumm about this, and they were of the opinion … the greatest problem was trying to undo the damage already done from the invasion *(of Russia)*[43] forward with regard to the civilian populations, especially the mass executions, which had not been handled very well. (Heaton, 2001:106)

Further to this, according to Wolff, Steiner was involved with Bach-Zelewski in deciding how the partisan threat could be met (Heaton, 2001:128). This clearly indicates that at the very least senior officers of the Waffen-SS who were in charge of front-line fighting units were aware of the atrocities being committed. Indeed the fact that the many senior Waf-fen-SS commanders were aware of the killing operations taking place is evidenced by the comments of *SS-Gruppenführer* Bittrich at a meeting of 15 Waffen-SS Generals in 1941, where he criticised the racial cleansing in the East being undertaken by Himmler (Heaton, 2001; Yerger, 1997). This is ironic given that Bittrich went on to command the SS Calvary Division in 1942, a unit that, was responsible for many atrocities on the Eastern

Front. Indeed this is the same SS General Bittrich who in April 1938 had taken over an apartment in Vienna with his wife that had been confiscated from a Jew (Von Lang, 2005:115). One could perhaps surmise that his concern arose out of the military implications of these actions, rather then any moral concern for the victims themselves. Certainly Bittrich never attempted to resign his commission or bring to justice any of the personnel of the SS Calvary Brigade involved in the cleansing actions. As one author has noted, the cleansing actions of units such the *Einsatzgruppen* and others were to be "… given the highest priority: no exigency of war, no economic consideration, no shortage of supplies would diminish the necessity of completing the assignment down to the last Jew" (Littman, 2003:35).

Also present at this meeting were such SS notables as Sepp Dietrich (*Leibstandarte SS Adolf Hitler* Division), Paul Hausser (*Das Reich* Division), Theodor Eicke (*Totenkopf* Division), Karl Wolff (Himmler's adjutant) and Felix Steiner (*Wiking* division) among others, all generals of frontline Waffen-SS units (Heaton, 2001). Yet at Nuremberg Hausser made the following claim that he did not "… remember a single case in which the front troops of my division had ever taken hostages or destroyed villages as a punishment" (The International Military Tribunal, 1946: Vol 20:363). Such a claim would not seem to match the recollections of other Waffen-SS generals and other facts.

As noted by Birn at the conclusion of her study, "… all actions of extermination were the common responsibility of the security police, order police and the Waffen-SS" (Birn, 1991:364). This claim is supported by Buchler who argues that "… units of both the police (Orpo) and the Waffen-SS played a very active role in the mass murder of Jews in Soviet territory" (Buchler, 1986:19). One of the arguments raised by defenders of the Waffen-SS is that units such as the 1st and 2nd SS Brigades and the SS Calvary Brigade were not part of the Waffen-SS as such. This claim can be rejected. Waffen-SS officers commanded these units, they contained members of the Waffen-SS and these units were later used as the cadres to form other Waffen-SS units such as the 18th SS Panzergrenadier Division *Horst Wessel* and the 8th SS *Florian Geyer* Division. They were engaged not only in anti-partisan duties, but also in combat duties on occasions. Perhaps the only difference that can be drawn between them and the front-line Waffen-SS units is that at times they came under the direct control of the *Reichsführer-SS,* rather the high command of the Waffen-SS and the Army. Let us now turn our attention to the SS killing units that operated in the wake of the advancing army groups, the *Einsatzgruppen.*

The role and methods of the Einsatzgruppen

The *Einsatzgruppen* were mobile killing groups that operated behind the front lines on the Eastern Front conducting so-called cleansing operations where they would murder Jews and any others who were seen as a threat to the Nazi regime. These actions can be seen to be the first steps on the path to the final solution and the death camps. Waffen-SS General Bach-Zelewski gave the following insight into the mission of the *Einsatzgruppen* at the IMT trial at Nuremberg:

> COL. TAYLOR: Are you generally familiar with the operations of the so-called *Einsatzgruppen* of the SD?
>
> BACH-ZELEWSKI: Yes.
>
> COL. TAYLOR: Did these units play any important part in large-scale anti-Russian operations?
>
> BACH-ZELEWSKI: No.
>
> COL.TAYLOR: What was the principal task of the *Einsatzgruppen*?
>
> BACH-ZELEWSKI: The principal task of the *Einsatzgruppen* of the *Sicherheitspolizei* was the annihilation of the Jews, gypsies, and political commissars.
>
> (The International Military Tribunal, 1946: Vol 4:477)

Bach-Zelewski had first hand knowledge of the role of the *Einsatzgruppen*, he had personally directed *Einsatzkommando* 8 in the killing of some 1,100 male Jews on the 17th of July 1941 in the area of Slonim (Miller et al., 2006:42). The methods of killing used by the *Einsatzgruppen* included shooting, gassing, burning, bludgeoning and others. Some methods of execution were as sadistic as they were unique. Adolf Ruche, a former *SS-Hauptscharführer*, gave evidence during the *Einsatzgruppen* trial[44] that showed how occasionally there were executioners who devised original methods for killing their victims:

> On the occasion of an exhumation in Minsk, in November 1943, *Obersturmführer* Heuser arrived with a *Kommando* of Latvians. They brought eight Jews, men and women, with them. The Latvians guarded the Jews, while Harter and Heuser erected a funeral pyre with their own hands. The Jews were bound, put on the pile alive, drenched with gasoline and burned. (Nuremberg Military Tribunal, 1946: Vol 4:448)

By December 1942 the *Einsatzgruppen* had murdered at least some 1.1 million people[45] in less then six months in which they had been operating in Russia. In all there were four *Einsatzgruppen* that operated in concert with the German Army Groups behind the front lines in Russia and were responsible to Himmler. The groups were divided into smaller sub-units called *Sonderkommandos* or *Einsatzkommandos*. The *Einsatzgruppen* were required to report to the Reich Main Security Office (RSHA) and also to the HSSPF in their area of operations, whom Himmler would use to pass on orders directly to the *Einsatzgruppen*.

The use of the Waffen-SS in the Einsatzgruppen

In all some 3000 men served in the *Einsatzgruppen* and these were drawn from the Waffen-SS, SD, Security Police, Gestapo, Criminal Police and various other police services. The Waffen-SS provided significant forces to the *Einsatzgruppen*. As noted during the *Einsatzgruppen* trial "… the troops were largely made of emergency service draftees and of companies of the Waffen-SS and Order Police" (Nuremberg Military Tribunal, 1946: Vol 4:93). One author puts the figure at some 1500 Waffen-SS soldiers being active members of the *Einsatzgruppen* (Stein, 1966). As well as being members of the actual *Einsatzgruppen*, Waffen-SS units were sent as support units to help them achieve their aim of pacification and purification of the rear areas. As noted by Lower on August 7th 1941 at Zhitomir, men on the *Einsatzgruppen* "along with a Waffen-SS platoon … collaborated in the Mass shooting of 400 Jews at a horse cemetery on the outskirts of town" (Lower, 2002:4). Some of these units were the 1st and 2nd SS Brigades, the *SS-Sonderkommando Dirlewanger* and the SS Calvary Brigade as well as regular Waffen-SS units; the actions of these units have already been discussed to some degree.

Yet again the Waffen-SS witnesses denied any knowledge of the actions of these killing groups at Nuremberg, yet their complicity cannot be denied. One former *Einsatzgruppen* officer gave a guide to the make-up of a *SonderKommando,* which he stated consisted of 20 drivers, 15 Waffen-SS, five administrative officials, 15 Gestapo/Police, 10 SD officials and five interpreters (Headland, 1992:38).

Service	Number of men	Per centage of Einsatzgruppen A
Waffen-SS	340	34.4
Drivers	172	17.4
Administration	18	1.8
SD	35	3.5
Criminal Police Kripo	41	4.1
Stapo	89	9.0
Auxiliary Police	87	8.8
Order Police	133	13.4
Female employees	13	1.3
Interpreters	51	5.1
Telautograph operators	3	0.3
Wireless operators	8	0.8
TOTALS	**990**	**100**

Note: Sourced from (The International Military Tribunal, 1946:Vol 4:220)

The IMT also heard evidence of the actions of the *Einsatzgruppen* and their composition. The prosecution presented Activity and Situation report number six, which covered the actions of the Security Police and SD in Russia from the 1st to the 31st of October 1941 (The International Military Tribunal, 1946:Vol 4:217). These reports were similar to the Operational Situation Reports produced by the *Einsatzgruppen* (which will be discussed shortly), except they covered greater time periods. The report covered personnel details of *Einsatzgruppen* A at this time period. The table above indicates the number of personnel and the percentage of the total force.

Of interest to us is that some 34 per cent of this group were made up of Waffen-SS personnel. Other *Einsatzgruppen* also had a similar mix of Waffen-SS men and other staff. "*Einsatzkommando* 6 consisted of approximately 130-150 men, including a platoon of Waffen-SS..." (Lozowick, 1987:228). In his study Stein identified that:

> On the basis of the evidence at hand it may be concluded that at least 1500 members of the Waffen-SS served with the *Einsatzgruppen*, that at least some of the senior SS combat officers were aware of the manner in which they were employed, and that for these reasons the Waffen-SS must bear its share of responsibility for the cold-blooded murder of hundreds of thousands of civilians. (Stein, 1966:264)

It was not always necessary, or perhaps desirable, to place the Jews within the ghettos to effect their elimination. In the Baltic States a more direct course of action was followed. A report by *SS-Brigadeführer* Stahlecker to Himmler, dated 15 October 1941, entitled "Action Group A", was found in Himmler's private files and was tendered at Nuremberg (document L-180). It refers to the actions of *Einsatzgruppen* A. Stahlecker reported that 135,567 persons, nearly all Jews, were murdered in accordance with basic orders directing the complete annihilation of the Jews (The International Military Tribunal, 1946: Vol 4:219). This report also goes on to tell us that the Waffen-SS undertook cleansing actions on the Eastern Front:

> ... It shows further that the forces of the uniformed police and the Waffen-SS are active mainly in front of Leningrad, in order to take measures under their own officers against the streaming back of the population ... It should be mentioned that the leaders of the Waffen-SS and of the uniformed police, who are on the reserve, have declared their wish to stay with the Security Police and the SD.
> (The International Military Tribunal, 1946: Vol 4:219)

In addition to these enlisted men, a number of Waffen-SS officers also served in the Einsatzgruppen. Of all of the Einsatzgruppen officers, eight per cent served in the Waffen-SS. This is in contrast to some 43 per cent of concentration-camp officers who served in the Waffen-SS (MacLean, 1999b). Some 23 officers served in the Einsatzgruppen then transferred to the Waffen-SS, while seven served in the Waffen-SS and then transferred to the Einsatzgruppen (MacLean, 1999b). A number of officers also served in non-divisional Waffen-SS organisations and these include the 12th and 3rd SS Corps, 502nd SS Heavy Tank Battalion and the 2nd SS Flak Detachment (MacLean, 1999b).

No.	Name of division/formation	Number of Einsatzgruppen officers
1st	SS Panzer Division *Leibstandarte SS Adolf Hitler*	3
2nd	SS Panzer Division *Das Reich*	1
3rd	SS Panzer Division *Totenkopf*	1
4th	SS Panzergrenadier Division *SS-Polizei*	3
8th	SS Kavallerie Division *Florian Geyer*	1
9th	SS Panzer Division *Hohenstaufen*	2
12th	SS Panzer Division *Hitlerjugend*	1
14th	Waffen-Grenadier Division Der SS (Ukrainische NR 1)	1
16th	SS Panzergrenadier Division *Reichsführer-SS*	1
18th	SS Freiwilligen-Panzergrenadier Division *Horst Wessel*	1
19th	Waffen-Grenadier Division Der SS (Lettisches NR 2)	1
20th	Waffen-Grenadier Division Der SS (Estnische NR 1)	1
29th	SS Waffen-Grenadier Division Der (Russische NR 1) later to become the (Italienische NR 1)	1
36th	Waffen-Grenadier Division Der SS	1
38th	SS Grenadier Division *Nibelungen*	1
3rd	SS Corps	2
12th	SS Corps	1
502nd	Heavy Tank Battalion	1
2nd	SS Flak Detachment	1
2nd	SS Infantry Brigade	1
	SS Regiment *Der Fuhrer*	1
	SS Regiment Leibstandarte Adolf Hitler	1

While these numbers may be small when compared to the total number of men serving in the Waffen-SS, the salient point is this; the officers of the *Einsatzgruppen* were at the cutting edge of the genocide being conducted in Russia. They had full knowledge of the killing operations being undertaken in Russia, and they were widely dispersed through the Waffen-SS. The table above indicates the divisions/formations in which *Einsatzgruppen* officers served.[46]

This bearing of responsibility is even more so when one acknowledges that it is reasonable to assume that the generals and, other officers of the Waffen-SS knew about the *Einsatzgruppen* and what they were doing. This is indicated by the testimony of *SS-Obergruppenführer* Bach-Zelewski during the trials at Nuremberg when asked about his knowledge of their activities.

> BACH-ZELEWSKI: *Einsatzgruppe B* was located in Smolensk, and operated in precisely the same way as all the other *Einsatzgruppen*. One heard everywhere in conversation that the Jews were being rounded up and sent to ghettos.
>
> (The International Military Tribunal, 1946: Vol 4:481)

The link between the Waffen-SS and the extermination units was admitted by a commander of the *Das Reich* Division, *SS-Gruppenführer* Georg Keppler, who outlined that "... posting to the former was a part of Waffen-SS discipline", where the posting was used as punishment for infractions (Reitlinger, 1957:171). The movement of personnel was not one-way, however. After suffering grievous losses on the Russian front the *Totenkopf* Division transferred a whole company of soldiers from *Einsatzgruppen* A to its 3rd infantry regiment (Sydnor, 1973).

That senior SS officers knew about the actions of the killing groups is beyond doubt. An order dated 21st September 1939 from *SS-Obergruppenführer* Heinrich Heydrich, chief of the security police, was sent out to various *Einsatzgruppen* leaders and several HSSPF outlining the *special measures* to be taken in the occupied countries (Nuremberg Military Tribunal, 1946: Vol 4:127). Heydrich outlined these special measures were to be carried out:

> In a spirit free from bureaucratic and administrative influences and with an eagerness to assume responsibility. While the regulations and orders of the prisoners-of-war system were hitherto based exclusively on considerations of a *military* nature, now the *political* goal must be attained, namely, to protect the German people from Bolshevist agitators and to gain a firm grip on the occupied territory at the earliest possible moment.
>
> (Nuremberg Military Tribunal, 1946: Vol 4:127)

While this order was issued before the invasion of Russia it is useful in that it clearly sets out the way in which the Jewish question was to be solved in the occupied territories.

The Operational Situation Reports

The Germans were meticulous in their recording the actions of the *Einsatzgruppen,* with Operational Situation Reports regularly being submitted by the units in the field to the authorities in Berlin outlining their actions.

The reports catalogue the involvement of various Waffen-SS units in the atrocities committed during cleansing operations in Russia. During the *Einsatzgruppen* trials the authenticity of the reports were shown beyond doubt and no challenge to them was mounted by the defence. Operational Situation Report 19 dated the 11th of July 1941 outlines Waffen-SS involvement in the killing of Jews, "*Einsatzkommando 4b* ... In Zborov, 600 Jews liquidated by the Waffen-SS as a retaliation measure for Soviet atrocities" (Arad et al., 1989:19).

Waffen-SS and Police troops executed the entire Jewish council in the Russian town of Belzy on the 15th of July 1941 (Stokes, 2002). Operational Situation Report 37 stated that this was in relation to partisan attacks on German troops: "The precise number of shootings can not be ascertained ... the *Kommando* appropriately punished the Jewish Council of Elders in Belzy and other Jews for failing to comply with security police directives and a retribution for attacks on German military personnel" (Arad et al., 1989:57).

Operational Situation Report 58 dated the 20th of August 1941 outlines how the Waffen-SS were involved with the *Einsatzgruppen* in the area of Novoselye, "... an exchange of gunfire took place on August 15 1941 between partisans and two sub-units of the Waffen-SS platoon attached to the *Einsatzgruppe A* near Boskina near the H.Q. of the *Einsatzgruppe A*. Thirteen partisans were killed..." (Arad et al., 1989:94).

Operational Situation Report 59 dated the 21st of August 1941 outlines the actions of *Einsatzgruppen C* in the Novo-Ukrainka area. The report commences with information about partisan activity and the shooting of civilians deemed responsible for such. It then describes the involvement of the 1st SS Brigade in the killing of Jews. An extract of the report is show below:

> After the German troops entered Staro-Konstantinov (the present seat of the Higher SS, the Police Chief and the Military Commander of the Rear Area), Jews were employed for cleaning the barracks. Since the Jews did not report for work lately, the military authorities had to round up the Jewish labour force early in the day. The Jews were impertinent and even refused to work. Out of about 1000 Jews that were recruited for fieldwork, only 70 appeared on the following day. Moreover it was established that harvesters were sabotaged. Finally, the Jewish Council of Elders spread the rumour that the Russians were advancing again; whereupon the Jews publicly threatened and abused the Ukrainians. Finally it was established that the Jews were conducting a flourishing trade with stolen cattle

and goods. In reprisal, the 1 SS Brigade carried out an action against the Jews in the course of which 300 male and 139 female Jews were shot. (Arad et al., 1989:100)

In Operational Situation Report 86 dated the 17th of September 1941 we again find the 1st SS Brigade conducting cleansing operations in the Novo-Ukrainka area. In the town of Ushomir SS units were in action where the 1st SS Brigade "... shot all male Jews" (Arad et al., 1989:134). The 5th SS Panzer Division *Wiking* also assisted in the cleansing operations in occupied Russia by liquidating 600 Jews (Knopp, 2002; Reitlinger, 1957). *SS-Brigadeführer* Heinz Karl Fanslau was brought to trial in relation to this matter for actions when he was in command of the supply battalion for the division, but was acquitted due to lack of evidence (Nuremberg Military Tribunal, 1946: Vol 5:998). The evidence above however does without doubt show a clear link between the *Einsatzgruppen* and the Waffen-SS.

The arguments that the Waffen-SS were not major players in the anti-partisan operations and associated genocide do not ring true on the evidence presented. Without a doubt the Waffen-SS were heavily involved in the activities of the *Einsatzgruppen*. These units were the leading edge of the effort to destroy the Jews and other undesirable elements. As such it would seem to repudiate the claims by the Waffen-SS that they were just simple soldiers and distinct from the terror apparatus of the SS. When it was found that the *Einsatzgruppen* were not killing Jews fast enough the Nazi regime turned to another SS terror apparatus to complete the task, the concentration-camps. The Waffen-SS would also be linked to this system of terror.

5. The Concentration-Camps

It is not the purpose of this book to verify that the crimes against humanity were committed in the concentration-camp system under the Nazis. Several million people perished in this terror apparatus.[47] This I believe history and subsequent tribunals have shown beyond doubt. The NMT attempted to arrive at a rough estimate as to the human cost:

> As to the total number of prisoners delivered to the camps, only a reasonable estimate can be made. If the number of dead at Auschwitz alone is considered, amounting to at least 3.5 million, it is safe to assume that no less than 10 million human beings were at one time or another incarcerated in a concentration-camp.
>
> (Nuremberg Military Tribunal, 1946: Vol 5:222)

What I will show in this chapter is the involvement of the Waffen-SS in this enterprise. However, to not make some attempt to paint the enormity or callousness of this enterprise would be a failing to history. To this point the post-war television interview below, by SS Corporal Richard Boch paints a terrifying picture. Boch tells the story seemingly without emotion and in an almost detached fashion.[48] He was approached by a fellow SS soldier in relation to the killing of the Jews in the gas chambers:

> "Richard, you are interested in the actions?", I said, "Yes, very interested indeed." He said "I will take you with me this evening." The new arrivals had to get undressed and when a certain number got inside they shut the doors and that happens three times…they took out a sort of tin, one of the SS guards did that, and then he climbed up a ladder and then at the top there was a round hole and he opened a little iron door and held the tin there and shook it and then he shut the little door again. And then a fearful screaming started, approximately, I would reckon after about 10 minutes it suddenly went quiet. I said to Herblinger "Can we get a bit nearer when they take them out?" So we went a bit closer, they opened the door, that was the prisoner squad who did that. Then a blue haze came out and I looked in and I saw a pyramid, they had all climbed on top of each other

until the last one stood on the very top. All one on top of the other, it was a pointed heap, all came up to a point. And then the prisoners had to go in and tear it apart. They had to tug and pull very hard to disentangle all these people. Then we went back to the hall, then it was the turn of the last lot to get undressed, the ones who had managed to hang back a bit all of the time. Then the prisoners had to check where small children had been hidden and covered up, they pulled them out and opened the doors quickly again and whoosh, they threw all the children in and slammed the doors. "Uh, I'm going to be sick," I said. I said, "Oh, I've seen nothing like it in my life, oh it's absolutely terrible." And just imagine when they threw the children in how the people inside screamed because then the people inside suddenly realised what was happening. And I said, "Karl, can we leave soon, I can't stand it any more?", and he said, "You do get used to anything in time." (Bloomberg, 2000)

Boch later refused the orders to take part in such massacres. Of note is that he was not shot as a result; a claim often made by the SS in the defence of following orders. As noted by Sydnor regarding the involvement of the Waffen-SS in the camp system; "A number of men from the *Totenkopf* Division became active cogs in the greatest deliberate process of human destruction in the history of mankind" (Sydnor, 1973:361). I shall show that the links between the camp system and the Waffen-SS extend far beyond just the *Totenkopf* Division.

Let me justify why I am including the concentration-camps. These are included as there is a strong link between the Waffen-SS and the concen-tration-camps, second many of the death camps were situated in the con-quered Eastern territories and third the majority of the victims came from the conquered Eastern territories while others were subject to the actions of the *Einsatzgruppen* behind the front lines in the east. As Sydnor notes in his study of the *Totenkopf* division;

> … Among the officers and NCOs and SS enlisted men who fought in the ranks of the *Totenkopf* division there were many who had come from or later went to SS agencies or affiliates engaged in non-military tasks. Per-sonnel exchanges between the SSTK[49] and the extermination centres, the concentration-camps, the *Einsatzgruppen*, the SS anti-partisan units, the staff of the HSSPF, the SD, the domestic police forces of the Reich, the administrative personnel, and operational staffs of the SS, are all a matter of documentary record. (Sydnor, 1990:341)

He is supported in this claim by Wegner who states the following regarding the relationship between the Waffen-SS and the more insidious branches of the SS:

> The staffs of the concentration-camps were organisationally part of the Waffen-SS. Units and formations of the Waffen-SS were used behind the front as part of "anti-guerrilla actions" and assigned, in limited numbers to be sure, to *Einsatzgruppen...* (Wegner, 1985:222)

In handing down its judgement that the SS was a criminal organisation the IMT stated the following in reference to the Waffen-SS and its activities and guilt:

> There is evidence that the shooting of unarmed prisoners of war was the general practice in some Waffen-SS divisions. On 1 October 1944, the custody of prisoners of war and interned persons was transferred to Himmler, who in turn transferred prisoner-of-war affairs to *SS-Obergruppenführer* Berger and to *SS-Obergruppenführer* Pohl. The Race and Settlement Office of the SS, together with the *Volksdeutsche Mittelstelle*[50], were active in carrying out schemes for Germanisation of occupied territories according to the racial principles of the Nazi Party and were involved in the deportation of Jews and other foreign nationals. Units of the Waffen-SS and *Einsatzgruppen* operating directly under the SS Main Office were used to carry out these plans. These units were also involved in the widespread murder and ill-treatment of the civilian population of occupied territories. Under the guise of combating partisan units, units of the SS exterminated Jews and people deemed politically undesirable by the SS, and their reports record the execution of enormous numbers of persons. Waffen-SS divisions were responsible for many massacres and atrocities in occupied territories ... Units of the Waffen-SS were directly involved in the killing of prisoners of war and the atrocities in occupied countries. It supplied personnel for the *Einsatzgruppen*, and had command over the concentration-camp guards after its absorption of the *Totenkopf* SS, which originally controlled the system.
>
> (The International Military Tribunal, 1946: Vol 22:514)

I shall expand upon these arguments in the following pages, but suffice for now it provides the reader with some indication of how I intend to frame my arguments.

Creation and management of the camp system

In 1934 the SS took control of the concentration-camp system and *SS-Reichsführer* Heinrich Himmler was now the regulator of this apparatus of the Nazi state. Waffen-SS General, *SS-Obergruppenführer* Theodore Eicke, a man with a reputation for brutality, was given the role of Inspector of Concentration-camps. Eicke was the commandant of Dachau, and this camp was used as the model for future camps. It was Eicke who formulated a code of conduct for the SS guards and also the disciplinary and punishment regulations for the prisioners (Bracher, 1969; Sydnor, 1990). The disciplinary regulations became the standard for concentration-camps and remained in use until 1945. They included punishments such as forced labour, solitary confinement, corporal punishment and the death penalty for certain offences. The brutality of Eicke was demonstrated by the code of conduct for the SS guards:

> The code of conduct for the SS guards was based upon Eicke's demand for blind and absolute obedience to all orders from SS superior officers, and upon his insistence that each prisoner be treated with fanatical hatred as an enemy of the state. (Sydnor, 1990:11)

SS-Obergruppenführer **Eicke**

Eicke was later to command the 3rd SS Panzer Division *Totenkopf* before being killed on the Russian front. This division was recruited almost exclusively from camp guards during its formation. Eicke provided the Nazis with a concentration-camp system that was "… beyond the control of traditional law and authority, in which the enemies of the state were broken and destroyed by the organised, impersonal and systematic brutalities…" (Sydnor, 1990:23). This system was to burgeon from a mere six camps before the war to some 185 by 1944, and this figure did not include hundreds of sub-camps. Waffen-SS General Oswald Pohl boastfully reported this growth to Himmler in April 1944:

> In April 1944 the defendant Pohl informed Himmler that there were 20 concentration-camps and 165 labour camps in the Reich and German occupied territory. A postscript to this letter in Pohl's handwriting boastfully states that: "In Eicke's time there were altogether six camps. Now: 185!"
>
> (Nuremberg Military Tribunal, 1946: Vol 5:221)

That Pohl was aware of what was happening in the camps is evidenced by his comment during his trial when asked by the judges if he was aware of the deaths in the camps:

> Q. What Judge Phillips and I were endeavouring to ascertain, and I think now we have ascertained, is whether you knew the number of deaths occurring in the concentration-camps, and from this long interrogation we now conclude that you did know.
> A. Yes.
>
> (Nuremberg Military Tribunal, 1946: Vol 45:433)

Further to this is a diary entry by SS doctor Kremer at Auschwitz.

> 23 September 1943 Tonight sixth and seventh *Sonderatkion*.[51] In the morning *Obergruppenführer* Pohl and party arrived at the Waffen-SS quarters. A guard was standing outside the door and was the first to stand to attention before us. In the evening, at 20:00 hours, dinner with *Obergruppenführer* Pohl in the officers mess, a real feast… (Klee et al., 1988: 260)

The denials of the Waffen-SS

Often it has been argued that the Waffen-SS was a separate organisation from the concentration-camp system. During his testimony at the Nuremberg trials SS General, *SS-Oberstgruppenführer* Paul Hausser was asked by the SS defence counsel if there was a link between the Waffen-SS and the camp guards:

> HERR PELCKMANN: Did the Waffen-SS furnish the guard units and the so-called command personnel for the concentration-camps?
>
> HAUSSER: The guards of the concentration-camps and the personnel in the command did not belong to the Waffen-SS. Only in the course of the

war were these units designated as Waffen-SS in order to release them from military service and give them freedom to carry out their police duties. The members of the Waffen-SS considered this measure, which they learned of only after the war, a deliberate deception on the part of Himmler. We did not have anything to do with the men of the concentration-camps and the guard personnel.

HERR PELCKMANN: It has not become quite clear yet, Witness, just what you meant when you said "to release them from military service." Will you explain that in more detail?

HAUSSER: All persons who served at home and in the Police had to be exempted from military service in the Army by the *Wehrkreis* or district commander in order to carry out their police tasks. That did not apply when all guard units were designated as Waffen-SS, for these were a part of the Armed Forces. In the main offices in Berlin these units, in order to differentiate them, were designated nominal Waffen-SS. But all this I learned only here later.

(The International Military Tribunal, 1946: Vol 20:366)

Hausser's testimony is confusing to say the least. After initially stating that the camp guards were not linked to the Waffen-SS, in the next breath he then admits that they were part of the Waffen-SS organisation. It needs to be considered that Hausser was one of the most senior Waffen-SS officers and had served on various commands staffs and in various theatres of war, yet he purported to have no knowledge of Waffen-SS involvement in the camp system. Yet this is a man who oversaw the SS training schools that had cells built into the basements for concentration-camp inmates to see to the comfort of SS officers. Of even more importance is his claim that the Waffen-SS soldiers only became aware of the amalgamation of the camps with the front-line units after the war. *SS-Brigadeführer* Kurt Meyer, former commander of the 12th SS Panzer Division *Hitlerjugend*, also puts forward this argument regarding lack of knowledge in his post-war account of his wartime involvement. He claims that soldiers of the Waffen-SS have been tarred with the same brush as other elements of the SS:

> The Waffen-SS is now incriminated with events in the concentration-camps because leading individuals of the government have placed special formations in the same category as the frontline troops … The soldiers had neither more nor less knowledge of the events in Germany that the majority of the German people. (Meyer, 2001:392)

Clear evidence will be shown that the front-line Waffen-SS units had close and inseparable ties with the camp guards and camp system administration well before the end of the war, and with this the obvious requisite knowledge of the operations of the camps was also present. Not only this, but the Waffen-SS were clear financial beneficiaries of the camp system.

SS-Brigadeführer Heinz Karl Fanslau was one of Hausser's former adjutants. His role was to organise "... replacements, recruiting, discharges, promotions, assignments, and transfers. Within this field he dealt indiscriminately with the Waffen-SS personnel and also with that of the concentration-camps" (Nuremberg Military Tribunal, 1946: Vol 5:998; Reitlinger, 1957). Fanslau tried unsuccessfully to argue that even though he was responsible for personnel matters in the camps he had no knowledge of the crimes being committed. The tribunal rejected this claim outright and he was found guilty with the following judgement.[52]

> As the officer in charge of personnel, he was as much an integral part of the whole organisation and as essential a cog in its operation as any other ... He was in command of one of the essential ingredients of successful functioning. This has no relation to "group condemnation", which has been so loudly decried. Personnel were just as important and essential in the whole nefarious plan as barbed wire, watchdogs and gas chambers. The successful operation of the concentration-camps required the coordination of men and materials, and Fanslau to a substantial degree supplied the men. He was not an obscure menial; he was a person of responsibility and authority in the organisation, who was charged with and performed important and essential functions ... His claim that he was unaware of what was going on in the organisation and in the concentration-camps which it administered is utterly inconsistent with the importance and indispensability of his position. Whether or not he was aware of the cold-blooded program of extermination of useless concentration-camp inmates, he must have been aware that millions of human beings had been herded into concentration-camps, in violation of all their rights and solely because Germany needed their labour, to work under the most inhumane circumstances. The Tribunal finds without hesitation that Fanslau knew of the slavery in the concentration-camps and took an important part in promoting and administering it. This being true, he is guilty of war crimes and crimes against humanity.
>
> (Nuremberg Military Tribunal, 1946: Vol 5:998)

Personnel links between the camps and the Waffen-SS

This link between the Waffen-SS and the concentration-camp system can be shown by a number of factors. Eicke formed a number of *Totenkopf* Standarten or Death's Head regiments that were used in the guarding of the concentration-camps prior to the war. With the commencement of the conflict another 12 regiments were formed. A Hitler decree on the 18th of May 1939 provided that the Death's Head units (camp guards) were to be used as combat replacements for the Waffen-SS (Sydnor, 1990). *This established a ready exchange in personnel between the camp system and the Waffen-SS.* In 1941 nine Death's Head infantry and two cavalry regiments were transferred to the control of the Waffen-SS,. Three Death's Head infantry regiments were formed into a Waffen-SS battle group, SS Kampfgruppe *Nord,* and one regiment was transferred to the Waffen-SS Motorised Division *Reich* (later *Das Reich*) (Mollo, 1982).

The apologists claim that the Waffen-SS were not associated with the camp system. Contrary to this view, however, is an order from Himmler, which incorporated all of the Death Heads units into the Waffen-SS (Simpson, 1990; Sydnor, 1990). In fact, some of the duties that Eicke had performed as Inspector of Concentration-camps were given to the Waffen-SS command to oversee (Mollo, 1982; Sydnor, 1990:133). As early as 1940 Waffen-SS units sent personnel to camps for duty and wounded soldiers were sent there for recuperation. There was a flow of Waffen-SS soldiers who were unfit for service or wounded into the camps, however later in the war as manpower demands increased "… great numbers of concentration-camp guards were re-drafted into the field divisions of the Waffen-SS" (Reitlinger, 1957:266). One example of this is *SS-Sturmbannführer* Richard Baer who was attached to the 3rd SS *Totenkopf* Division. Baer served in the camps prior to the war and then undertook combat duties until he was wounded in 1942. He then was transferred back to the camp system where he went on to become commandant of Auschwitz (MacLean, 1999a; Segev, 1987).

When ordered to form a new tank battalion in 1942 for the *Totenkopf* division, *SS-Obergruppenführer* Eicke drew on personnel from "… the SS Mountain Division *Nord,* and from an additional gleaning of the various SS agencies – including the guard detachments of the concentration-camps" (Sydnor, 1990:259). Some camp commanders recalled that their men were sent off to the Waffen-SS divisions. From Auschwitz at least 2500 were sent between 1940 and 1943, and from Sachsenhausen between 1942 and 1945 some 1500 were sent (Stein, 1966). Former camp inmate Helmut Bickel had this to say about the interchange of SS soldiers to the camps and their character.

> I can only compare the actions of the SS men who came to us from the front lines and those SS men who had never been in the front lines: all of them acted alike. The SS man who was assigned as a guard in a

concentration-camp or as officer of the guard in a concentration-camp, the moment he entered that barbed-wire fence simply became a member of a group of murderers. In order to give an example, there was an *SS-Obersturmführer* who had just returned from front line duty and he had a small terrier and while working one of the inmates, a Jew, while pushing his little cart, unintentionally hit his little dog. The dog just gave a little yelp; that was all that happened. This SS man liked the dog so much, however, that for that reason, because the man had molested the little dog, he killed the inmate. That is how much he liked the animal and hated the human being. That was not his character. That was simply the outstanding position which he held and where he had power over life and death of the inmates. For the SS men it was the sacred duty towards the Führer to kill an inmate as brutally as possible.
(Nuremberg Military Tribunal, 1946: Vol 5:785)

An in-depth examination of personal files of over 950 SS officers who served in the camp system was conducted by MacLean (1999a), and it would seem to refute the testimony of Hausser regarding there being no links between the Waffen-SS and the camp system. This examination revealed that over 43 per cent of all concentration-camp officers had served in the Waffen-SS fighting units either before or after their service at the camps (MacLean, 1999a). Yet despite the fact that a multitude of officers from the camp system had served in the Waffen-SS, senior officers such as Hausser still attempted to distance the Waffen-SS when questioned by the defence for the SS at Nuremberg:

HERR PELCKMANN: The Prosecution asserts that the Waffen-SS was only a part of the whole SS organisation and that as such it was needed for the carrying through of the joint criminal conspiracy. Please comment on this.

HAUSSER: I believe that it can be gathered from all of my testimony that the Waffen-SS was a completely independent unit and connected with other organisations only through the person of Heinrich Himmler. This separation of the various branches was undoubtedly intensified during the war. Therefore, we could not have harboured common criminal plans with the others or participated in carrying them through.
(The International Military Tribunal, 1946: Vol 20:367)

Hausser went as far as to claim that "… There were neither official nor personal relations with the Death's-Head units, which had the task of guarding the concentration-camps" (The International Military Tribunal, 1946: Vol 20:360). Indeed it has been suggested by some ex-Waffen-SS veterans that Himmler was careful to try and keep the Waffen-SS separate from the camps for the sake of its image and also the to avoid the soldiers confronting matters that "… they could not understand or judge" (Reitlinger, 1957:265). At least one author attempts to portray the Waffen-SS as being innocent and only victims by association with the concentration-camp guards. This was because the *Totenkopf* carried the same pay books, wore the same uniform as the true Waffen-SS which, had never been implicated in the terror regime of the concentration-camps (Hohne, 1969). This is clearly not the case, as I will show evidence that the Waffen-SS were involved in, and had knowledge of, the camp system.

During the preparation for his television documentary for the Thames television company on the SS, author Andrew Mollo came across this denial of association. He had contacted *SS-Obersturmbannführer* Richard Schulze-Kossens[53] for the purpose of an interview; Kossens had been an officer in the *Leibstandarte SS Adolf Hitler* and was also the Waffen-SS adjutant to Hitler for part of the war. Schulze-Kossens was briefly the commander of the 38th SS Grenadier Division *Nibelungen*, the last Waffen-SS division formed before the end of the war (Westwood, 2001; Williamson & Andrew, 2004b). Upon finding out that the television series was to cover all aspects of the SS, including the camps, Schulze-Kossens had this to say:

> If this report is correct, I must inform you that I am not prepared to give an interview which begins with the events in the concentration-camps, which will inevitably stir up feelings against the SS. As an officer of the former Waffen-SS I am not interested in allowing myself to be defamed again in England if our troops are again to be associated with the events in the concentration-camps. Our statements which would distance us from such events would only create the impression of a cover-up … I want to take this opportunity to say how deeply it would offend me to have our troops portrayed once again as a sort of "soldateska" who committed a string of war crimes… (Mollo, 1982:2)

This is a crucial argument raised by many Waffen-SS apologists; that they were in fact separate from the camp system and had nothing to do with the personnel of the system and had no knowledge of the crimes committed therein. At Nuremberg Hausser argued the following:

> HERR PELCKMANN: To what extent were the crimes in concentration-camps, such as the extermination of the Jews, known to the Waffen-SS? I should like you to remember that you speak not only for yourself as a highly placed general, but that you also speak for the simple SS man, based on your own experience, of course.
>
> HAUSSER: It sounds quite unlikely, and foreign countries do not wish to believe that the members of the Waffen-SS as well as myself knew noth-

ing of the crimes of which we have heard here. This perhaps may serve as
an explanation: At home only those who had victims in the concentration-
camps learned, anything about them; only the ever-present secret opposition spread stories and rumours. This was kept from the SS man. If he
happened to hear something by chance, he thought that it was hostile propaganda. Foreign radio broadcasts or newspapers were unknown to him
for they were forbidden at home. The bulk of the Waffen-SS was facing
the enemy. The war tasks grew from year to year and the efforts became
more intense. The SS man did not have the time or opportunity to check
rumours, and like myself he was surprised and indignant about all these
things which Himmler had done contrary to what he had preached to us
in peacetime.

(The International Military Tribunal, 1946: Vol 20:369)

I will present clear evidence that it would have been almost impossible
for officers such as Hausser not to be aware of what was going on in the
camps. As well as administrative ties there were also personnel links
between the camps and the Waffen-SS. Camp officers served throughout
the divisions of the Waffen-SS including the divisions commanded by
Hausser such as the *Leibstandarte SS Adolf Hitler, Das Reich* and the
Totenkopf divisions. These camp officers served in every division of the
Waffen-SS except for the 28th SS Division *Wallonien*, 37th SS Division *Lut-
zow* and the 38th SS Division *Nibelungen* (MacLean, 1999a). Examples of
this interaction are not hard to find, for instance Hilmar Wackerle became
the first commandant of Dachau in 1933. He later went on to serve in the
5th SS *Wiking* Division until being killed at Lvov in Poland in 1941
(MacLean, 1999a; Segev, 1987). Otto Foerschner was an *SS-Sturmbannführer* who served in the 5th SS *Wiking* Division and later went on to command the Dora sub-camp at Buchenwald (MacLean, 1999a; Segev, 1987).
He was executed on the 28th of May 1946. This lack of distance between the
two groups is supported by the observation that:

> ... the total separation between the battlefield units of the Waffen-SS and
> even more sinister organisations such as the *Einsatzgruppen* and the
> *Totenkopfverbände*[54] a separation of which post-war apologists make
> much – does not stand up to detailed examination, there was a division,
> but it was somewhat porous. (Windrow et al., 1982:6).

Further to this not only did hundreds serve in the front line Waffen-SS
divisions, but six former concentration-camp officers also rose to become
divisional commanders in the Waffen-SS. It was not the case that these officers just served at the minor labour camps, rather many of them served at

the major extermination camps such as Auschwitz, Sobibor, Belzec, Belsen, Dachau and Mauthausen, etc (MacLean, 1999a). Yet despite the fact that officers with knowledge of the atrocities that were being committed in the camps were woven throughout the fighting units of the Waffen-SS, senior Waffen-SS officers such as Hausser claimed no knowledge of the activities of the concentration-camps.

Just as with the *Einsatzgruppen*, the Waffen-SS used transfers between the front-line units and the camps as a form of punishment. *SS-Obersturm-bannführer* Karl Kuenstler is an example of this type of treatment. As commandant of the Flossenburg concentration-camp he came into disrepute due to his drinking, as a result he was transferred to the 7th SS *Prinz Eugen* Division where he was later killed during combat duties (MacLean, 1999a; Segev, 1987). Hans Maubach was an SS officer on the staff of SSPF Odilo Globocnik in Lublin and had an intimate knowledge of the killing camps through the administrative role he played on the staff of the SSPF. In October 1941 he had a falling out with Globocnik and was sent to the Waffen-SS where he served in the *Leibstandarte SS Adolf Hitler* (Poprzeczny, 2004). There were other reasons for sending officers from the front to the camps and vice versa. These included incapacitation by injury, incompetence and specific expertise that could be utilised in the camp system (Sydnor, 1973).

Hausser was not alone in his claim of lack of knowledge of the camps. Waffen-SS officer, Robert Brill, who served in the *Leibstandarte SS Adolf Hitler* and also at the Waffen-SS training centre, gave the following testimony:

> MR. COUNSELLOR SMIRNOV: And you contend that the Waffen-SS did not participate in the killings in the concentration-camps?
>
> BRILL: I said that I and countless comrades of the Waffen-SS knew nothing about them. The defendant's counsel told me that killings were carried out. I did not deny it.
>
> (The International Military Tribunal, 1946: Vol 20:352)

Note that Brill does not deny what occurred in the camps, but merely not having knowledge of such actions. Brill seems to be unaware of the fact that at least 16 officers from the camp system served in the *Leibstandarte SS Adolf Hitler*. The list below of officers and the Waffen-SS divisions they served in render such claims regarding this lack of knowledge as ridiculous.

No.	Name of Division	Number of camp officers
1st	SS Panzer Division *Leibstandarte SS Adolf Hitler*	16
2nd	SS Panzer Division *Das Reich*	39
3rd	SS Panzer Division *Totenkopf*	159
4th	SS Panzergrenadier Division *SS-Polizei*	29
5th	SS Panzer Division *Wiking*	45
6th	SS Gebirgs Division *Nord*	57
7th	SS Freiwilligen-Gerbirgs Division *Prinz Eugen*	23
8th	SS Kavallerie Division *Florian Geyer*	28
9th	SS Panzer Division *Hohenstaufen*	22
10th	SS Panzer Division *Frundsberg*	20
11th	SS Freiwilligen-Panzergrenadier Division *Nordland*	12
12th	SS Panzer Division *Hitlerjugend*	6
13th	Waffen-Gebirgs Division Der SS (Kroatische NR1) *Handschar*	9
14th	Waffen-Grenadier Division Der SS (Ukrainische NR 1)	5
15th	Waffen-Grenadier Division Der SS (Lettische NR 1)	5
16th	SS Panzergrenadier Division *Reichsführer-SS*	17
17th	SS Panzergrenadier Division *G_tz Von Berlichingen*	15
18th	SS Freiwilligen-Panzergrenadier Division *Horst Wessel*	7
19th	Waffen-Grenadier Division Der SS (Lettisches NR 2)	3
20th	Waffen-Grenadier Division Der SS (Estnische NR 1)	7
21st	Waffen-Gebirgs Division Der SS (Albanische NR1) *Skanderberg*	4
22nd	Freiwilligen-Kavallerie Division Der SS *Maria Theresia*	3
23rd	Waffen-Gebirgs Division Der SS *Kama* later to become Panzer division *Nederland*	5
24th	SS Gebirgs Division *Karstjager*	1
25th	Waffen-Grenadier Division Der SS (Ungarische NR1) *Hunyadi*	2
26th	Waffen-Grenadier Division Der SS (Ungarische NR 2) *Hungaria*	3
27th	SS Freiwilligen-Panzergrenadier Division (Flamische NR 1) *Langemarck*	5
28th	SS Freiwilligen-Panzergrenadier Division *Wallonien*	0
29th	SS Waffen-Grenadier Division Der (Russische NR 1) later to become the (Italienische NR 1)	3
30th	SS Waffen-Grenadier Division Der (Weissruthensche NR 1)	2
31st	SS Freiwilligen-Grenadier Division	2
32nd	SS Freiwilligen-Grenadier Division *30 Januar*	
33rd	Waffen-Kavallerie Division Der SS (Ungarische NR 3) later to become Waffen-Grenadier Division Der SS (Franzosische NR 1) *Charlemagne*	1
34th	Waffen-Grenadier Division Der *SS Landstorm Nederland*	6
35th	SS Polizei Grenadier Division	1
36th	Waffen-Grenadier Division Der SS	7
37th	Freiwilligen-Kavallerie Division *L_tzow*	0
38th	SS Grenadier Division *Nibelungen*	0

The concentration-camp system was just too big, and the Waffen-SS too closely entwined for the soldiers of the Waffen-SS not to have known about the activities that were going on there. For instance, *SS-Obersturm-bannführer* Jochen Peiper was a leading figure in the Waffen-SS. Many would say that he was the epitome of the Waffen-SS, officer being resourceful, tough and brutal. He would rise to prominence in the public eye after the war when brought to trial for the massacre at Malmedy in Belgium of American soldiers. From November 1939 he performed the role of military adjutant to Himmler before going to become one of the most well-known officers of the *Leibstandarte SS Adolf Hitler*. Although not directly associated with the camps, there is no doubt that he had knowledge of the camps and their function:

> As personal adjutant he would have been privy to virtually everything in Himmler's office and he could not have failed to be aware of Hitler's and Himmler's policies for ethnic cleansing of the Greater Reich, the organisation and establishment of concentration-camps and the overall policy for the genocide of the Jewish race. Indeed, there is photographic evidence of Peiper with Himmler at Mauthausen during a visit to this, the most deadly of all the existing concentration-camps, at the end of May 1941. (Reynolds, 2002:27)

His case highlights the fact that as well as those directly involved in the camps system there would have been hundreds of Waffen-SS soldiers involved in the administration or supply of such a system. In addition to these officers who actually served in the fighting divisions of the Waffen-SS, in excess of 50 SS officers also served in other Waffen-SS non-divisional organisations such as corps headquarters, independent regiments, etc (MacLean, 1999a).

Economic links between the camps and the Waffen-SS

In April 1941 Himmler issued a directive that instructed all existing concentration-camps were, for economic and administrative reasons, to be listed as part of the Waffen-SS establishment (Hohne, 1969; Stein, 1966). Further reorganisation of the SS departments took place in 1942 which placed the concentration-camps within one unified economic administration for Police, Waffen-SS and General SS (Koehl, 1983). So not only was there a link in personnel, but also a link along administrative and economic lines. This was indicated by the evidence given by Waffen-SS officer Brill when confronted with a report by the Russian prosecutor Mr Smirnov, outlining the usage of seven tons of human hair taken from 140,000 female prisoners at the Auschwitz camp (document number USSR-511). The letter was sent from Waffen-SS General Glucks to the various camps administrations:

> The chief of the SS Economic and Administrative Main Office, *SS-Obergruppenführer* Pohl, on the basis of a report submitted to him, has ordered that all human hair cut in concentration-camps be appropriately utilised. Human hair is to be used for the manufacture of industrial felt and to be spun into yarn. Out of combed and cut hair of women, hair-yarn socks for

U-boat crews are to be made, as well as hair-felt stockings for employees of the Reich railways ... The hair gathered in all the camps will be utilised by creating a special production unit in one of the concentration-camps. More detailed instructions as to the delivery of the collected hair will be given separately. Reports on amount of hair gathered each month, male and female recorded separately, must be submitted on the 5th of each month, beginning with 5 September 1942. Signed: Glucks, *SS-Brigade-führer* and Major-General of the Waffen-SS.

(The International Military Tribunal, 1946: Vol 20:353)

Brill is then questioned about Waffen-SS involvement in the camp system.

MR. COUNSELLOR SMIRNOV: Now, Witness, I would like you to look at the stamp. Do you see this stamp? It says, "Waffen-SS Commandant, KL Sachsenhausen." Do you still assert that the command of the camps was not composed of the Waffen-SS?

BRILL: Yes. I will explain that. The commands of the Waffen—SS-the commands of the concentration-camps were officially on the budget of the Waffen-SS...

MR. COUNSELLOR SMIRNOV: So they were on the budget of the Waffen-SS, were they not?

BRILL: I said they were on the budget of the Waffen-SS. For economic reasons it was necessary that the commands, in their dealings with the Reich, operate under the name of an organisation, which had the possibility of working with Reich funds and with the Reich authorities.

(The International Military Tribunal, 1946: Vol 20:353)

Brill attempts to discount this link between the camps and the Waffen-SS as being of no importance, it was merely economic and administrative; but none-the-less they are linked. Camps like the one at Majdanek were designed hold prisoners who would work for industries owned by the SS and operated primarily for the benefit of the SS, in accordance with Himmler's plans to make Lublin the industrial centre of an SS empire. Like any military organisation the Waffen-SS could not have functioned without economic support and administrative support. Himmler himself espoused how the camps would be used to the economic and material benefit of the Waffen-SS. Examples of the economic links between the Waffen-SS and the camp system are not hard to find. SS clothing works were set up in the camps in Lublin. These acted as subsidiary of the main Waffen-SS clothing workshops at Ravensbruck concentration-camp (Arad, 1987; White, 1990). Indeed the camp at Majdanek was "... intended to produce supplies necessary to feed, clothe, house, fuel, transport and arm the SS" (White, 1990:13).

In April 1943 Himmler made a speech to officers of the *Leibstandarte SS Adolf Hitler* at Metz. He explained how the SS would benefit from the work in the camps (document 1918-PS):

> The apartment-building program, which is the prerequisite for a healthy and social basis of the entire SS, as well as of the entire leadership corps, can be carried out only when I get the money for it from somewhere. Nobody is going to give me the money. It must be earned, and it will be earned by forcing the scum of mankind, the prisoners, the professional criminals, to do positive work. The man guarding those prisoners serves harder than the one on close-order drill. The one who does this and stands near these utterly negative people will learn within three to four months-and we shall see. In peacetime, I shall form guard battalions and put them on duty for three months only. They will learn to fight the inferior beings; and this will not be a boring guard duty, but if the officers handle it right, it will be the best indoctrination on inferior beings and inferior races ... This in turn is necessary because we stand or die with this leading blood of Germany; and if the good blood is not reproduced, we will not be able to rule the world.

(The International Military Tribunal, 1946: Vol 4:202)

Again Himmler is clearly outlining racial and ideological messages. Of note is Himmler again goes to lengths to state how the role of the camp guard is just as important and perhaps more onerous than that of the fighting SS soldier, this again being a message used by him to forge the SS into one organic body.

The camps were run with chilling economic efficiency. At Nuremberg a report (document d-960) was tabled that clearly shows the callousness with which human life was treated. It was put to *SS-Oberführer* Gunther Reinecke, who was chief judge of the Supreme SS and Police court. It clearly shows the link between the camps and the Waffen-SS.

> Waffen-SS, Natzweiler Concentration-camp, Commander's office, 24 March 1943.
>
> Bill to the Security Police and SD, Strasbourg.
>
> For the 20 prisoners executed and cremated in this concentration-camp, costs amounting to 127,05 Reichsmark arose. The Commander's office of the Natzweiler Concentration-camp requests the early payment of the above-mentioned sum.

(The International Military Tribunal, 1946: Vol 20:459)

This economic wrangling over the costs to be born for the destruction of human lives is also clearly illustrated in a letter from the President of the Reich Research Department to the Reich Finance Minister relating to whether the SS is entitled to payments for experiments conducted on camp prisoners (document 002-PS):

> The Reich Surgeon SS and Police, in a personal discussion, told me that the budget claim, which he looked after, is used primarily in the pure military sector of the Waffen-SS. Since it is established on a smaller scale for the enlarging of scientific research possibilities, they pertain exclusively to such affairs, which are carried out with the material (prisoners), which is only accessible to the Waffen-SS and are therefore not to be undertaken by any other experimental office. I cannot object therefore on behalf of the Reich Research Council against the budget claim of the Reich Surgeon SS and Police. The letter is signed, "Mentzel, Ministerial Director."
>
> (The International Military Tribunal, 1946: Vol 4:210)

Reports such as the above clearly show both the type of actions being undertaken in the camps and the administrative and economic links the Waffen-SS had with such.

Not only were there the personnel links in regards to the camps, but there was also the issue of property and material taken from the Jews and others who were evacuated to the camps. The Waffen-SS were clear beneficiaries from the concentration-camp system. War records of the *Totenkopf* Division indicate that they received numerous supplies from the workshops of the camps such as Dachau and Oranienburg (Sydnor, 1973). On the 13th of May 1943 *SS-Obergruppenführer* Frank wrote to Himmler and informed him of the "… utilisation of Jewish concealed and stolen goods" (Nuremberg Military Tribunal, 1946: Vol 5:709). In the letter Frank suggests that some of the property, in particular men's watches, be distributed in the following manner.

> I suggest to distribute the repaired men's watches as follows:
>
> (a) Each combat division receives immediately — 500 items, beginning 1 October 1943, "*Leibstandarte Adolf Hitler*", once more 500 items, division "*Das Reich*", "*Totenkopf Division*", (once received already 500 watches each).
>
> (b) The submarine service receives immediately 3000 items beginning 1 October 1943, once more 3000 items.
>
> (c) Concentration-camps receive for squads on outside duty, guard-commanders etc, according to the decision of the commandant, 200 items. This is a total of about 25,000 watches; remainder 2,000 items.

Fountain pens — Each combat division receives 300 items; the submarine service receives 2000 items; remainder 1500 items.

(Nuremberg Military Tribunal, 1946: Vol 5:710)

Waffen-SS units received winter clothing that had been confiscated in the camps and ghettos in the East. These units included the *Leibstandarte* and *Totenkopf* Divisions (Reitlinger, 1957; Sydnor, 1990; Weingartner, 1974). Here is conclusive proof that the Waffen-SS were beneficiaries of the looting that was being done of the Jewish populations. One would wonder what the 500 soldiers of the *Leibstandarte* thought when they received 500 watches with Jewish names inscribed on the back? In his reply on the 3rd of December 1943 Himmler agreed with the distribution of watches but added the following:

> The Reich Leader SS has agreed that you, according to your proposition, distribute pocket watches, wristwatches and fountain pens among the individual divisions. He merely requests that the police division should not receive 700 pocket watches, but only 500. Those 200 watches are to be distributed, 100 watches each, among the divisions, "The Reich", and "Death's Head." I have reported to the Reich Leader SS immediately because I thought that would be better as you suggested to put the watches and fountain pens in his name at the disposal of the divisions for the yuletide celebration.
>
> (Nuremberg Military Tribunal, 1946: Vol 5:713)

The Waffen-SS undertook the administration of the camps and ensured that its rigid discipline code was enforced, as can be seen from the letter from two Waffen-SS Generals (document 2189-PS). It is dated the 11th of August 1942 and is from *SS-Brigadeführer* Glucks, on behalf of *SS-Obergruppenführer* Pohl, to the commandants of the concentration-camps.

> The *Reichsführer-SS* and Chief of the German Police has ordered that punishment by beating will be executed in concentration-camps for women by prisoners under the ordered supervision. In order to co-ordinate this order the Main Office Chief SS of the Economic Administration, *SS-Obergruppenführer* and General of the Waffen-SS Pohl, has ordered, effective immediately, that punishment by beating will also be executed by prisoners in concentration-camps for men.
>
> (The International Military Tribunal, 1946: Vol 4:201)

There was little mercy from the Waffen-SS soldiers for those camp inmates who could no longer function or committed minor infractions. For example, Waffen-SS soldiers executed prisoners during evacuation marches from the Hersbruck concentration-camp to Dachau and shot one prisoner for daring to steal a potato[55] (Ruter et al., 2004: Vol 6).

The links between the medical experiments and the Waffen-SS

But even worse atrocities took place within the camp system in the name of medical advancement, so-called advancement that the Waffen-SS was to play a pivotal role in. In a post-war interview SS General Karl Wolff claims:

> Never would I have thought; it never occurred to us that we might arrogantly talk about exterminating anybody who didn't happen to have been born with the right skin or who was culturally inferior to us, or was undesirable. (Bloomberg, 2000).

Yet in a letter to the State Secretary of the Reich Ministry of Transportation Wolff expressed his thanks for the assistance being given in transporting the Jews to the extermination camps. This document formed part of the prosecution evidence during the Pohl Trial, and reads as below:

> Thank you very much, also in the name of the Reich Leader SS, for your letter of 28 July 1942. I was especially pleased to learn from you that already for a fortnight a daily train; taking 5000 members of the Chosen People every time, had gone to Treblinka... I have contacted the departments concerned myself, so that the smooth carrying out of all these measures seems to be guaranteed.
> (Nuremberg Military Tribunal, 1946: Vol 5:777)

When this was put to Wolff, who up to that point had denied any knowledge of the actions in the camps, he had the following to say:

> I admit without any reservation that this had slipped from my memory. However, it is not possible for a human being to remember every letter which I wrote during a number of years. I gave the answers according to the best of my belief and knowledge and to the best of my recollection.
> (Nuremberg Military Tribunal, 1946: Vol 5:778)

During the Pohl Case, Wolff was questioned in relation to his knowledge of the actions taking place at the camps and elsewhere:

> Q. Well, did you ever hear about Russians and Poles, who were not Jews, being exterminated and killed, did you ever hear about that?
> A. No. I have never heard anything about extermination. I know that in the cases of combating partisans, and in cases of attempts at life, harsh mea-

sures were taken and people would be shot, but what your Honour is probably referring to is systematic and planned extermination.
(Nuremberg Military Tribunal, 1946: Vol 5:681)

   This is the same SS general who was convicted after the war of being
responsible for the deaths of 300,000 Jews at Treblinka and for the conduct
of medical experiments at the Dachau concentration-camp (Gutman, 1990).

SS- Obergruppenführer Wolff

   It would seem that Wolff was not surprised, however, when he signed
off on many of the reports from the concentration-camps outlining the
deaths of the culturally inferior or the disposal of property taken from camp
inmates to SS formations. Film footage of the period shows Wolff visiting
a concentration-camp near Minsk in 1941 looking anything but surprised as
he toured the concentration-camp with Himmler looking at the camp
inmates consisting mainly of Russian POWs. This is the same SS general
who had knowledge of and assisted with the administration of the cruel and
abhorrent medical experiments being conducted at Dachau, that resulted
in inmates being subjected to fatal cold weather and high-pressure

experiments. At Nuremberg a letter was produced which shows complicity of Wolff and the senior Waffen-SS administration beyond doubt (document 343-PS). It is from *Luftwaffe* Field-Marshal Milch to Wolff thanking him and the SS for their assistance in conducting the experiments.

> Dear Wolff
>
> In reference to your telegram of 12 May, our sanitary inspector reports to me that the altitude experiments carried out by the SS and Air Force at Dachau have been finished. Any continuation of these experiments seems not to be necessary. However, the carrying out of experiments of some other kind, in regard to perils on the high seas, would be important … The low-pressure chamber would not be needed for these low-temperature experiments. It is urgently needed at another place and therefore can no longer remain in Dachau. I convey the special thanks from the Supreme Commander of the Air Corps to the SS for their extensive co-operation. I remain with best wishes for you in good comradeship and with Heil Hitler! Always yours, E. Milch.
>
> (The International Military Tribunal, 1946: Vol 4:204)

Himmler himself later wrote to Milch and begged him to allow the doctor responsible for these terrible experiments, Dr. Rascher, to be transferred to the Waffen-SS so that experiments in relation to frost-bite, etc could be carried out. He was duly transferred to the Waffen-SS. The Medical Case revealed that Waffen-SS doctors participated in a number of experiments involving camp inmates as human guinea pigs for issues such as freezing, incendiary explosive injuries, poison, malaria, mustard gas, jaundice, bone and nerve transplants and regeneration and typhus, etc. Without going into the detail of such it is sufficient to say that they were held to be the most grave of crimes against humanity by the tribunal, which resulted in the deaths of thousands of camp inmates.

These experiments included shooting prisoners in the leg with an infected or poisoned bullet and then calmly watching them as they died an agonising death. The below is an excerpt of a report prepared by the Reich Surgeon for the SS and Police (document L-103). I have included the letter in full as I think it is important to understand the callous way in which the SS undertook these experiments. The SS doctors reported on how they shot prisoners with poisoned bullets"

> On 11 September 1944, in the presence of *SS-Sturmbannführer* Dr. Ding, Dr. Widmann, and the undersigned, experiments with aconite nitrate bullets were carried out on five persons who had been sentenced to death. The calibre of the bullets used was 7.65 millimetres, and they were filled

with poison in crystal form. Each subject of the experiment received one shot in the upper part of the left thigh, while in a horizontal position.

(The International Military Tribunal, 1946: Vol 4:208)

The SS Doctor then goes on to outline in great deal the fatal sufferings of the prisoners:

> In the case of two persons, the bullets passed clean through the upper part of the thigh. Even later no effect from the poison could be seen. These two subjects were therefore rejected. The symptoms shown by the three con- demned persons were surprisingly the same. At first, nothing special was noticeable. After 20 to 25 minutes, a disturbance of the motor nerves and a light flow of saliva began, but both stopped again. After 40 to 44 min- utes, a strong flow of saliva appeared. The poisoned persons swallowed frequently; later the flow of saliva is so strong that it can no longer be con- trolled by swallowing. Foamy saliva flows from the mouth. Then a sensa- tion of choking and vomiting starts. At the same time there was pronounced nausea. One of the poisoned persons tried in vain to vomit. In order to succeed he put four fingers of his hand, up to the main joint, right into his mouth. In spite of this, no vomiting occurred. His face became quite red. The faces of the other two subjects were already pale at an early stage. Other symptoms were the same. Later on the disturbances of the motor nerves increased so much that the persons threw themselves up and down, rolled their eyes, and made aimless movements with their hands and arms. At last the disturbance subsided, the pupils were enlarged to the maximum, the condemned lay still. Rectal cramps and loss of urine was observed in one of them. Death occurred 121, 123 and 129 minutes after they were shot.

(The International Military Tribunal, 1946: Vol 4:208)

It may seem hard to comprehend how doctors, supposed to save life, could in fact take it in such abhorrent circumstances. One SS doctor, Hans Munch, who served at Auschwitz, gave this insight in a post-war interview as to the SS psyche and their racist views, "… that was their religion, they believed that by eliminating the Jews they were not only improving Ger- many, but also the whole world" (Halliley, 2003).

It is of interest that the camps served as a training ground for Waffen- SS medical staff, with some 152 Waffen-SS medical staff having served in one or more camps (MacLean, 1999a). *SS-Obergruppenführer* Ernst Grawitz was the doctor who recommended to Himmler that poison gas be used to kill the Jews, he also served with the 1st SS Infantry Brigade and the *Wiking* Division (Miller et al., 2006:468). Johannes Kremer was a *SS-Ober-*

sturmführer in the Waffen-SS reserve.[56] He held a doctorate and was also a doctor of medicine. In 1942 he received orders to proceed to the Auschwitz concentration-camp where he kept meticulous diaries as to the events that occurred there (Weitz, 2003). He attended his first action and recorded the following diary entry:

> ... 3.00AM attended my first *Sonderatkion* (gassing of camp inmates). Dante's inferno seems to me almost a comedy compared to this. They don't call Auschwitz the extermination camp for nothing. (Weitz, 2003)

Kremer later relates how he selected inmates from the camp sick bay, administered them a lethal injection and then used their organs for research (Weitz, 2003). Another example of Waffen-SS involvement is that SS officers from the Main Hygienic Office of the Waffen-SS were responsible introduction of Zyklon B gas as the main instrument of killing in the camps (Arad, 1987). In the Medical case[57] before the Nuremberg Tribunal, of the 23 defendants indicted in this case, some seven were members of the Waffen-SS.

> KARL BRANDT — Personal physician to Adolf Hitler; *SS-Gruppenführer* and *General-Leutnant* in the Waffen-SS; Reich Commissioner for Health and Sanitation and member of the Reich Research Council.

> KARL GENZKEN — *SS-Obergruppenführer* and *General-Leutnant* in the Waffen-SS; and Chief of the Medical Department of the Waffen-SS.

> KARL GEBHARDT – *SS-Gruppenführer* in the SS and *General-Leutnant* in the Waffen-SS; personal physician to *Reichsführer-SS* Himmler; Chief Surgeon of the Staff of the Reich Physician SS and Police and President of the German Red Cross.

> JOACHIM MRUGOWSKY — *SS-Oberführer* in the Waffen-SS: Chief Hygienist of the Reich Physician SS and Police and Chief of the Hygienic Institute of the Waffen SS.

> VIKTOR BRACK — *SS-Oberführer* in the SS and *SS-Sturmbannführer* in the Waffen-SS; and Chief Administrative Officer in the Chancellery of the Fuehrer of the NSDAP.

> FRITZ FISCHER — *SS-Sturmbannführer* in the Waffen-SS; and Assistant Physician to the defendant Gebhardt at the Hospital at Hohenlychen.

> WALDEMAR HOVEN — *SS-Hauptsturmführer* in the Waffen-SS: and Chief Doctor of the Buchenwald Concentration-camp.

> (Nuremberg Military Tribunal, 1946: Vol 1:8)

All were found guilty of war crimes and crimes against humanity. Brandt, Gebhardt, Mrugowsky, Brack and Hoven were sentenced to hang, while the others were sentenced to various terms of imprisonment.

Other crimes linking the camps and the Waffen-SS

Many of the concentration-camp officers saw themselves at "… first and foremost soldiers", indeed up to two-thirds of concentration-camp officers had some kind of military background (Segev, 1987:60). Of note is that MacLean's analysis is only concerned with officers who actually served in front-line Waffen-SS units. He does not take into account officers of the Waffen-SS who did not complete active military service at the front. These officers included the likes of *SS-Hauptsturmführer* Amon Goeth a member of the Waffen-SS. Goeth, who was commander of the Cracow concentration-camp, was tried after the war in Poland[58] and hung in 1946. He was found guilty of the murder of 8000 inmates at the Cracow camp, the liquidation of the Cracow ghetto, which resulted in the deaths of 2000 people, the closing down of the Tarnow ghetto and the sending of the survivors to Auschwitz and the closing down of the forced labour camp at Szebnie, which resulted in the deaths of several thousand people (The United Nations War Crime Commission, 1946 Vol 7:1). Goeth would go,

> … on to the balcony of his villa in the morning with a rifle and binoculars and scan the campground. When he saw a prisoner doing something that displeased him – pushing a cart too slowly, standing rather than moving, or committing some other unfathomable crime, he would shoot the prisoner. (Staub, 1989:138)

It is beyond belief to try and state that despite the fact that hundreds of officers from the camp system were in daily service with the units of the Waffen-SS, the Waffen-SS were not aware of the crimes that had and were being committed. *SS-Sturmbannführer* Per Sorenson, commander of the 24th SS Panzergrenadier Regiment *Danmark*, recounted how during his officer training for the Waffen-SS he and others were taken on an excursion of the Dachau concentration-camp and of a mental asylum to reinforce the ideological and racial messages of the SS (Smith et al., 1999). Indeed the actual existence of the concentration-camps could hardly be denied by certain units, when, for example, all new officers of the *Leibstandarte* received their tactical training in the same area as the Dachau concentration-camp (Reynolds, 1999:3). The 24th Waffen-SS Division *Karstjager* was formed in 1942 using the SS training camp at Dachau (Nafziger, 2001).

In addition to this a number of Waffen-SS atrocities have been catalogued since the end of the war. I have included just a few of these. On the 3rd of November 1943 Operation *Harvest Festival* was commenced. This resulted in the shooting of some 42,000 inmates of the Majdanek concentration-camp by units of the Waffen-SS (Arad, 1987; Scheffler, 1985;

White, 1990). These executions were not allowed to be carried out by the camp personnel, rather "… but were carried out by Police and Waffen-SS units brought from other areas of the General Government for this purpose alone" (Scheffler, 1985:45). In April 1945 racial German recruits of the Waffen-SS, who were from an armoured warfare school, were seen to be indiscriminately shooting the inmates of the Belsen concentration-camp (Reitlinger, 1957:266). Waffen-SS soldiers were convicted of shooting prisoners during an evacuation march from the Hersbruck concentration-camp to the Dachau concentration-camp[59] (Ruter et al., 2004: Vol 6). A soldier of the 11th SS Infantry Regiment was found guilty of shooting Jews at a detainment camp near Radom in Poland[60] (Ruter et al., 2004: Vol 6). Soldiers of the Ukrainian 14th Waffen SS Division were involved in the "… shooting of Soviet prisoners of war at Szebnie, the liquidation of Poles, Gypsies and Jews in the town of Moderowka and the reinforcement of German units guarding the concentration-camp at Szebnie" (Littman, 2003:73). Soldiers of the SS *Gotz Von Berlichingen* Division were convicted of shooting foreign concentration-camp prisoners as the war drew to a close[61] (Ruter et al., 2004: Vol 3). Members of the *Das Reich* division shot Jewish camp inmates and a Russian POW near Melk in Austria in 1945[62] (Ruter et al., 2004: Vol 26). These examples serve to illustrate the involvement of the Waffen-SS in the crimes committed in the camp system.

It can be seen beyond doubt that the Waffen-SS perpetrated some of the worst atrocities of World War II. Most of these were committed on the Eastern Front in the whirlwind of the brutal campaign there. It was on the Eastern Front that the Waffen-SS gave full vent to their ideological and political crusade to create an Aryan utopia and rid it of undesirable elements.

While not examining every minute action carried out by the Waffen-SS, I believe I have shown that the conduct of the Waffen-SS in committing atrocities can be considered systemic. They were involved in atrocities in combat; they were involved in the *Einsatzgruppen* and their deadly campaigns of mobile genocide. They conducted themselves with utter brutality in the fight against partisans, and last but not least, they were irrevocably entwined in the twisted terror that was the concentration-camp system and its associated genocide. We have seen what the Waffen-SS did; I must now address the next crucial question, why did they do it?

6. The Waffen-SS as a criminal organisation

"Soldaten wie die anderen auch"

Just soldiers like the others. This is the claim made by veterans of the Waffen-SS and their supporters. In 1953 West German Chancellor Konrad Adenuaer uttered these very words in describing the Waffen-SS. Legitimacy was lent to the Waffen-SS claim of innocence when US President Ronald Reagan visited a war cemetery containing Waffen-SS graves in an effort to put the past to rest. Veterans continue to claim that they were no different to the other armed forces of Germany during the war. *Das Reich* Division veteran, *SS-Obersturmbannführer* Otto Weidinger stated in his history of the *Der Führer* Regiment; "… the truth will be served by the statement that the soldiers of the Waffen-SS and the *Der Führer* Regiment in particular never considered themselves a special force or guard. All felt that they were just German soldiers" (Weidinger, 1998:20). Weidinger neglects to mention that he joined the Nazi Party in 1933 and served in the SS guard unit at Dachau in 1934 (Yerger, 2000). While indeed the Waffen-SS were German soldiers, there was a great difference between them and the members of the *Wehrmacht*. As noted by Huffman: "Waffen-SS troops were the most radicalised and politicised troops in the German armed forces, and the fanaticized military elite and political soldiers of Nazi Germany" (Huffman, 2005:iv)

A leading spokesman for former Waffen-SS veterans, *SS-Brigadeführer* Kurt Meyer, a former commander of the 12th SS Panzer Division *Hitlerjugend*, was just one of many to claim the innocence of the Waffen-SS. In a speech to Waffen-SS veterans after the war he claimed that the Waffen-SS "… committed no crimes except the massacre at Oradour[63] and that was the action of a single man. He was scheduled to go before a court martial, but he died a hero's death before he could be tried" (Stein, 1966:255). Through these efforts of former veterans and others the

Waffen-SS has been able to gain acceptance despite the fact that large-scale atrocities continue to tarnish its image.

When giving evidence at Nuremberg SS Colonel *SS-Oberführer* Gunther Reinecke, who was chief judge of the Supreme SS and Police court, made the following claim in relation to the atrocities of the SS being systematic when questioned by the defence counsel for the SS.

> HERR PELCKMANN: ... Did the Waffen-SS commit crimes against the civilian population in the occupied territories and at the front, and were these crimes committed systematically and in violation of international agreements, in violation of the penal law existing in the countries concerned, and in violation of the general principles of penal law of all civilised nations?
>
> REINECKE: No, there can be no question of that. It is clear that on the part of the Waffen-SS violations of international law occurred in individual cases, just as they took place on the other side also. But all these were isolated occurrences and not systematic...
>
> (The International Military Tribunal, 1946: Vol 20:430)

Reinecke's argument is supported to some degree by comments from authors such as the following regarding the liability of the Waffen-SS; "The doctrine of criminal conspiracy and collective guilt formulated during the Nuremberg era no longer satisfies serious investigators" (Stein, 1966:vii). Other authors argue that the criminality of the Waffen-SS is not outstanding. "The Waffen-SS as a group had a record no worse than that of the Western Allies" (Rikmenspoel, 1999:vii). However, as I have shown in the last chapter the claim that the Waffen-SS did not commit systematic violations is bankrupt. Still "... even outside the circles of SS apologists, however, many Germans insist that criminal acts committed by the Waffen-SS personnel were exceptions to person and condition" (Koehl, 1962:278). This would seem to suggest that rather then being seen from an individual standpoint, the crimes of the Waffen-SS should be viewed from an organisational one. This statement brings with it the following question. Is the application of collective guilt and group responsibility appropriate in this case?

Group Responsibility or Collective Guilt?

Is it feasible to hold the entire Waffen-SS responsible for the evils acts committed, when not all of the members of the Waffen-SS were directly involved? This was just the proposition put forward by Lieutenant-Colonel

Murray Bernays, who was a Jewish lawyer in the US War Department's Special Projects Branch, which was responsible for deciding how war criminals would be dealt with. Bernays argued that central to the plan should be the notion of collective criminality, in which the crime of membership would make each member of a criminal organisation liable for the acts committed (Ball, 1999; Van Sliedregt, 2006). This was an approach fraught with danger. Levinson notes, "Great difficulties emerge when one considers the question of criminal responsibility for actions occurring within an organisational context. If we wish to engage in communal condemnation, whom should the opprobrium be directed?" (Levinson, 1973:371). Fletcher succinctly surmises the core question in relation to collective guilt:

> As the fight over collective guilt is won or lost, so are larger stakes decided: Is the individual the ultimate unit of action and responsibility, or are we, as individuals, invariably implicated by the actions of the groups of which we are a part? (Fletcher, 2002:1499)

The Waffen-SS was declared a criminal organisation by the IMT. However, despite the fact that the leadership corps of the SS was seen as criminal "... the question is not only whether an organisation can have a criminal purpose, but whether its members can be guilty by virtue of association or membership or something more is required?" (Bassiouni, 1999:389).

The notions of group responsibility and collective guilt become much more relevant when the crimes committed have everything to do with the group and not the individual. In other words, when the crimes committed are systematic, the issue of group accountability comes to the fore. While the prior discussions have shown that the Waffen-SS did commit systematic violations of international law and acts that this book may well consider evil, there is one important premise to this conclusion. That is that not every soldier of the Waffen-SS committed atrocities. As noted by Sydnor "... it would be puerile to assume the reverse of the apologist book; namely that all or a majority of the officers and men who served in the Waffen-SS were criminals" (Sydnor, 1973:341). In his study Wiggers supports this view by arguing the below:

> By the same token, this paper does question the wholesale classification of Waffen-SS members as criminals who were ideologically seduced or mentally ill, or volunteer members of a physical, racial and ideological elite ... A careful and comprehensive analysis of the war-time Waffen-SS organisation, its character and activities, indicates that the picture of the criminal organisation presented by the prosecution at Nuremberg and post-war critics was overblown, a result of heightened post-war emotion,

and a victim of a failed legal innovation concerning collective guilt. (Wiggers, 1990:178)

Certainly the IMT recognised the importance of knowledge of the crimes that were committed, as distinct from just pure membership of the organisation being required to entail criminal guilt:

> A criminal organisation is analogous to a criminal conspiracy in that the essence of both is co-operation for criminal purposes. There must be a group bound together and organised for a common purpose. The group must be formed or used in connection with the commission of crimes denounced by the Charter. Since the declaration with respect to the organisations and groups will, as has been pointed out, fix the criminality of its members, that definition should exclude persons who had no knowledge of the criminal purposes or acts of the organisation and those who were drafted by the state for membership, unless they were personally implicated in the commission of acts declared criminal by Article 6 of the Charter as members of the organisation. Membership alone is not enough to come within the scope of these declarations.
>
> (The International Military Tribunal, 1946: Vol 22:500)

From a pure legal viewpoint the above arguments may have credence in limiting the ability to apportion blame or guilt to the Waffen-SS in its entirety. On the other hand, it must also be remembered that the atrocities committed by the Waffen-SS were not just isolated events conducted by a few psychotic personalities. The crimes are simply too widespread and enormous in their undertaking for this to be a valid argument. It is beyond the scope and purpose of this book to conduct a full exploration of the nuances of collective guilt from a legal standpoint. I will, however touch on some issues that will justify my inclusion of the entire Waffen-SS membership in regards to responsibility for the actions committed by the organisation more from a moral than legal viewpoint.

The crimes committed by the Waffen-SS were spread throughout the organisation and its formations, they were legitimised and condoned by the command and control elements of the organisation, and finally on the evidence presented, they must have been well-known to the majority of those serving in the Waffen-SS. The crimes were planned and carried out at every level of war. From the strategic level where Himmler and his command structures planned the genocide, to the operational level where divisional commanders and HSSPFs issued orders in compliance with strategic goals, to the tactical level where the soldiers committed the killings. With this comes the issue of group responsibility and collective guilt. I would argue that the Waffen-SS should be held morally responsible (as against legal, criminal, or collective guilt) as a group. I will discuss this in depth presently, as well as the prerequisites for such responsibility. However, it is worth noting that moral responsibility ensuing from moral condemnation does not necessarily coincide with legal responsibility. My major purpose in coming to the above conclusion is that I am not posturing in the realm of punishment, rather I am looking to apportion responsibility (in this case moral rather than legal), and these are two key, but entirely different concepts.

The major question posed is that if these persons are acting as agents for the rest of the group (i.e. the Waffen-SS), does it follow that Waffen-SS should also be held responsible for the actions of the agents? It was this type of thought process of letting others act as agents that allowed many civilians in Germany to one way or another condone the dirty work that was being done by others. However, letting others commit the atrocities does not necessarily absolve the others from the dominant group from responsibility (moral rather then legal) for what is occurring:

> When some major evil such as genocide is said to be committed by some large collectivity such as the German state, each individual German is, as it were, under a sort of moral cloud, a presumption that he or she probably or possibly had something to do with it. (Narveson, 2002:188)

In situations such as this there is a denial of the victim, which is created when individuals rationalise actions in such a way that reduces the immorality of the action against a certain individual (Day & Vandiver, 2000). A soldier from the 22nd Panzer Division serving on the Eastern Front upon seeing a train containing Jews heading to a concentration-camp highlights this vilification of certain groups:

> All of us had heard about concentration-camps, but the generally accepted understanding was that only anti-social and anti-German elements, like Communists, homosexuals, Jews, thieves, bible punchers, gipsies and such like were being kept there and forced to do a decent day's work for the first time in their lives. (Metelmann, 2001:31)

Coser (1969) argues that society is aware of roles and actions that are distasteful, yet society condones the acts that are completed by others. In other words, we allow others to act for us as agents. This I would argue was the situation in the Waffen-SS, the vast majority of soldiers must have been aware of the genocidal actions that were taking place and as such tacitly approved of such. Previous discussions have shown that Waffen-SS troops "… were some of the most highly motivated on the German side. They had all been thoroughly indoctrinated with Nazi racial superiority theories. To the members of the Waffen-SS, their Russian enemies were racial inferiors to be treated as subhumans" (Ripley, 2004:58). This attitude towards the Russian soldiers being seen as a primitive subhuman can be seen in the post-war comments of SS General Max Simon, who stated the following when writing about the Russian soldier: "The Russian peasant… he cannot think independently, a deficiency not found among West European peasants…" (Simon, 1949:9). *SS-Obergruppenführer* Lothar Debes described how in fighting, "… cunning, cruelty and malice appeared…" among the Russian enemy (Debes, 1947:34). This was a common view held of the Russian opponent.

In an attempt to shift blame members of the Waffen-SS have often fallen back on the defence that only a few men committed atrocities when the issue of responsibility for atrocities is raised. When questioned about the issue of killing prisoners at Nuremberg, SS General Paul Hausser had the following to say in regards to group responsibility:

> HAUSSER: Yes. These incidents are not the result of training, but rather the failure of individuals, perhaps the giving way of nerves when in difficult situations deep in enemy territory. But these accusations should not be generalised. Even if there had been 10 instead of only two cases, the ratio as applied to the entire membership of the Waffen-SS of one million men would mean there would be one case to every 100,000 men. Such incidents are the results of the intensification of combat on the ground and in a long war; incidents which have occurred on both sides and will always continue to occur. You cannot hold the bulk of the Waffen-SS responsible.
>
> (The International Military Tribunal, 1946: Vol 20:367)

Even if only a handful were committing atrocities, the knowledge of this must have gravitated out in an ever-expanding circle of knowledge. This was exactly the proposition put to *SS-Obergruppenführer* Wolff during the Pohl Trial.

> Q. Well, the circle of people who knew about the gassings, and the mass liquidation of people, certainly was more than just a handful, wasn't it? It was not just a few people you told us about yesterday? A. I don't think that I used the expression "a few people". I would like to give you a proportional number, then I would assume that the people who had knowledge and who participated in the planning and execution of these monstrosities were merely tenths of one per cent, and I would say

that this itself is a good percentage, and to a number of one million members of the Waffen-SS, or the General SS, that it is an infinitely small proportion. For the majority of the SS it is incomprehensible that the entire
group collectively were sentenced as criminals, although they neither
played any part in this nor did they have any knowledge.
(Nuremberg Military Tribunal, 1946: Vol 5:775)

During Wolff's trial for war crimes, fellow Waffen-SS General Bach-
Zelewski gave evidence that "… he found it highly improbable that an SS
officer of his rank and position would know nothing about the crimes" (Von
Lang, 2005:184). This assumption could safely be applied to the entire
Waffen-SS leadership on the evidence that has been discussed in the previous chapter. It is of interest that Wolff was clearly aware of the actions that
were taking place, as were others who chose not to pursue the subject. The
following incident during the Russian campaign, recounted by Hitler's *Luftwaffe* adjutant, Nicolaus Von Below, illustrates this.

> During the stay at Winniza a young lieutenant of the FHQ[64] signals train
> told me that he had witnessed a terrible massacre nearby. While working
> on communications equipment he had come to a gorge, where he discov-
> ered an SS troop shooting a large number of men and women. He was
> very distressed by what he had seen and thought that he ought to report it.
> I spoke to the SS liaison officer, *Gruppenführer* Wolff, and asked him to
> investigate and report back. After a few days he supplied me with a very
> ambiguous answer and hinted at sabotage in the rearward areas. I was
> requested to take no further steps in the matter. I was satisfied with the
> explanation and forgot the incident… (Von Below, 1980:155)

Von Lang completed an exhaustive work on Wolff's career and he notes
that "At the very least, however, he must have discovered what was really
happening to the Jews during his service for Hitler and Himmler at the
Führer's headquarters between 1939 and 1943" (Von Lang, 2005:1). The
above highlights an important point, the genocide that was being committed must have been widely known to the membership of the Waffen-SS,
especially the command elements.

I would argue against the statements of Hausser and Wolff that the bulk
of the Waffen-SS cannot be held accountable in the sense of group responsibility. I base this argument on the following. As a pure legal concept the
notion of collective guilt may fail. Indeed it has been discredited as being
unfair since the war. It has been noted that "Collective criminal punishment
is in principle open to the charge that it violates fundamental standards of
fairness by being over inclusive: the category of individuals actually stig-

matised or otherwise treated as criminal would include some who could successfully defend themselves" (Levinson, 1973:374). The result of the IMT declaring the Waffen-SS as being criminal has been criticised because it was a "... completely lopsided approach ... intended to serve only one purpose and that was to brand as criminal such organisation as the SS" (Bassiouni, 1999:384). This is supported to some degree when one considers that: "Being the member of an identity group does not by itself constitute a crime, and the law abhors collective responsibility" (Barkan, 2004:311). However, I would draw upon the associative notion put forward by Fletcher; I would argue that members of the Waffen-SS bear some responsibility by virtue of association with the organisation.

This view is supported by the following comment: "Whilst individual criminal responsibility can be regarded an emancipation from collective responsibility, this does not mean that collective responsibility has become obsolete and irrelevant to modern criminal law" (Van Sleidregt, 2006:81). As Berglund stated in his article there is great difficulty in approaching the notion of collective guilt:

> ... to agree upon a response to the Nazi crimes, one which acknowledged a link between the German people and the acts of their leaders, while not admitting to collective guilt, anticipated the struggles that the Germans and other nations have had with their histories of ethnic violence. As the debates in post-war Germany have shown, the search for a conception of national responsibility that does not equate with punishable collective guilt is precarious...(Berglund, 2000:239)

If one looks at the International Criminal Court (ICC)[65] in its current form it can be seen that although its legislation is designed to deal with individual criminality, it has to deal with crimes that can only be completed by collective co-operation by individuals. The IMT and NMT, both courts which dealt with the Waffen-SS, were no different. Fletcher outlines this notion further in relation to the ICC:

> The four crimes over which the Court has jurisdiction, aggression, crimes of war, crimes against humanity, and genocide are deeds that by their very nature are committed by groups and typically against individuals as members of groups. Whatever the pretence of liberal international lawyers, the crimes of concern to the international community are collective crimes. It is true that as a formal matter only individuals are prosecuted, but they are prosecuted for crimes committed by and in the name of the groups they represent. Once the collective nature of these crimes comes into proper focus, once we overcome the liberal bias that has prevailed since Nuremberg, we should be able to see the influence of collective action in domes-

tic law as well. I argue below that the innovation of hate-crime laws in the United States reflects a similar turn towards collectivist thinking in the law ... My point is to show that although the orthodox view stresses individual responsibility, the heart of international criminal law remains collectivist in nature. (Fletcher, 2002:1510)

This is one of my key arguments. Although legally the individual may be the preferable unit to deal with, on the issue of moral responsibility it is crucial to take a group or organisational standpoint. In this case I would suggest that the Waffen-SS has a group or organisational responsibility that is defined and evidenced by the previous discussions. This responsibility has a much narrower focus than a broad-based national responsibility or guilt; the Waffen-SS was a much smaller specific group that had specific aims and tasks. As such I would suggest that the Waffen-SS does bear group responsibility for the actions undertaken on the part of the organisation. This responsibility is clearly differentiated from collective guilt by Schaap:

> ... Attribution of collective guilt is unjust because it imputes blame without regard to the actions and intentions of individual group members. Attribution of collective responsibility on the other hand, is just since it refers only to a liability predicated on the duties of citizenship. (Schaap, 2001:750)

In this case it is liability predicated on membership; membership of the Waffen-SS. As a moral concept I see the issue of group responsibility being acceptable. The members of the Waffen-SS had much more than just passing or innocent knowledge of the evil acts being committed; they had intimate knowledge. They were responsible for the concentration-camps, they contributed to the *Einsatzgruppen*, and they controlled the anti-partisan conflict. But more then just mere knowledge, they contributed as an organisation to the evil actions undertaken. Indeed, group responsibility becomes more applicable in situations where the perpetrators form a significant part of the dominant group and where the victims are chosen for belonging to a different group (Radzik, 2001). Certainly this is the case with the Waffen-SS. They were seen as an elite of the Nazi state, their victims were predominately chosen on racial and ideological grounds. The members of the Waffen-SS could hardly argue that they were not aware of its racial and ideological nature, especially given that in the early years of the war the formation was all volunteer and the group members self-selected themselves. In the later years of the war where the volunteer concept diminished and conscription was introduced there was still a large hard core of committed idealists within the Waffen-SS. Even in the later years of the war the new conscripts were still embraced into the idealism of the Waffen-SS to some degree. As one veteran of the *Totenkopf* Division recalls:

> When the former *Luftwaffe* men joined us as replacements they asked what is the spirit of the *Totenkopf* division. The answer must have been – it was just simple and plain – steadfast in modesty, the stubbornness and unshakable belief in what we thought was right and we were willing to give our lives for. (Volkner, 2004:150)

Former operations officer of the 12th SS *Hitlerjugend* Panzer division, *SS-Obersturmbannführer* Hubert Meyer, gave the following insight into the late-war ethos of the Waffen-SS:

> Into the place of German victory had moved the conviction that one could not unconditionally surrender, especially not to the enemy in the East. On the contrary, it was paramount to guard the homeland from that in particular. Above all, the spirit of comradeship and espirit de corps held the troops together. Even the replacements, which had come from the *Luftwaffe* and the *Kriegsmarine* before and after the Ardennes offensive, were, in the majority, caught up in that spirit. (Meyer, 2001:383)

The issue of group responsibility also would seem to apply when one considers that the Waffen-SS as a whole was a beneficiary in term of goods and economic support from the camp system; a system of terror in which many of the Waffen-SS had worked in and had knowledge of. This is despite the claims made by senior officers such as Hausser.

> HERR PELCKMANN: Do you consider that the Waffen-SS, in its majority, participated in the crimes which indubitably were committed?
>
> HAUSSER: No. The Prosecution chains the Waffen-SS to the fate of Heinrich Himmler and a small circle of criminals around him. The Waffen-SS is taking this quite bitterly for it believes that in its majority it fought decently and fairly. It is far removed from these crimes and from the man who is responsible for them. I should like to ask the High Tribunal to please listen to the accounts and the judgments of the front soldiers on your side. I believe that they will not fail to show us respect. Wherever specific incidents occurred they were exceptions. The Waffen-SS considers it quite unjust that it is being treated differently from the mass of the German Armed Forces and it does not deserve to be outlawed as a criminal organisation.
>
> (The International Military Tribunal, 1946: Vol 20:370)

Many of the Waffen-SS worked in the camp system; undeniably they had knowledge of its workings, yet none of the senior officers ever protested against them. They were aware of and committed atrocities in combat and during anti-partisan operations. They were an integral part of the *Einsatzgruppen* and their genocide. Yet never did the senior officer corps as a group prevent their men for serving in these units or committing these atrocities. Never did they as an elite group band together to stop this carnage. In fact the only time complaints were made in relation to the ethnic cleansing being conducted was when it was seen as not assisting the war effort.

It was not the case that the senior officer corps of the Waffen-SS could not have protested against the actions Hitler and Himmler were undertaking. After all, many of the senior officers went to great lengths after the war to say that Himmler was insignificant and that they did not listen to him. In fact, this is the very picture Hausser attempted to paint at Nuremberg.

> HERR PELCKMANN: What influence did Heinrich Himmler actually have on the moral attitude of the members of the Waffen-SS?

> HAUSSER: Heinrich Himmler most assuredly tried in peacetime to exert his influence on the small *Verfügungstruppe*. During the war this was practically impossible. He did not address troops of the Waffen-SS. On occasion he did talk to some officers and commanders of some divisions in the field. It was generally known that Heinrich Himmler, who had done only one year's military service, had no conception of the military and underestimated the military tasks and the work involved. He liked to play the role of the strong man through exaggeration and through superlatives. If someone comes along with big words, the soldier on the front does not pay much attention. Therefore, the influence of Himmler was very insignificant during the war. He wore his uniform, of course, but the reputation of the Waffen-SS was established by its officers, by the example they set and by their daily work.

> HERR PELCKMANN: Was the influence of Himmler on the commanders perhaps stronger than on the masses of SS soldiers?

> HAUSSER: Quite the contrary. The commanders, of course, were under him so far as military obedience was concerned. But they had the right to criticise through their own experience of life and of the world, and as a matter of fact this criticism was necessary in the face of Himmler's extravagant and romantic ideas. These men had enough experience so that they could translate his statements into the language and manner of thought of the soldier. The critical attitude toward Heinrich Himmler increased continually during the war. In most cases he believed that he could dispense with the advice of an experienced soldier. Objections were cut off short with the words, "This is the typical viewpoint of a general" - viewpoints which he opposed.

(The International Military Tribunal, 1946: Vol 20:368)

They did not challenge him to stop the atrocities. They obeyed orders to send men to the camps or *Einsatzgruppen*. They obeyed orders to conduct brutal cleansing operations as part of the anti-partisan effort. They obeyed orders to accept into their ranks those who had been part of the terror apparatus. It was not the case that they could not choose to disobey orders. In 1943 when the 1st SS Panzer Corps was threatened with destruction at Kharkov, Hausser disobeyed a direct order from Hitler to hold the town (Darman, 2004; Nipe et al., 2002; Ripley, 2000, , 2004). Nothing was done to him; in fact he was later awarded the Knight's Cross. In 1945 *SS-Obergruppenführer* Steiner refused to come to Berlin to save Hitler, again nothing was done to him (Darman, 2004; Read & Fisher, 1992; Ryan, 1994). It seems that when military considerations dictated, the Waffen-SS could resist and disobey orders if it suited.

Why then did they not revolt against the genocide and murder being committed? I would argue that this was due to the fact that the Waffen-SS held and displayed a collective view and attitude that approved of the actions being committed. It has been suggested that underlying such attitudes "... very often is a philosophical theory of collective virtue, collective spirit, collective significance, that purports to authorise the doing of great evils by individuals" (Narveson, 2002). I believe that the evidence I have previously discussed shows that the Waffen-SS held such a collective view. As such I would argue that the Waffen-SS, should, as a group, be held morally responsible for the acts committed in its name.

Just Ordinary Soldiers? The Waffen-SS and Demonisation

Whilst the Waffen-SS may not have just been ordinary soldiers like any others, they were ordinary people. I would argue against any notion that the Waffen-SS should be viewed as some sort of grouping of evil men who did evil for the sake of it. As noted by Morton.

> The average reader of this book is not unimaginably different from many of the perpetrators of evil deeds, and a large proportion of the evil in the world is the result of the actions of people well within the range of normal routines of social life. (Morton, 2004:4)

Morton in his review of evil clearly enunciates that evil actions do not necessarily mean that there are evil people. Human actions are often understood in terms of their explanations. The ability of evil acts to defy rational explanation has often led to the power of evil being invoked in an attempt to explain these acts as the result of some kind of pure or radical force, for instance the person did it because they are evil. When talking of genocide and other atrocities:

> It is probably difficult to read or hear about accounts of genocide without at least fleetingly concluding that the killers were twisted and evil human beings who bear very little resemblance to oneself or one's friends, neighbours and loved ones. (Newman, 2002:43)

There has been a tendency to explain away atrocious behaviour as being the actions of someone outside the norm, a *them* who have no implications for the rest of society. When trying to deal with massive human rights violations such as genocide as committed on the Eastern Front, we often see the people committing these acts as evil, an aberration from the norm:

> Thus the preference for attributing participation in atrocities to an evil, hateful, or even obedient nature is entirely consistent with the way human beings typically explain events. As a result, people may be predisposed by their cognitive makeup to endorse such personality-based explanations even when there is little evidence to support them. (Kressel, 2002:148)

After the war this process was undertaken against the SS. They were made to appear different to ordinary Germans, so in this way Germany could account for the crimes that were committed. The SS in fact became the alibi for Germany. Indeed after the war when looking at the phenomenon of the Nazis it was more comforting to believe that no normal or healthy person would be able to engage in such atrocities against humanity. In regards to the SS an overly simplistic view was held. It was commonly assumed that these persons completely identified with their roles and in fact enjoyed them. As a consequence the SS are viewed as utterly evil and sadistic, and, no allowance for explanations other than the evil personality was made. In the past it has been easy to dismiss evil actions as the result of evil personalities however as Waller points out;

> Most of the perpetrators of the Holocaust and other cases of mass killing and genocide were extraordinary only by what they did, not by who they were. They could not be identified, *a priori*, as having the personalities of killers. Most were not mentally impaired. Nor were they identified as sadists at home or in their social environment. Nor were they victims of an abusive background. They defy easy demographic categorisation ... In short the majority of perpetrators of extraordinary evil were not distinguished by background, personality, or previous political affiliation or behaviour as having been men or women unusually likely or fit to be genocidal executioners. (Waller, 2002:8)

The logic of the demonic individual diminishes when one considers that the majority of Waffen-SS members showed an "... exceedingly low crime rate" after the war (J. Steiner, 1963:441). In other words, when placed in the situation of an ideological war they were capable of great crimes, yet when returned to a normal societal situation they behaved normally. The argument on the demonic individual would dictate that these soldiers should have continued their depraved behaviour into their civilian lives; but they did not. Indeed, the vast majority of men and women responsible for the slaughter of their fellow human beings have not been sadistic or psychopathic, rather they are just ordinary people capable of evil acts. Society finds that hard to accept as people want psychological distance from the perpetrators of atrocities; "... they did not want to believe that the potential to act like a Nazi could exist in them or their neighbour" (Waller, 2002:63). Public perceptions "... require our evildoers to be major figures, with something of the demonic about them, rather than pathetic figures in the grip of impulse" (Darley, 1992:202). This need for demonising of the perpetrator can lead to the erroneous assumption that behind an evil act must lay an evil individual. This assumption has been clearly rejected by a number of authors; it is also rejected by this study.

> Do not bother to demonise people as being inherently evil. That's not how it works. Instead, we should view evil as opportunistic, passing like an electrical current through the world and through people: or wandering like an infection that takes up residence in individuals or cultures from time to time. (Morrow, 2003:17)

This need to demonise has led to some people being classified as being the embodiment of evil, such as Hitler or *Reichsführer-SS* Heinrich Himmler (Berkowitz, 1999). Himmler was one of the main architects of the Holocaust and other mass atrocities that were committed by the SS; as such it is easy to demonise him as an evil person.

> However, as soon as we peel off a few layers from the demonised image we lay bare the far simpler features of a romantically eccentric petty bourgeois who, under the specific conditions of a totalitarian system of government, attained exceptional power and hence found himself in a position to put his policies into bloody practice. (Fest, 1970:172)

This quote encapsulates two core arguments of this book, first that evil is an interaction between personality and situation, and second, the evil person does not exist. Indeed the case of Himmler can lead to a whole host of questions:

Was Heinrich Himmler mad, bad or just confused when he complimented his SS Generals in 1943 for remaining "decent fellows" while overseeing the slaughter of the Jews? What concept of decency could the SS Reichs-führer possibly have in mind here? How could he describe the deaths of thousands of men, women and children as simply a means of cleansing the soil to allow new fruit to grow? (Scarre, 1998:436)

His actions seem to defy rational understanding and this makes it easy to use the label evil in dealing with Himmler. However, in contrast to the main players in the Nazi Party we have the thousands that joined the Nazi Party; by all accounts the were not crazed bloodthirsty monsters. This view can be seen after World War II when the argument was raised that many of the German soldiers were just following orders when they were liquidating the Jews.

Some, however, seemed to derive a specific pleasure from the act. The actions of *SS-Oberführer* Dirlewanger in torturing the young girls as previously mentioned would seem to indicate that Dirlewanger might be possessed of an evil power given the extreme pleasure he took from unnecessarily demeaning the Jewish women prior to their execution. The torture of the girls would appear to a rational person to serve no purpose; they were going to be killed very shortly anyway. This would have us believe that some people undertake actions for no other purpose than to be evil, or in other words, evil for the sake of evil. Baumeister (1999) refers to this as the myth of pure evil. However,

> The disturbing psychological truth is that participation in mass murder need not require emotions as extreme or demonic as would seem appropriate for such a malignant project. Or to put the matter another way, ordinary people can commit demonic acts. (Lifton, 2000:5)

During World War II, German soldiers on the Eastern Front "… engaged in heinous and repugnant acts of slaughter …. they *(the German soldiers[66])* looked perfectly normal, but committed extraordinary atrocities" (Bartov, 1999:9). One Waffen-SS veteran of the *Leibstandarte SS Adolf Hitler* Division, Gerhard Stiller, outlined how some of his fellow soldiers came to be able to commit horrendous acts: "After a few years they became so desensitised that they did not even notice anymore. Given that they were capable of just bumping someone off without batting an eyelid. Let's just say they would need to develop a lot of their humanity again" (Halliley, 2003). This concept of ordinariness or banality of perpetrators was the conclusion reached in Arendt's (1963) study of SS bureaucrat Adolf

Eichmann: He was just an normal person who carried out extraordinary acts of evil.

The idea of a pure or radical evil personality or person is rejected by this book. To illustrate this point let me return to the SS officers of the *Einsatzgruppen*, the mobile killing groups that operated behind the front lines on the Eastern Front liquidating Jews and others. MacLean (1999b) identified 30 Waffen-SS officers[67] who had performed service in these death units. An analysis of the details provided by him shows the following. Of the 28 officers examined some 93 per cent were agnostic with 7 per cent being of Protestant religion. As far as occupations were concerned 31 per cent were businessmen, 20 per cent were lawyers, 11 per cent were each doctors or police. Other occupations held included university student and professor, farmer and an engineer, with three officers of unknown occupation prior to joining the *Einsatzgruppen*. Regarding education, 57 per cent had high school or equivalent, 14 per cent had tertiary-level qualifications and some 29 per cent possessed doctorate-level education. As for political affiliation some 89 per cent were members of the Nazi Party, the rest were non-members. Of the Nazi Party members, some 52 per cent joined the Nazi Party prior to them coming to power in 1933. What this analysis shows is that this group of officers were diverse in occupation and overall well-educated. Indeed many came from occupations where you just would not think genocidal killers would come from, such as doctors, police officers and lawyers. The political affiliations to the Nazi Party would appear strong. However, of note is that only 46 per cent of the officers overall could be classified as *old* party members (i.e. pre 1933). *Nothing stands out among this group of officers: Their backgrounds do not appear out of the ordinary.* Certainly there is nothing to suggest that they would readily become mass murderers.

Indeed, as Bartov noted "… a great deal has been said, and some written, on the potential of everyone to become a serial killer under certain circumstances, as well as the potential of all human societies to develop genocidal trends" (Bartov, 2003b:82). Certainly social psychologists by and large do not see evil actions as the result of evil personalities (Berkowitz, 1999). There is agreement with Baumeister's dismissal of the myth of pure evil and the proposition that people exist for pure evil *per se*. Rather,

> When one probes behind evil actions one normally finds, not an evil individual viciously forwarding diabolical schemes, but instead ordinary individuals who have done acts of evil because they were caught up in complex social events. (Darley, 1992:204)

The above quote raises the question why do only some ordinary individuals act in this way? Is there something about their personality or the particular dynamics of the complex social events that they found themselves in that causes them to act this way? To be sure, many writers have commented on the fact that many of the most notorious evil acts have not been committed by demonic individuals, but rather by ordinary human beings (Arendt, 1963; Browning, 1998). It has been suggested that to rely on a concept of evil being derived from some kind of satanic metaphysical force is a akin to "... an intellectual hangover from a religious past" (Garrard, 2002:326). This comment reinforces the view that often it is indeed ordinary people who carry out acts of evil for quite mundane reasons. It has been argued that ordinary people, simply doing their jobs and without any particular hostility on their part, can become agents in a terrible destructive process. In fact, a number of studies have shown that ordinary human beings have the capacity to kill other human beings and experience the event as being nothing extraordinary (Lifton, 2000).

Take the following for example. Anti-partisan operations were common during the war on the Eastern Front, as a large number of civilians and Russian soldiers trapped behind the front lines took up arms against the German invaders. It was a war often fought with little pity on either side as seen by the experience of one Waffen-SS soldier:

> Our lines of communication were overextended and had to be kept open to supply the great armies at the front ... all we could do was mount the occasional sweep with what men we had ... We let fly with grenades and went in firing and several men and three women threw out their guns and surrendered. They were searched and marched off out of the wood, taken back to base and interrogated. All were roughly handled and then shot. (Blandford, 1994:95-96)

In this case the shooting of the surrendered partisans was seen as necessary to enable the German war effort to be successful, a small evil for a greater good. It is often the case that the factors causing the commission of acts that are evil are quite ordinary and are committed by ordinary people, not demonic monsters. Indeed we need to look beyond the explanation of demonisation to find the real reasons why ordinary people, such soldiers of the Waffen-SS, were capable of committing extraordinarily evil acts.

In summary I would argue that the notion of an evil individual is not conducive to understanding human behaviour in the light of evil acts. The sense of evilness should attach to the act and not the actor. To put forward the concept of an evil individual may impinge on our understanding and attempts to find rational causes for the behaviour of people who commit evil acts. It is with this in mind that I shall attempt to show why the Waffen-SS were capable of committing the evil crimes they did.

7. An examination of Waffen-SS actions

The purpose of this chapter is to examine the actions of the Waffen-SS and try to determine the causative factors of theirs actions. This is important for two reasons; first it allows us to objectively discount any defences that the Waffen-SS apologists may raise to justify the acts committed. Second it allows us to fully analyse the actions of the Waffen-SS.

As has been noted there is no evidence to suggest that actions undertaken by the Waffen-SS can be attributed solely to "... pathological personalities or group psychoses among SS personnel" (Kren et al., 1976:96). It will be my argument that an interactive approach of both personality and situation will best explain why the Waffen-SS committed acts I would consider to be evil. I would argue that the crimes they committed were caused by the following factors; First, the situational influence of a regime that legitimised criminal orders and actively devalued the target groups that were to be the victims of genocide. Second there was a ready acceptance by Waffen-SS soldiers of this victim devaluation. Third, the situational context of absolute obedience by Waffen-SS soldiers and the preparedness of these soldiers to blindly obey orders that would appear to be obviously criminal in their nature contributed to the Waffen-SS committing war crimes. Fourth the mentality or disposition of the Waffen-SS, in particular the aspect of "hardness" both on themselves and towards enemies of the Reich made them more prepared to carry out atrocities. And lastly the brutalising effect that difficult life conditions on the Eastern Front had on the Waffen-SS, both in relation to the climatic events and the nature of the fighting made the Waffen-SS soldier brutal in the extreme.

In any genocidal action however there are a number of common factors that are usually present. There is a bureaucracy/regime that is prepared to undertake evil acts. In this case it was the SS, and later the Waffen-SS. There are individuals present in society who are prepared to surrender their moral responsibility to commit these actions. The early and even later recruits into the Waffen-SS exhibited this willingness, but more importantly perhaps was that the command and control elements of the Waffen-SS were clearly prepared to do the above. The following of these directions from the regime was part of the creation of distance between the perpetrator and the victim. This is shown by the preparedness of the Waffen-SS to do what was necessary for the Nazi state so as to ensure its survival. The perpetrator does not have to be concerned with the moral implications of the act because this moral role has been assumed by the regime. The radical views held by the Waffen-SS in regards to Jews and other subhuman elements reflected this moral discharge of responsibility to the state. There is usually some kind of difficult life conditions present in society that make society more susceptible to this type of action. In this case the economic hardship of the Great Depression, and the sense of betrayal and loss following the humiliating conditions imposed by the victors after World War I. With these conditions in place the scene was set for the Waffen-SS to engage in an orgy of murder and mayhem.

Learning to hate: Seeing the evil enemy

> ... every man should be trained to be a fanatical hater ... It doesn't matter which front our divisions engage in combat, the unyielding hate towards every opponent, Englishmen, American, Jew or Bolshevik, must make every one of our men capable of the highest deeds. (Wegner, 1990:207)

These were the words used by *SS-Brigadeführer* Treuenfeld to describe the conduct expected of the troops of the 9th SS Panzer Division *Hohenstaufen* in 1943. The term highest deeds is suggestive of using whatever means are necessary to achieve the military aim. The comments of this Waffen-SS general would seem to fly in the face of propositions by apologists such as Theile who argue that, "Ideology never, or rarely, played a role on the battlefield" (Theile, 1997:125). First-hand accounts from Waffen-SS soldiers would also seem to suggest otherwise. For instance one veteran of the *Das Reich* Division described the hate of one of his fellow troopers, a volunteer from Switzerland; "He hated Bolshevism from the depths of his soul, and this hate had driven him to our forces" (Gunther, 2004:116). As noted by Williamson: "Certainly no effort seems to have been spared to build up a hatred for Bolshevism, and so it may be assumed that a hatred of the ideological enemy would play a part in the attitudes of some Waffen-SS men during the campaign in the East." (Williamson, 2003:213). This hatred of the opponent's political system is reflected in the oath of allegiance sworn by foreign troops in the Waffen-SS, such as the Latvian 15th SS Grenadier Division:

> I swear by God this holy oath, that in the struggle against Bolshevism I will give the C-in-C of the German Armed Forces, Adolf Hitler, absolute obedience and as a fearless soldier if it be his will I will always be prepared to lay down my life for this oath. (Bender et al., 1975:70)

Himmler emphasised this in a pamphlet called *"Die Schutzstaffel als antibolschewistiche Kampforganisation"* or SS Defender against Bolshevism. In this he outlined how, "Many even believe that Bolshevism – this Jewish organised and led struggle of subhumanity, is totally new in world history. We believe it is important to establish that as long as there has been men on earth, the struggle between humans and subhumans has been the historical rule" (Pruess Publishing, 2001:7).

In most genocidal actions there is a progression along a continuum of destruction that begins with small actions that progress to the final act of extermination of the target group. This proposition can be likened to the concept of momentum building as put forward by Milgram. The men of the *Einsatzgruppen* are a good example of killing becoming progressively easier and more efficient over time. Zukier (1994:435) refers to a similar process termed murder by instalments in which there is a pivotal encounter with evil, the first unlawful act. After this the person then progressively increases their involvement, and this progression is facilitated by the overcoming of internal and external obstacles and the illusion of minimal change in actions "… the next step is a mere adjustment, not that different from its predecessor" (Zukier, 1994:435).

To achieve this momentum target groups are often devalued, which can lead to the victims being excluded from the benefit of normal moral considerations. This devaluation can occur through two processes, first by dehumanising the victims and second by blaming the victims for the perceived sufferings of society. An example of this can be found in a speech that *Reichsführer-SS* Heinrich Himmler gave to recruits of the Waffen-SS on July 13th, 1941 as they were preparing to go to the Eastern Front:

> This is an ideological battle and a struggle of races…on the other side stands a population of 180 million, a mixture of races whose very names are unpronounceable, and whose physique is such that one can shoot them down without pity and compassion. (Stein, 1966:126)

It is also important that the target groups or victims are clearly identified and devalued so that the process of curing the perceived ills of the
nation can be undertaken. This necessitates that the cause is totally
removed. Moral considerations of the victims are replaced by higher ideals
that are aimed at protecting the needs of the majority. In fact, as part of their
victim devaluation the Germans made good use of lingual manipulation to
portray and stereotype the Jews as various diseases or disease carriers to the
extent that it assisted in the facilitation of the genocide against them. The
psychology of genocide has been likened to a society suffering from an illness, and the antidote or cure to this illness is the action that results in genocide.

In his history of the *Leibstandarte SS Adolf Hitler,* Weingartner (1974)
argues that by the time of the Russian conflict war had become a struggle
of moral absolutes. In this type of war "… the enemy became the faceless,
dehumanised embodiment of evil with whom no compromise was possible.
Evil had to be annihilated so that good might triumph" (Weingartner,
1974:165). This allows behaviour that would otherwise be considered as
unacceptable to become acceptable to attain these higher ideals. The following example shows how the genocide of European Jews was ideologically driven and carefully thought out. During dinner in February, 1942
Hitler explained to *Reichsführer-SS* Heinrich Himmler and a *SS-Sturmbannführer* of the 5th Waffen-SS Panzer Division *Wiking* his view and solution
of the Jewish problem:

> The discovery of the Jewish virus is one of the greatest revolutions that
> have taken place in the world. The battle in which we are engaged today
> is the same sort of battle waged during the last century by Pasteur and
> Koch. How many diseases have the origin in their Jewish virus ... We shall
> regain our health only by eliminating the Jew. Everything has a cause,
> nothing comes by chance. (Trevor-Roper, 2000:332)

The issue of victim devaluation flows on to the actions of a soldier in
combat. War arouses psychological traits within the human psyche. Certainly it has been seen as essential to have soldiers hate and despise the
enemy, for this reason "… all modern nations have attempted in one way or
another to instil in their soldiers a picture of the enemy sufficiently repugnant or evil to inspire this hatred" (Stein, 1966:127). Waffen-SS veteran
Gisberg Pohl justified his involvement in suppressing the Warsaw Ghetto
uprising in the following way; "Being a young man one easily made too
much of it. We had after all gone to Russia, we wanted there to destroy sub-
humanity – that is, I was strongly convinced of my task, that I was right"
(Bartov, 2003a:29).

War also brings forward the need to depict your enemy as evil. To see one's enemy as evil allows the average soldier to justify their aggression and the acts this aggression can lead to. This perception of the enemy as the other by demonising or dehumanising the enemy can generate a fear that results in complete commitment to the state that engages in total war and its consequences. An example of this is the use of euphemisms in describing innocent civilians or racially unacceptable groups as partisans or bandits who were killed in counterinsurgency operations in Russia. For Waffen-SS soldiers undertaking anti-partisan duties this had the benefit that "... as long as the men believed that they were eliminating a legitimate and viable threat, the chance of any negative psychological and morale problems was lessened" (Heaton, 2001:127). Indeed by portraying target groups as potential partisans, "... this conceptual integration of Jews and partisans was quickly internalised by a receptive SS and by German Army soldiers and provided the mass murder of the Jews with the legitimisation of a war against the partisans" (Buchler, 1986:14).

The soldiers of the Waffen-SS 3rd Panzer Corps received indoctrination in the form of a paper "... in which it was stated that the Russian was a mixture of animal and man, and that extreme caution should be shown towards Russian prisoners. The reason for this was that they were capable of committing every possible cruelty" (Smith et al., 1999:88). It is this ability to depict the enemy as evil that often allows troops to free themselves of normal constraints and to pursue the conflict as an ideological crusade on behalf of the regime. The war of the Eastern Front during World War II was a war of ideologies of political and racial origins. In this context it was necessary to have the Waffen-SS soldier see the Russians as *untermenschen* or subhumans. The Nazis were highly successful in depicting the Russians as evil:

> During the war in Russia the process of dehumanisation of the enemy was probably more successful than in any other war in modern history – the Russians, Slavs, Jews, Mongols, all had lost any relationship to the human race, and were nothing more that satanic monsters trying in vain to appear human, impostors whose identity had to be exposed and whose existence endangered everything which civilised men held dear. (Bartov, 2001:83)

This dehumanisation of the enemy works best with an obviously foreign or physically different enemy (Bourke, 1999). It is argued that:

> This almost obligatory dehumanisation of the enemy is particularly pronounced when there are radical ideological differences between the opponents, differences which ... may portray the enemy as the foe of civilisation and the enemy of progress... (Holmes, 1985:366)

Cultural and racial differences raise obstacles that make it difficult for soldiers to interact with the enemy with any affection. This was shown by the ability of American soldiers to more readily identify with their German opponents as compared to the Japanese (Stouffer et al., 1949; Weingartner, 1996). The enemy can be depicted as evil, by portraying them as being sub-human and preternaturally brutal (Weingartner, 1996). It is recognised that "... combat in theatres where the enemy was of a different race, was portrayed as different, was particularly hateful and liable to involve atrocities" (Bourke, 1999:143).

What this depiction of evil allows is an *us versus them* mentality, in which the enemy is seen as being some type of foreign being. It is this us and them thinking that is often a precursor to genocidal actions. This thinking can lead to a distinction between us (the internal group) and them (the external group), and with this comes a related separation of internal and external morals that are applied to each party. Hitler made the following speech to his generals on 30th of March 1941, prior to the invasion of Russia:

> ... our tasks in Russia: destroy the armed forces, dissolve the state ... We must distance ourselves from the standpoint of soldierly comradery. The Communist was not a fellow soldier before captivity; neither will he be one afterward. This is a battle of annihilation ... This struggle will be very different from the battle in the West. In the East, harshness is gentleness for the future. (Bartov, 1999:30)

From the speech above one can see that Hitler was already attempting to show the Russian soldier as being outside of the universe of moral obligation and therefore not deserving of compassionate treatment which in turn helps to remove the normal restraints that individuals have against aggression. It has been argued that the German officers and men had; "... internalised a view of humanity that categorised it not only racially into Slav and Jewish *untermenschen* and Aryan superman ... depriving them of the right to live" (Bartov, 1997:332). Indeed the commander in chief of the army, Field-Marshal Von Brauchitsch, instructed senior officers that the coming conflict on the Eastern Front would be "... a struggle between two different races, requiring the troops to act with all necessary harshness" (Forster, 1985:308).

An evil enemy is seen as not being deserving of the protection of the normal rules of conflict. The ideological views of Hitler and the Nazis found their way down to the lower ranks of the Waffen-SS where many soldiers accepted and agreed with the idea that the war against the Soviet Union was to be pursued under different conditions and using different methods from those of a normal war. A soldier of the 1st Panzer Division *Leibstandarte SS Adolf Hitler* wrote a letter to his parents shortly before the invasion, where he talked of the *Leibstandarte* and its coming role:

> ... But in the *Leibstandarte* we think ourselves a cut above the rest. We are the only ones. The Führer's own to do with as he will. This is our creed, that we will go forward over a precipice to death if need be, but without question. It is a glorious feeling to be ready to get at the enemy, to bash his brains out on his own filthy floor ... it will be all right. We must defeat the subhuman. (Wykes, 1974:117)

So successful were the Nazis in their indoctrination that the Waffen-SS soldiers' perception of war and society was quite possibly a distortion of reality. After the invasion of Russia ideological indoctrination was used in the Waffen-SS in an attempt to increase the combat effectiveness of the troops (Wegner, 1990). An increase in indoctrination in 1943 was also coupled with "Hitler's declaration of total war ... to reinforce the motivation of front-line troops to fight the Slav and Jewish subhumans in the East ... they were locked in a life or death struggle with their enemies" (Ripley, 2003:272; Wegner, 1990). Members of the 10th SS Panzer Division *Frundsberg* were instructed on being members of the German Volk who were involved in a continuing struggle against internal (the Jews) and external enemies (the Russians) in an effort to allow the Führer to "... achieve the historic unity of all Germans" (Wegner, 1990:206).

Of importance here is that the ideological instruction given to the soldiers included both internal and external enemies of the Reich. The SS newspaper, the *Das Schwarze Korps,* regularly ran stories that racially vilified the Jews and other undesirables; "... it labels such Jews, degenerate subhumans. Another article classified the Jews in Polish ghettos as dirty lousy Eastern Jews and commented about their skinny legs and pimpled faces" (Combs, 1986:130). In their study of the Waffen-SS Kren and Rappoport found that the Waffen-SS soldiers typically believed the ideological messages that were given to them with the result that they had "... no difficulty in performing acts that would be regarded as barbaric and atrocious by regular armies" (Kren et al., 1976:95). As one Danish volunteer in the Waffen-SS said in a letter to home; "Yes, we'll eradicate these Jews from the surface of the earth, because while there are Jews, there is also war. Now, I can imagine there are some who would say that the Jews are humans too. My answer would be that rats are also animals" (Christensen et al.,

2003:22). This letter serves to illustrate the attitude held by many in the Waffen-SS.

In this conflict the military actions of gaining additional living space and the police and political actions resulting in the extermination of racial inferiors were seen as different aspects of the same war. This extermination was made possible by the ideology that was held and believed at the time. The post-war comments of a veteran of the 5th Waffen-SS Panzer Division *Wiking* show how the problem was Bolshevism and the cause was the Jew. This was a connection accepted by many German soldiers:

> Jewish Bolshevism, you see, that was the big enemy ... and these were the people to fight against because they meant a threat to Europe, according to the view at the time ... and the Jews were simply regarded as the leadership class or as those who were firmly in control over there in the Soviet Union (Rees, 1999:51)

This view is one that can be attributed to the worldview held in general by SS men who attributed "... at least four typical characteristics to their Jewish victims. They were seen as communists, dangerous, spreaders of disease and insolent" (Lozowick, 1987:230). Even when giving evidence in the *Einsatzgruppen* trial, SS officer Otto Ohlendorf attempted to argue that Jews and communists were synonymous with each other. Ohlendorf was a lawyer who was placed in charge of *Einsatzgruppe* D, which was attached to the German 11th Army in Russia:

> It was obvious that the number of Jews in the general population in Russia, in relation to their number in the higher administration, was very, very small. The prosecution has submitted a report from my *Einsatzgruppe* to the army. In this report in enclosure No. 2 it explained the situation of Jewry in the Crimea. Unfortunately, this enclosure was not available. It would have shown that in the Crimea, for example, up to 90 per cent of the administrative and leading authoritative positions were occupied by Jews ... For us it was obvious that Jewry in Bolshevist Russia actually played a disproportionately important role. Three times I was present during executions. Every time I found the same facts which I considered with great respect, that the Jews who were executed went to their death singing the "International" and hailing Stalin. That the Communist functionaries and the active leaders of the Communists in the occupied area of Russia posed an actual continuous danger for the German occupation the documents of the prosecution have shown.
>
> (Nuremberg Military Tribunal, 1946: Vol 4:248)

So not only were the Jews involved in Bolshevism, they were the leadership class of it according to the SS mentality. This mentality was reflected in an SS pamphlet titled "Bolshevism – Jewish Subhumanity", which was made available to SS officers It stated, "The mask is off. Behind it visible to all, stands the eternal Jew. Rightly one does not view Bolshevism as a manifestation of the modern period. It is instead the product of Jewish thought…" (Pruess Publishing, 2005:12).

Just prior to the invasion of Russia men of the SS *Wiking* division were issued an instruction which:

> … warned the soldiers that fighting in the East was different, and that all kinds of undercover attacks and hostilities could be expected from enemy civilians and POW. Therefore caution and quick and ruthless use of weapons was the best way of preventing such events. (Smith et al., 1999:87)

This clearly implied that the execution of POW's and suspect civilians would be tolerated and in fact encouraged. Certainly, as has previously been discussed, the Nazis were very successful in portraying the Russians as an enemy to be despised. In particular Hitler was adept at entwining his anti-Jewish and anti-communist ideals as part of justified military measures. The SS newspaper *Das Schwarze Korps* linked its anti-Semitism and anti-Bolshevism so closely that the two themes became nearly inseparable. The Jews and communists were portrayed as the backbone of the partisan activity behind the front lines in Russia, which meant that it did not require Nazified zealots, merely conscientious and politically obtuse professional soldiers to carry them out.

The Russian soldier was depicted as being an evil individual who raped women and destroyed civilised society. This kind of ideological training or propaganda allowed soldiers to be "… reassured that the enemy was too evil to warrant survival" (Bourke, 1999:217). Many German soldiers believed this type of propaganda. The Waffen-SS soldiers were fed a continual diet of indoctrination in relation to the Russians through the form of training, leaflets and regular publications. The result of this being that; "When the enemy is regarded as a repulsive and evil animal, an *untermensch*, a subhuman, the result is an unmatched brutalisation of warfare, for the soldier is generally set free from feelings of guilt or remorse for his grisly deeds" (Stein, 1966:128).

When Bach-Zelewski, Waffen-SS General and for many years a member of the Nazi Party, was asked to explain the phenomenon of the *Einsatzgruppen* killings, he replied "I am of the opinion that when, for years, decades, the doctrine is preached that the Slav race is an inferior race, and Jews not even human, then such an outcome is inevitable." (Nuremberg Military Tribunal, 1946: Vol 4:474). So successful was this indoctrination that the average German soldier continued to fight vigorously up until the end of the war in an effort to "… defend hearth and home against the barbarians from the East", even though all hope of victory was gone (Strachan, 2000:356). Bartov (1997) and other authors also comment on the remarkable ability of the German forces to keep fighting to the end. The men of the Waffen-SS were tenacious in the defence of the Reich to the end due in no small part to the fact that they had been taught and believed that the Russian soldiers were little more than subhuman.

The fact that German forces, in particular the *Ostheer*,[68] were able to maintain cohesion to the very end has been attributed to "… the view shared by a large number of officers and soldiers regarding their own mission in the war, the character of the enemy confronting them…" (Bartov, 1997:333). In his examination of the 1st SS Panzer Corps, Reynolds argues that the Waffen-SS soldiers fought hard on the Eastern Front due to a number of reasons, which included:

> Their experiences on the Eastern Front had strengthened the resolve of the German military to protect their homeland for as long as possible and at whatever cost. Stories circulating at the time concerning the fate of German civilians in the territories captured by the Russians were of course exploited by Joseph Goebbels and did much to strengthen the resolve of both those who had experienced the Eastern Front and the younger members of the Corps who had yet to see battle. (Reynolds, 1999:39)

When interviewed after the war German General Tippelskirch observed that, "Our infantry lost their fear of the Russian infantry in 1941, but they remained fearful of being taken prisoner – and sent to Siberia or worse. This fear helped to stiffen their resistance…" (Liddell Hart, 1975:221).

Not all of the Waffen-SS soldiers were happy to die the hero's death, however. In November 1944 reports from the 18th SS *Horst Wessel* Division describe many of the conscripted soldiers fleeing or surrendering to the Russians, with the division having little combat value. Other SS Divisions also showed signs of disintegration. The commander of the German Army Group South, Colonel-General Friessner, had this to say; "In the 4th SS

Panzergrenadier Division some commanders have shot themselves because their soldiers had run away. The 18th SS Panzergrenadier Division has been a total failure" (Ungvary, 2005:18). This illustrates the fact that by the end of the war some of the SS Division had very limited combat capabilities, perhaps in part due to the dilution of the elite qualities that they possessed at the beginning of the war. While units such as the *Leibstandarte SS Adolf Hitler* kept the cohesion and combat ability to the end, some of the Waffen-SS units formed towards the end of the war were of little if any combat value, especially when it is considered that many of the personnel for these units had been conscripted into the ranks.

None-the-less, many of the SS Divisions continued to fight in a competent manner and commit atrocities up to the very end and past the point when it should have been obvious to all involved that the conflict could not possibly be won by Germany. The cohesion of the Waffen-SS can be seen to rely on two main factors. The first factor being the faith in the Hitler as a leader who would lead Germany to victory despite the odds that Germany faced. Indeed after the war when speaking to Waffen-SS veterans, Steiner claimed that only a handful out of some 300 claimed not to be affected by the charisma of Hitler (J. Steiner, 1963). As late as March 1945 one-third of German prisoners taken still maintained confidence in the abilities of Hitler (Shills & Janowitz, 1948).

Many senior Waffen-SS commanders outlined how the morale of the men was good even in the closing stages of the war. Waffen-SS Colonel, *SS-Standartenführer* Adolf Ax commanded the 32nd SS Grenadier Division *Januar* and was also the chief of staff of the 16th SS Corps (A. Munoz, 2001; Westwood, 2001). Ax had the following to say about the 15th SS Latvian Grenadier Division in early 1945: "The personnel of the division was of excellent calibre. Health was generally good, morale was high…" (Ax, 1947:8). *SS-Gruppenführer* Karl Brenner, commander of the 6th SS Mountain Division *Nord*, described his men as follows in late 1944; "Morale and fighting spirits were outstanding, caused by the successful battles against the Russians and the Finns" (Brenner, 1947a:5).

The comments of Waffen-SS soldier, Jan Munk, during the formation of the 38th Waffen-SS Division *Nibelungen* in April 1945 gives insight into how soldiers still believed in the ultimate victory despite the situation they found themselves in: "I was given a company of Volkssturm[69] personnel – boys and old men – who were then trained mostly in the use of the new panzerfaust[70]… We had no materials and morale in the ranks was poor. I was, however, still convinced that Germany would win the war" (Williamson, 1995:124). This fanaticism and belief in the leader and the final victory allowed SS soldiers of this division to justify acts like the execution of 16 German soldiers who had deserted their posts in March 1945[71] (Ruter et al., 2004: Vol 4). This type of blind belief is echoed by Wilhelm Tieke, a Waffen-SS officer who in the last days of the war served in SS Panzer Brigade *Westfalen*. He had this to say as to why he kept fighting:

> It was a combination of youthful idealism, of blind trust in the leadership, a sense of duty, the execution of an oath, the fear of draconian punishment and a belief in final victory through the introduction of new weapons, which were always part of conversation. (Tieke, 2004)

In fact German generals after the war when asked about the morale of the German soldier stated that "… they had and kept such extraordinary confidence in Hitler that they remained confident of victory in the face of all the facts" (Liddell Hart, 1975:257). SS General Bach-Zelewski was present at a military conference after the failed Ardennes offensive[72] in early 1945 where Hitler berated his generals. He recalled that "Field Marshal Von Rundstedt thanked him *(Hitler[73])* for his hard but just criticism and promised in the name of all generals present to take Hitler's instructions to heart to do his utmost in the coming battles" (Bach-Zelewski, 1946:8).

There was, however, some criticism of Hitler from Waffen-SS officers. For example, during the siege of Budapest in which two Waffen-SS Divisions and various army units were surrounded and destroyed. One Waffen-SS officer had the following to say in relation to Hitler's refusal to allow them to break out of the encirclement and reach the German lines; "Now I know that our men are meant to be sent to the slaughter in Budapest" (Ungvary, 2005:172). Of note is that despite the criticism the Waffen-SS soldiers followed Hitler's orders to defend Budapest until it was beyond all hope, either to hold the town, or be relieved by other German forces.

The second reason that the Waffen-SS fought on until the end of the conflict was "… extreme dehumanisation and demonisation of the enemy, a process which terrorised the troops to such an extent that anything, including death, seemed to them better then falling into Soviet hands" (Bartov, 1997:336). Indeed after the hard winter of 1941-42 and the shock of the first Russian counter-offensive, the morale of German troops took a battering. However, desertion and surrender were not viable options "… since either might lead to unspeakable torture at the hands of a seemingly inhuman foe" (Glantz & House, 1995:105). The reality of the situation was that as the Waffen-SS had embarked on an ideological war that they were now losing, this in itself created a fear of what the victors might do to them.

As the following accounts illustrate there was an inordinate fear among the Waffen-SS in falling into the hands of the Russians. *SS-Oberschar-führer* Sollhammer of the *SS Leibstandarte* Division recalls: "The Russian tanks divided into two groups, surrounded us on both sides, and then advanced on our column from the rear. With that we were hopelessly sur-rounded ... I saw *Oberscharführer* Gratz, *Oberscharführer* Burgstaller and *Oberscharführer* Gantiola shoot themselves with their pistols" (Lehmann, 1990:310). Sollhammer later heard shots, which he claimed to be the Russ-ian soldiers shooting surrendered Waffen-SS soldiers in the back of the neck.

SS-Brigadeführer Oskar Hock, chief medical officer of the 2nd SS Panzer Corps, outlined how Waffen-SS wounded could not be left behind: "We could not risk capture by the Russians, knowing their total disregard for the Red Cross. It was better to transport even those casualties that were not in a condition to be transported and have them die en route than to have them killed by the Russians" (Hock, 1947:10). Eduard Jahnke, of the *Das Reich* Division, outlined the attitude held by soldiers of the Waffen-SS: "We counted on the fact, especially we from the Waffen-SS, that they wouldn't take any prisoners. That they would stand us up against the wall, and so we fought until the last bullet" (Halliley, 2003). This is perhaps best evidenced by my discussion in the previous chapters where a noticeable number of Waffen-SS senior officers committed suicide. Large numbers of Waffen-SS soldiers in fact chose to commit suicide rather then fall into Russian hands during the siege of Budapest in 1944 (Ungvary, 2005).

This was a fight to the death; surrender was not an option. This fear was supported to some degree by the discovery of mutilated corpses of both *Wehrmacht* and Waffen-SS soldiers early in the campaign in Russia, photos of which were made available to the troops. Members of the *Leibstandarte SS Adolf Hitler* came across murdered German soldiers early in the conflict on the 3rd of July 1941:

> Kurt Meyer came across the gruesome scene of murdered German sol-diers for the first time. Their hands had been tied and they were all naked. The officers who were nearby had also been trampled on and dismem-bered. The LAH's official history stated that Dietrich strictly forbade any reprisals. (Mooney, 2004:63)

SS-Brigadeführer Oskar Hock recalled events in 1941: "The Russians had gained control of the only supply line and evacuation route ... the Russians attacked small groups of vehicles in particular. Even single ambulances with wounded were forced to stop after driver and assistant were shot. At times the wounded were shot and sometimes left lying on the road" (Hock, 1947:6). This fear of the enemy was not limited to the German side. A veteran of the artillery regiment of the *SS Leibstandarte* division recalls how upon wiping out the Russian 962nd rifle regiment, "... the regimental commander and most of the officers had shot themselves already" (Fischer, 2004:51). Max Simon, *SS-Gruppenführer* and officer in the *Totenkopf* Division, had this to say as to the finality of the conflict:

> ... the Russian infantryman always fights to the last, each man in his foxhole. Tank crews whose tanks were burning continued firing with every available gun as long as there was life in them. Our success was never secure until we could be sure that no living enemy was left in the position. Even wounded who had lost consciousness picked up their weapons again as soon as they recovered their senses. (Simon, 1949:15)

I would argue that the factors that enabled these killings by the Waffen-SS include the demands of authority, that being the command elements of the Waffen-SS. The predisposition of the killer, that being the soldiers of the Waffen-SS. The distance from victim, target attractiveness of victim and group absolution attained by the devaluing of the target groups. The issue of distance plays a greater role in conflicts of this century given the advances society has made in the technical and mechanical way in which the slaughter of soldiers and civilians can be conducted so much more efficiently. During his evidence at Nuremberg, *Einsatzgruppen* Commander Ohlendorf made comment of the importance of distance in carrying out evil acts:

> OHLENDORF: Some of the unit leaders did not carry out the liquidation in the military manner, but killed the victims singly by shooting them in the back of the neck.
>
> COL. AMEN: And you objected to that procedure?
>
> OHLENDORF: I was against that procedure, yes.
>
> COL. AMEN: For what reason?
>
> OHLENDORF: Because both for the victims and for those who carried out the executions, it was, psychologically, an immense burden to bear.
>
> (The United Nations War Crime Commission, 1946: Vol 4:320)

This perception of distance can be related to both *physical* distance and *psychological* distance from the enemy. The concept of victim devaluation as discussed previously ensures a degree of psychological distance between the perpetrator and their acts of evil doing. Psychological distance is referring to the ability of the soldier to identify or empathise with the enemy; the greater this connection the less able is the soldier to hate. The converse of course is true; the less one sees a reflection of the self the more one is readily able to commit acts of evil without associated feelings of guilt. This links in with the previous discussion that differences in race, appearance and culture make this connection more difficult between combatants. It is this ability to see an evil enemy that allows soldiers to justify and follow criminal orders.

Loyalty is my honour: Obedience to evil

> Many atrocities are crimes of obedience, but many more are crimes of agreement and even initiative. (Kressel, 2002:169)

The above quote would indicate that the committing of evil acts is interactional. The soldier is not only subject to the situation, which requires obedience, but they are also subject to their own actions. Obedience is a key factor in any discussion of evil acts committed during war where we are dealing with groups of individuals. The Waffen-SS, especially those led by old party comrades like Josef Sepp Dietrich, commander of the *Leibstandarte SS Adolf Hitler,* could be relied upon to do their duty, when army units may not have proved as reliable.

It is perhaps the willingness of the individual to submit to the will of the state rather than modern effects of weaponry that has led to the experiences of total war in the 20th century. Certainly as argued by Huffman "… many Waffen-SS troops jettisoned their humanity, severing their accountability and morality" (Huffman, 2005:23). Guilt was only something that is felt later, and often this guilt was directed towards their comrades (i.e. a perception of having let them down, of a friend getting killed and not them), rather than a guilt for actions taken against the enemy. The soldiers of the Waffen-SS had in fact become morally anonymous. This, particularly in military situations, can create potential for people to commit evil acts.

The whole structure of military organisations leads to a diffusion of responsibility for evil actions that are undertaken. Orders are given and followed. There are a number of links in the military chain of command, each of which fragments responsibility for the human act. This results in the dilemma that "… no one man decides to carry out the evil act and is confronted with its consequences" (Milgram, 1974:11). Baumeister cites four principles that come into play when talking about group responsibility and the lack of individual guilt and responsibility. They include diffusion of responsibility, deindividuation, and division of labour and separation of the decision-makers from those who carry out the acts (Baumeister, 1999:325).

It was this deindividuation alluded to by Baumeister that allowed the SS soldier to reduce their moral prohibition to committing evil acts by relying on the group membership of the SS to relieve them of this responsibility. When referring to the ability of the soldier to hate the enemy and obey the state it is important for the purpose of this case study to remember that the German soldier was influenced not just by German anti-Semitism or Nazi indoctrination, but also the traditions of obedience and identification with the state, which characterised German culture at least since the late 19th century.

A high level of obedience and fanaticism were demanded by the SS, and those that did not meet the accepted standards were either not admitted or eased out of the organisation (Staub, 1989; J. Steiner, 1963). Indeed, in a pamphlet titled SS "Defender against Bolshevism", both loyalty and obedience are singled out as important virtues for the SS man (Pruess Publishing, 2001). The SS not only demanded strict obedience, but also presented the security and refuge found in submerging oneself in a strong in-group. This obedience was needed "... because without it, there was no guarantee that one would have the necessary discipline or the will to struggle to fulfil the commands of the Führer and dictates of National Socialism" (Hatheway, 1999:38). It was seen that the obedience was to be unconditional "... not upon official matters, but on ideological matters" (Krausnick et al., 1965:367). It was for this reason that Himmler could boast that the SS man "... hesitates not for a single instant but executes unquestioningly any order coming from the Führer" (Ziegler, 1989:4). The individual was freed of responsibility for himself, the SS man saw himself as just following orders. He became a tool of the Nazi regime, not only carrying out his orders, but anticipating them, by virtue of their shared ideology.

On June 14th 1941 SS-Obergruppenführer Theodore Eicke, commander of the 3rd SS Panzer Division Totenkopf, outlined to his officers that the conflict in the East had to be "... fought as an ideological conflict, a life and death struggle between National Socialism and Jewish-Bolshevism – a fact that would demand the most ruthless and uncompromising conduct"

(Sydnor, 1990:153). These criminal orders were used as a basis for making it clear to German soldiers that "The communist was to be annihilated using all means – i.e. particularly illegal ones" (Schroder, 1997:321). Indeed "… the series of directives which surfaced via OKW, OKH and SS circles…" before and shortly after the invasion left little doubt as to the ideological nature of the coming conflict (Headland, 1989:402).

It was a result of these orders that certain sections of the Russian society such as Commissars and Jews were singled out for destruction in orders issued by Hitler and the High Command. *SS-Obergruppenführer* Eicke instructed his regimental and battalion commanders that the "… principal carriers of the enemy ideology, the political commissars attached to Red Army units, were to be killed immediately after their capture of surrender, regardless of the circumstances" in accordance with instructions from the Führer (Sydnor, 1990:153). A veteran of an SS Calvary Regiment outlined how these illegal orders were rationalised:

> We knew that Bolshevism was the world enemy number one … and we were told that the aim *(of Bolshevism)*[74] was to overrun Germany and France and the whole of Europe … that's why we had to fight … when we caught any of them *(i.e. Commissars)*[75] they just had to be killed. (Rees, 1999:51).

Indeed the SS was held together by a moulding of the personality and a communal sharing of a certain mental outlook and a certain mode of life. *SS-Brigadeführer* Otto Kumm had this to say on the attitude and loyalty of the soldiers of the Waffen-SS and their commitment when engaged in combat; "This is where you have been placed, and this is where you are to stand and if need be die. There was no mercy" (Halliley, 2003).

His sentiment is echoed by *SS-Standartenführer* Leon Degrelle who claims that: "Right through the war the Waffen-SS never retreated. They would rather die then retreat" (Degrelle, 1983:32). In reality the Waffen-SS did retreat. When whole German armies were smashed by the Russians the Waffen-SS divisions had little choice but to retire with the German Army units. What these comments do highlight is the fanatical zeal with which some Waffen-SS commanders were prepared to fight for the Nazi cause. Indeed as one author points out that for Danish members of the Waffen-SS who felt "… more or less imprisoned as volunteers, the mentally easiest way of coping with the situation was after all to identify themselves with the cause they were fighting for" (Smith et al., 1999:89). Staub also identified this type of behaviour with SS soldiers who progressively identified with the system they were in:

SS-Brigadeführer **Kumm**

The evolution of the SS into a system devoted to mass murder in the context of changes in the larger system of Germany, and learning though participation, the psychological condition of many SS members came to fit the role they were to fulfil. (Staub, 1989:137)

Undeniably it has been recognised that the SS obeyed the orders given to them by the Nazi bureaucracy:

… because their deeds did not violate any deep personal values and because they had merged psychologically and socially with the organisation. Large numbers, too, identified with the goals of the Nazi Party and more important the person of Adolf Hitler. All probably felt some inclination to obey authorities that they wrongly accepted as legitimate. (Kressel, 2002:164)

The reason for this obedience can be seen that "… when the NSDAP and the SS as its praetorian guard came to power, the hereto deviant, but politically successful, new social methods were legitimised and institutionalised" (J. Steiner, 1963:429).

One point worth discussing is that ideology by itself may not be the sole or main cause why a soldier chooses to fight or commit atrocities (Kellett, 1987; Peppers, 1974). Rather an interactional approach is best used to explain why ordinary soldiers such as the above could commit the atrocities that they did. The situational aspect of the ideological indoctrination in concert with other situational forces (i.e. obedience to authority, difficult life conditions) and personal dispositions (i.e. anti-Semitism, sadism, greed) combined to allow actions such as the above to occur. The training programs of the *SS Junkerschulen* were designed to ensure that the Waffen-SS officer corps would be capable of carrying out whatever orders were given to it:

> Himmler's armed SS sought to project the image of a disciplined, highly trained racial *Führerkorps* of a New Order ... Within this context it was essential that the leadership corps of the armed SS consist of professionally trained SS officers who would have the physical, mental and moral courage necessary to carry out whatever needed to be accomplished in order to further the goals of the National Socialist Revolution. (Hatheway, 1999:10)

It was for this reason that often in SS reports civilians and Jews were referred to as bandits, partisans, criminals, etc; it allowed the soldiers to believe that they were killing legitimate targets that were a viable threat to them with the associated benefits of lessening any negative psychological and morale It has been suggested that soldiers can often overcome feelings of personal guilt for combat actions by centring these actions on the premise that they were obeying orders from a legitimate authority. The argument has been raised that perhaps rather than being seen as committing acts of evil, these soldiers were in fact just following orders. After all, generally the entire code of the German military, and especially the SS, emphasised complete, unquestioning obedience. It was this unquestioning obedience that many Waffen-SS veterans would argue dictated that they had to follow criminal orders.

Just following orders

The justification for barbarity in conflicts has often been that the issue is resolved swiftly and decisively and this in itself is a more humane act. This is often the evil logic upon which total wars are based upon. Some would argue that evil is a necessary part of warfare. But does this proposition entail that to ensure victory one needs to embrace evil and embark upon warfare without restraint? Does one need to unquestioningly follow orders that are obviously evil? If one common theme comes out of the episodes of history it is the concept of *total war*, which so often in recent decades has led to the committing of evil acts in the name of war.

This targeting of civilians contravenes accepted war conventions and moves the conflict into the bounds of evil acts. Judge Parker highlighted this link between war crimes and total war in his judgment of the major war criminals before the IMT:

> The truth remains that war crimes were committed on a vast scale … by every conceivable circumstance of cruelty and horror. There can be no doubt that the majority of them arose from the Nazi conception of "total war", with which the aggressive wars were waged. For in this conception of "total war", the moral ideas underlying the conventions which seek to make war more humane are no longer regarded as having force or validity. Everything is made subordinate to the overmastering dictates of war. Rules, regulations, assurances and treaties all alike are of no moment, and so, freed from the restraining influence of international law, the aggressive war is conducted by the Nazi leaders in the most barbaric way. Accordingly, war crimes were committed when and wherever the Führer and his close associates thought them to be advantageous. They were for the most part the result of cold and criminal calculation.
>
> (The International Military Tribunal, 1946: Vol 1:227)

In total war the civilian nation is exposed to attack. As a result of this the whole nation is mobilised for warfare. For example, during the conflict on the Eastern Front the Russians' ability to use civilian groups to form partisan groups became a serious problem for the German forces. As a result mopping-up operations were conducted to eradicate suspected partisan groups. This notion of partisan groups or bandits was a loose definition that included unwanted elements of society such as Jews and intellectuals and gave the Germans the excuse to target civilians as well as the military during the conflict.

In the area of the Pripet Marshes the 1st and 2nd SS Calvary Regiments[76] conducted mopping-up or pacification operations (Wilson, 2000). These regiments were combined to form the SS Cavalry Brigade in August 1941 and answered directly to Himmler's staff (Bender et al., 1972; Buchler, 1986; Trang, 2000). The brigade came under the control of Waffen-SS General, *SS-Gruppenführer* Hermann Fegelein, who later married Gretl Braun (sister of Hitler's mistress Eva Braun). In the last days of the war in 1945 Hitler had Fegelein arrested and shot as a scapegoat for Himmler's disloyal conduct. On the 12th of August 1941 *SS-Sturmbannführer* Magill of the 2nd regiment reported that:

Jewish marauders were shot. Only a few manual labourers employed by the *Wehrmacht* repair shops were spared. Driving the women and children towards the marshes did not have the desired effect as the marshes were not deep enough to ensure drowning … The total number of marauders and others shot by the *reitende Abteilung* stands at 6526 men. About 10 prisoners were taken away … Overall, the operation may be described as a success. (Trang, 2000:32).

SS-Gruppenführer **Fegelein**

Magill went on to serve in the 14th *Galicia* Grenadier Division (Westwood, 2001). He was later convicted by a German court[77] of the mass shooting of thousands of Jews in the Pripet area, among them at least 4500 Jews from the Pinsk ghetto (Ruter et al., 2004). He was sentenced to five years' imprisonment with three other SS soldiers.

It was perhaps ominous that over dinner in August 1942 Hitler likened the fight against the partisans in Russia to the American Indian conflict; "The struggle we are waging against the partisans is very much like the struggle in North America against the Red Indians. Victory will go to the strong, and strength is on our side. At all costs we will establish law and order there" (Trevor-Roper, 2000:621). When one considers this it is clear that the end in any conflict is victory. Does this then justify the contention that victory must be achieved by any means? This was the logic used by the German Army on the Eastern Front. Its Commander in Chief, Von Brau-chitsch, argued that in the fight against partisan groups "... the essential rapid pacification of the country can be achieved only if every threat on the part of the hostile civilian population is dealt with ruthlessly. All pity and softness are weakness and constitute a danger" (Forster, 1985:313). The above examples give rise to the claim of military necessity. Military neces-sity being the pursuit of strategic or tactical advantage/disadvantage that can allow "... destructive interests to come to the fore to the detriment of individual protection" (Streim, 1997:305). The problem of justification re the military action arises when the use of such tactics, if carried to an extreme, are disproportionate to the military results obtained. Strictly speaking the principle of military necessity outlaws useless violence. The judgment of the Nuremberg Trials made it clear that "... egregiously harm-ful actions that are not justified by military necessity..." were to be seen as war crimes (Wilkins, 2001:51).

During the conflict on the Eastern Front the German forces resorted to brutal tactics, which were more than a means to an ends, but rather the only way to conduct the struggle. After all, given the impressive early victories of the Germans using their traditional military doctrines, it was hardly a necessary military measure for them to kill Russian prisoners or allow the *Einsatzgruppen* to rampage behind the front lines. This type of action was not necessary for success in the Western campaign, so why were they in the Eastern campaign? In the East the aim of the conflict was the total destruc-tion of the enemy.

When Hitler invaded Russia he was not of a mind to only go so far then seek political finalisation to the conflict. This might have left the commu-nist regime intact. Rather, he was intent on the destruction of the commu-nist system of government and the perceived cause of this system, the Jews, and a nation that was racially abhorrent to him. Hitler clearly outlined what he expected from the conflict in the East:

> St. Petersburg must therefore disappear utterly from the earth's surface. Moscow too ... It is not by taking over the miserable Russian hovels that we shall establish ourselves as masters in the East ... As for the ridiculous 100 million Slavs, we will mould the best of them to the shape that suits us and we will isolate the rest of them in their pigsties; and anyone who

talks about cherishing the local inhabitant and civilising him, goes straight off into a concentration-camp. (Trevor-Roper, 2000:617)

This quote reinforces the contention that the total war concept not only applies to the application of force to the enemy, but also to the notion of blind obedience of the citizens of the nation conducting the war. Indeed Hitler was well aware that the war on the Eastern Front would entail the mass slaughter of Jews and Communists: moreover, he was not the only German who knew it.

Many soldiers of the Waffen-SS relied on the claim that they were just following orders and as such should not be held liable for their actions. For any defence of superior orders to succeed the defendant must prove two parts; first that the orders were acted on under duress, and second that the person carrying out the order was ignorant of their illegality. That members of the Waffen-SS were aware of the illegality of the orders they were following would seem to be confirmed by the comments of *Wiking* Division veteran, Hendrik Verton, who claimed:

> The ten pledges in the pay book of every German soldier gave very strict guidelines over our treatment of prisoners. For instance number 3. It is an offence to kill prisoners who have surrendered, including partisans or spies. 4. Prisoners are not to be abused or mishandled. 6. Wounded prisoners are to be humanely treated. (Verton, 2007:111)

The illegality of many of the orders that the Waffen-SS executed would seem to be beyond argument, so it is worth examining the issue of duress and following superior orders. At Nuremberg, Chief SS Judge Gunther Reinecke claimed that there was no latitude for members of the Waffen-SS to avoid the tasks they undertook when questioned by the defence counsel for the SS.

> HERR PELCKMAN: Was it possible for members of the Waffen-SS to leave the Waffen-SS if they did not agree with the tasks which they were given or the orders which were issued?
>
> REINECKE: A possibility of this sort did not exist at all. Service in the Waffen-SS was military service, legally established and legally recognised. Even members of the Waffen-SS who had joined as volunteers were later subject to general conscription and bound by compulsory military service. It was therefore possible to leave the Waffen-SS only by means of desertion, and then the deserter would have had to expect the full consequences of the law.
>
> (The International Military Tribunal, 1946: Vol 20:445)

SS-Gruppenführer Otto Ohlendorf put this same proposition forward during the *Einsatzgruppen* trial:

> I would like to say the following: The men of my group who are under indictment here were under my military command. If they had not executed the orders which they were given, they would have been ordered by me to execute them. If they had refused to execute the orders they would have had to be called to account for it by me. There could be no doubt about it. Whoever refused anything in the front lines would have met immediate death. If the refusal would have come about in any other way, a court martial of the Higher SS and Police Leader would have brought about the same consequences. The jurisdiction of courts martial was great, but the sentences of the SS were gruesome.
>
> (Nuremberg Military Tribunal, 1946: Vol 4:249)

When asked again about the issue of following orders Ohlendorf stated the following:

> DR. ASCHENAUER. The concluding question concerning the set of questions concerning Russia — What was your power of decision concerning execution orders?
>
> OHLENDORF. I do not think I have to repeat this. As to the orders for execution, even if applying the harshest standard, I had no possibility whatever to circumvent them.
>
> (Nuremberg Military Tribunal, 1946: Vol 4:267)

On the face of it the proposition that soldiers were just following orders may appear a valid argument, yet this is exactly the type of contention that the subjects in Milgram's experiment relied upon. That being that they were merely following the directions of a legitimate authority (the experiment supervisor) to justify the undertaking of wrongful acts. They relied on the false claim that they had no choice but to act as directed by the experimenter. The exception here is that those who joined the Waffen-SS, in the early years at least, did so in a voluntary capacity. As noted by Kressel "… unlike the Milgram subjects, many Nazis sought out their destructive roles, entering the party, attending rallies and joining the SS" (Kressel, 2002:162). Members of the SS were in effect involved in self-selection, with a preference for military activities and a belief in Nazi ideology (Staub, 2002).

There is criticism of the principle of obedience to orders absolving the men following them. Gewirth (2001) suggests that those who give the orders are guilty of primary criminality, while those who obey orders that they know to be wrongful have a secondary guilt attached to them. On the Eastern Front the German soldiers were not mere victims of their own military tradition. The relationship between the Waffen-SS and Hitler with regard to the Soviet Union was determined in large measure by a consensus on both ideological matters and Germany's role in Europe and world politics. In other words, we have the interaction between the soldier's disposition and the situation of the ideological conflict.

The argument has been raised that the failure to follow orders may result in some worse punishment for the individual involved. As this book is examining the Waffen-SS as its case study it will concentrate on this situation as it applies in this context of German soldiers during World War II. The example of the soldiers in Waffen-SS clearly refutes this thinking. They were involved in actual cleansing operations on the Eastern Front, yet of those few who refused, none were shot out of hand. Wolfgang Filor of the *Das Reich* Division recounts how he was ordered to shoot a fellow SS soldier but refused:

> Today, when someone for the SS says: "If I hadn't done it, I'd have been shot", I say: that's simply not true, or else he had a superior officer with no humanity or comradeship. For example, in October 1942 in Stralsund, I was ordered to take part in the execution of an NCO in the SS. I went to my superior officer and said: "I volunteered to fight at the front. I don't want to execute anyone." He asked me, "Are you refusing to obey an order?" but he let me go. Twenty others did volunteer the next day because they got a bottle of wine and the next day were given a pass to walk around Stralsund. (Knopp, 2002:253)

The stories of the SS would have us believe that Filor would have been hauled off and shot for his refusal, but he was not. Even *Einsatzgruppen* officer Otto Ohlendorf was forced in his later testimony to admit under questioning from the prosecution that he had successfully refused orders from security chief Reinhard Heydrich.

> Q. You were ordered three times to join the *Einsatzgruppen*, were you not?
> A. Yes.
> Q. And twice you refused?
> A. Yes.
> Q. The order in the first instance came from Heydrich?
> A. Yes.
> Q. The second order for you to become a member of the *Einsatzgruppe* came from Heydrich?

A. Yes.

Q. You refused both the first and the second order?

A. Yes.

(Nuremberg Military Tribunal, 1946: Vol 4:276)

It is clear that few, if any, German soldiers were shot for failing to obey orders to shoot civilians. Investigations by the Central Office of the German Lander Justice Department after the war showed that "... there is no known case where refusal to shoot the Jews resulted in damage to life and limb" (Birn, 1997:283). When giving evidence at various post-war German trials expert, Hans Gunter Seraphim, declared that the "... closest scrutiny of all available SS records does not reveal one single instance where some objector to following criminal orders had endangered his own life" (Wolfson, 1965:568).

In his graphic account of the Holocaust Klee (Klee et al., 1988) gives voice to many veterans whose accounts show that the disobedience of criminal orders did not and would not result in any kind of draconian punishment. The following are just some of the responses in relation to the argument that failure to obey criminal orders would have resulted in terrible punishment. "I carried out the orders not because I was afraid I would be punished by death if I didn't ... my chances of promotion would be spoilt or I would not be promoted at all" (Klee et al., 1988:79). When a reservist from a Police battalion refused to shoot innocent victims, his commander; "... called me a coward and sissy and the like ... Finally he said 'He is not even worthy of that kind of duty', by which he wanted to emphasise my uselessness for 'tough action" (Klee et al., 1988:79). When asked about what disciplinary action would be taken against those who refused to take part in the mass executions an SS officer remarked "Not a lot. I never knew of such a case..." (Klee et al., 1988:79).

A top-secret document prepared for the SS and Police courts showed that between 1939 and 1944 only some 1000 SS men were shot as punishment for various infractions (Wolfson, 1965). When one considers that up to 900,000 men served in the Waffen-SS, the number of executions indicate that less than 0.1% were executed by the SS courts. Further to this, the SS Statistical Annual gave the figures in relation to discharges from the SS. In 1938 alone some 8033 SS members were discharged out of the SS. Of these some 5104 obtained an honourable discharge at their own request (Wolfson, 1965). What this shows is that it was entirely possible to achieve exit from the SS if the individual wanted such. Some 14 SS men were discharged for refusal to obey orders, they were not executed. These figures strongly rebut the contention of those SS members who have argued that release from the SS would have involved punishments, reprisals and possibly death. Indeed, many of the West European volunteers for the SS were allowed to return to their home countries at the end of their enlistment period, they were not forced to stay in the Waffen-SS.

Even some of the SS doctors involved in the euthanasia of patients in German mental institutions were able to quit their horrible task with no mention of punishment. The salient point raised, however, is that many of the soldiers *believed or claimed to believe* that they could be shot and here lies the justification for their actions. Even today the same claim is made, as one Waffen-SS veteran stated in a recent documentary:

> We grew up as Nazis, Hitler Youth of course … I was enthusiastic, there was no opportunity for employment, but at that time I could not see the connections. Today of course I can see it differently. I must say we are guilty, very guilty. Except the individual soldier, as such he just did his duty. And if we had said, "We don't want to do it any more" we would have been shot immediately, they did that often enough. (Carruthers, 2001)

This belief can perhaps be equated to the soldiers claiming that they perceived they had no choice but to conduct objectionable acts. This belief led many of the killers to try and mount a defence under the guise of *duress*.

For this defence to succeed the soldier must be able to show that the threat to their wellbeing must be imminent, real and inevitable. Many killers argued that they held a sincere belief and acted in accordance of this belief that to fail to obey an order would lead to death. This thinking falls into difficulty, however, if one considers that while:

> … such fears under the totalitarian Nazi regime might sound logical, there is evidence to show that several policemen did refuse to obey such repugnant orders and that they suffered no punishment. Indeed, some were subsequently promoted, showing that neither their lives nor their careers were threatened. Once it became clear that no ill befell those who refused similar orders, there was little or no excuse for those who did obey and took part in the massacre of innocent civilians. (Williamson & Vuksic, 2002:14)

The testimony of *SS-Gruppenführer* Otto Ohlendorf at Nuremberg is a good example of this type of thinking. When questioned as to why orders to kill innocent civilians were followed he gave the following responses:

HERR BABEL: You personally were not concerned with the execution of these orders?

OHLENDORF: I led the *Einsatzgruppe*, and therefore I had the task of seeing how the *Einsatzkommandos* executed the orders received.

HERR BABEL: But did you have no scruples in regard to the execution of these orders?

OHLENDORF: Yes, of course.

HERR BABEL: And how is it that they were carried out regardless of these scruples?

OHLENDORF: Because to me it is inconceivable that a subordinate leader should not carry out orders given by the leaders of the state.

HERR BABEL: This is your own opinion. But this must have been not only your point of view, but also the point of view of the majority of the people involved. Didn't some of the men appointed to execute these orders ask you to be relieved of such tasks?

OHLENDORF: I cannot remember any one concrete case. I excluded some whom I did not consider emotionally suitable for executing these tasks and I sent some of them home.

HERR BABEL: Was the legality of the orders explained to these people under false pretences?

OHLENDORF: I do not understand your question; since the order was issued by the superior authorities, the question of legality could not arise in the minds of these individuals, for they had sworn obedience to the people who had issued the orders.

HERR BABEL: Could any individual expect to succeed in evading the execution of these orders?

OHLENDORF: No, the result would have been a court martial with a corresponding sentence.

(The United Nations War Crime Commission, 1946: Vol 4:353)

This argument can be soundly rejected. Ohlendorf's own testimony refutes the proposition that one could do nothing but obey orders given. It has been contended that many of the German executioners were fully aware that they did not have to conduct the killings as ordered, the men simply knew that they did not have to kill. In fact "… even in the army, enlisted soldiers and high officers often could avoid participation in the murder of unarmed civilians" (Zukier, 1994:429). This proposition is supported by testimony from killers themselves and also various studies of units involved in the killing processes (Browning, 1998; Goldhagen, 1997; Krausnick et al., 1965; Williamson et al., 2002). Browning (1998) goes on to argue that there is a clear lack of evidence in any of the post-war trials that indicates that soldiers were shot for refusing to obey orders to kill unarmed civilians.

Indeed, former Federal German Senior Chief State Prosecutor Alfred Spiess conducted a detailed study of SS and Police crimes. He outlines one case in which a police reservist refused to carry out the shootings of civilians; no punishment was given to the soldier. Spiess was curious about this and spoke to a number of SS judges to see why in situations such as this the soldiers were not court martialled. The SS judges stated the following to him:

> The explanation is very simple. If these people had been brought before an SS and Police court, it would have to establish which order had been disobeyed. What sort of order was it? In one case it would have been an order for the mass murder of Jews, and in another the shooting of women and children. But these were both criminal orders, and according to the Military Penal Code, paragraph 47, clause 3, which was still valid in those days, a soldier was not obliged to carry out a criminal order. You see, that meant that this Military Penal Code was also applicable to the SS and Police, and so when a man is brought before a court, the court has to ascertain if the order was criminal and who gave the order. One would have found the chain of command ending up with Hitler himself - and that was simply out of the question, wasn't it? (Mollo, 1982:68)

Paragraph 47 of the German Manual of Military Law limited the notion of unconditional obedience with two moral justifications. First, that the order "... must be confined to the pursuit of some military objective..." and second, "... pursuit of the military objective is only justified if it serves some higher national purpose and if the military organisation as a whole forms an integral part of a wider state organisation. If a military command runs counter to the general state system it has neither purpose nor justification..." (Krausnick et al., 1965:306). This raises two important points, first, many of the orders given and obeyed by the Waffen-SS served no military purpose and second, the Waffen-SS was not part of the general state apparatus. It was designed to serve ideological and extra-state political purposes.

If one examines Ohlendorf's responses carefully he himself admits that he allowed soldiers who found the task unsuitable or who were incapable of performing the task to return home, with no mention of any form of punishment. The judges of the *Einsatzgruppen* case also noted this fact and in their judgement stated:

> One may accuse the Nazi military hierarchy of cruelty, even sadism if one

will. But it may not be lightly charged with inefficiency. If any of these *Kommando* leaders had stated that they were constitutionally unable to perform this cold-blooded slaughter of human beings, it is not unreasonable to assume that they would have been assigned to other duties, not out of sympathy or for humanitarian reasons, but for efficiency's sake alone. In fact Ohlendorf himself declared on this very subject — "In two and a half years I had sufficient occasion to see how many of my *Gruppe* [group] did not agree to this order in their inner opinion. Thus, I forbade the participation in these executions on the part of some of these men, and I sent some back to Germany." Ohlendorf himself could have got out of his execution assignment by refusing cooperation with the army. He testified that the Chief of Staff in the field said to him that if he, Ohlendorf, did not cooperate, he would ask for his dismissal in Berlin.

(The United Nations War Crime Commission, 1946: Vol 4:481)

The judges rejected the SS defence proposition that the soldiers were following superior orders under duress.

During a killing action undertaken in occupied Russia in 1941 a number of Order Police "... dropped out because they personally knew some of the 201 victims or could not stand the mental pressure" (Matthaus, 1996:136). No mention is made of any of these soldiers being disciplined or shot for failure to participate in the shootings. Field Marshal Von Rundstedt and General Blaskowitz, both senior commanders of the *Wehrmacht,* refused to allow or criticised the cleansing operations being undertaken in Poland, yet neither were marched off and shot (Zukier, 1994). During the initial occupation of Poland, Von Rundstedt forbade *Einsatzgruppen* to operate in his area of control. Himmler gave into this stand against his cleansing actions. Blaskowitz went so far as to prepare a written list of atrocities committed by the SS in Poland and sent such to the Führer demanding that action be taken. By 18 November 1939 the Blaskowitz memorandum was on Hitler's desk. Part of the memorandum requested that executions only be carried out after a proper court had delivered a sentence. Hitler rejected this notion outright as childish ideas on behalf of such generals (Hohne, 1969:306). Blaskowitz was not drummed out the door and shot, rather he was shortly moved to the Western Front, and Poland was put under the control of more reliable party and SS elements. This clearly shows that senior officers did and could have protested against the cleansing actions undertaken on the Eastern Front, and done so without the threat of being shot.

Some soldiers in the 101st Police Battalion refused to commit the killings. None were punished for this (although they were ostracised). One officer in fact was transferred to a safer assignment in Germany (Browning, 1998). Some members of the Order Police when involved in killing actions in occupied Russia in 1941 later "… among themselves, raised doubts about the legality of the execution" (Matthaus, 1996:136). Matthaus cites an example of a small Gendarme detachment stationed in occupied Russia whose actions were observed by a Jewish interpreter. The Gendarmerie were part of the German Order Police and is best described as being the equivalent to a village policeman. In occupied Eastern Europe Gendarmerie personnel were used to supervise and control static local native police units. The unit referred to by Matthaus was commanded by an individual who disliked carrying out killing actions against Jews. As such his men "… were able to abstain from participating in the shooting, if they so desired" (Matthaus, 1996:141).

This raises the issue of initiative. Initiative to do or not do the evil act, this was clearly a choice that was available to men of the Waffen-SS on the Eastern Front. The distances were simply too vast for the top Nazi bureaucrats to personally enforce their extermination policies. They had to rely on their subordinates to this on their own initiative on receipt of general orders in this regard. *SS-Gruppenführer* Odilo Globocnik for instance decided to kill all the Jews in his area. Later he presented this proposal to Himmler for approval (Lower, 2002). This type of behaviour can be termed as anticipatory obedience This example leads us back to the interactional approach to the explanation of evil acts. In the above case it is clear that despite their being a situation that was conducive to evil acts being conducted (the state having authorised killing actions of the Jews), much still depended on the individual's disposition as to how and if the action was undertaken. Indeed in military terms one could frame the policies of Himmler as a strategic evil (the situation) and the actions of the subordinates as tactical evil (the dispositions and actions of the individual).

The testimony of *SS-Brigadeführer* Franz Six shows that there was clear scope for soldiers of the Waffen-SS to question and take responsibility even when involved in some of the worst activities on the Eastern Front. Six was convicted in 1948 and sentenced to 20 years' imprisonment, which was later commuted to 10 years. He was released in 1952. *SS-Brigadeführer* Six, a former university professor, was attached to *Einsatzgruppe* B as commander of the *Vorkommando Moscow,* which operated as part of Army Group Centre in 1941-1942. Six served in the 2nd Waffen-SS Panzer

Division *Das Reich*. He was later transferred to the Foreign Office and went on to become head of the information department there (Klee et al., 1988; MacLean, 1999b). He puts paid to the myth that men of the *Einsatzgruppen* were victims of their situations with no choice but to obey orders:

> During the war a person could at least try to have himself transferred from an *Einsatzgruppe*. I myself managed to do this successfully … there were without doubt cases where people who were transferred from an *Einsatzgruppe* suffered disadvantage. I can no longer recall any individual cases. Nonetheless, as far as I know, nobody was shot as a result. One could apply to the RSHA[78] for a transfer to the front or to be released for service in another field. (Klee et al., 1988:83)

The testimony would seem to render the claim of Reinecke and other Waffen-SS apologists of having no choice but to commit evil acts as not being true. Further to this, *SS–Obersturmbannführer* Albert Hartl, a former Catholic priest and university graduate, was an officer attached to *Einsatzkommando* C gave evidence of how it was possible to avoid committing these atrocities. The judges in the *Einsatzgruppen* case made specific reference to it:

> The witness Hartl testified that Thomas, Chief of Einsatzgruppe B, declared that all those who could not reconcile their conscience to the Führer Order, that is, people who were too soft, as he said, would be sent back to Germany or assigned to other tasks, and that, in fact, he did send a number of people including commanders back to the Reich.
>
> (The United Nations War Crime Commission, 1946: Vol 4:482)

There is a capacity to question orders that appear to be immoral. How does one show that the individual soldier does indeed bear moral responsibility for their actions? Does the need to obey superior orders justify the individual soldier in surrendering or restricting their personal moral judgements and responsibilities? This study would argue no. A clear indication of how bankrupt the above argument is can be seen in Article 33 of the *Rome Statute*[79]:

> Superior orders and prescription of law 1. The fact that a crime within the jurisdiction of the Court has been committed by a person pursuant to an order of a Government or of a superior, whether military or civilian, *shall not relieve that person of criminal responsibility*[80] unless:
>
> (a) The person was under a legal obligation to obey orders of the Government or the superior in question;
>
> (b) The person did not know that the order was unlawful; and
>
> (c) The order was not manifestly unlawful.

2. For the purposes of this article, orders to commit genocide or crimes against humanity are manifestly unlawful.

This is unmistakable proof that the international community expects soldiers to exercise moral responsibility and judgement when involved in combat duties. While the Rome Statute may be a relatively new legal instrument of the United Nations, one can find the same principles outlined in more relevant laws of the time. Take for example Articles 43 and 46 of the Hague Conference of 1907, Laws and Customs of War on Land (Hague IV); October 18, 1907, which outline the duties of an occupying force:

> Article 43. The authority of the legitimate power having in fact passed into the hands of the occupant, the latter shall take all the measures in his power to restore, *and ensure, as far as possible, public order and safety[81]*, while respecting, unless absolutely prevented, the laws in force in the country.

> Article 46. Family honour and rights, *the lives of persons*, and private property, as well as religious convictions and practice, *must be respected*.[82]

The preamble to this convention clearly outlines the objectives sought by the conference:

> ... These provisions, the wording of which *has been inspired by the desire to diminish the evils of war[83]*, as far as military requirements permit, are intended to serve as a general rule of conduct for the belligerents in their mutual relations and in their relations with the inhabitants.

The Geneva Convention of 1929 also set out to ensure that warfare was conducted in an orderly manner and resulted in humane treatment of combatants and civilians alike. An example of this is Article 2 that dealt with the treatment of prisoners of war:

> Article 2. Prisoners of war are in the power of the hostile Power, but not of the individuals or corps who have captured them. They must at all times be humanely treated and protected, particularly against acts of violence, insults and public curiosity. Measures of reprisal against them are prohibited.

Of note is that Germany was signatory to both the Hague and Geneva Conventions as to the conduct of war and the laws and customs of war on land, yet when it suited them the Germans ignored these treaties at will. The formation of the Nuremberg Trials at the conclusion of World War II demonstrated a decision by the Allies that individual officials bear personal responsibility for outrageous conduct towards their own citizens and foreigners during wartime. To step outside the boundaries of what is acceptable military conduct places blame for the act clearly on the shoulders of the individual committing the act. There can be no reliance on the claim that they were just carrying out a military activity with no room for individual moral judgements. Indeed the war crime categories outlined at Nuremberg showed that society requires individual obedience to higher moral principles than that of just following orders.

The IMT Charter at Nuremberg denounced the defences under the heads of superior orders, command of law and acts committed in the name of the state. These principles were adopted by later war-crime trials (Peppers, 1974; Ratner & Abrams, 1997). The judges in the *Einsatzgruppen* case made the following comment in their judgement:

> The *Einsatz* battalions were not being called upon to face shot and shell. They were not ordered to charge into the mouths of cannon. They were called upon to shoot unarmed civilians standing over their graves. No soldier would be disgraced in asking to be excused from so one-sided a battle. No soldier could be accused of cowardice in seeking relief from a duty which was, after all, not a soldier's duty. No soldier or officer attempting escape from such a task would be pleading avoidance of a military obligation. He would simply be requesting not to be made an assassin. And if the leaders of the *Einsatzgruppen* had all indicated their unwillingness to play the assassin's part, this black page in German history would not have been written.
>
> (Nuremberg Military Tribunal, 1946: Vol 4:484)

Perhaps the most damning evidence that those committing atrocities knew what they were doing was wrong is in their own reactions to the acts they performed. Perpetrators of evil acts often suffer both physically and mentally as a result of the actions they undertake. It is of interest that despite claims by some perpetrators of atrocities that they were merely following orders, they suffered enormous side-effects from the trauma of what they did. This, it could be argued, is clear evidence that despite what the perpetrators state, one can perhaps infer their true state of mind by the unconscious physical and psychological reactions they had to the acts they were committing. It is of interest that of the some 105 Waffen-SS army, corps and divisional commanders studied by Yerger, some 11 per cent committed suicide at the end of the war (Yerger, 1997, , 1999). Another five per cent were executed for war crimes on the Eastern Front (Yerger, 1997, , 1999).[84] This high suicide rate could perhaps be argued as a side-effect of the enormous crimes that the Waffen-SS commanders were required to undertake.

There are problems associated with calling upon individuals to perform evil actions. The committing of atrocities can place those who were involved under massive psychological stress. To avoid this SS officer Ohlendorf of *Einsatzgruppen* D gave orders "… for several people to shoot simultaneously, in order to avoid any individual having to take direct, personal responsibility" (Klee et al., 1988:60). Indeed the search for more efficient killing procedures was driven by the need to increase the cleansing of the target groups and also lessen the psychological impact on the men doing the killings (Lifton, 2000; Rhodes, 2002). The conduct of the killing actions in occupied Russia required the perpetrators to have a high level of contact with the victims prior to and while the killings took place. This psychological strain placed on the perpetrators was thus extraordinary and of an altogether different kind than in situations of military combat.

Even one of the main architects of the slaughter found it difficult to deal with. In August 1941 Himmler visited Minsk on the Eastern Front, and there requested that members of *Einsatzgruppen* B conduct a cleansing action so that he could witness the executions. As a result some 100 prisoners were taken to the outskirts of the city and shot. *SS-Obergruppen-führer* Karl Wolff, a general on Himmler's staff, was present and gave this account of the incident after the war:

> It was of course inevitable that Himmler had a look, and from these shots, shots to the head, bits of brains spurted out and splattered in a high arc on to his coat. He trembled, didn't he? Of course he was nauseated by what he saw. Then he began to stagger and reel. (Halliley, 2003)

Himmler's doctor was called to attend him. So disturbed was he by what he had seen that Himmler sought a better way to kill that would involve less stress on the perpetrators and also be more efficient. The use of the gas chambers was seen as one way of depersonalising the killings and introducing the concept of *distance* between victim and perpetrator (Lifton, 2000; Zukier, 1994). In modern times the increase in the types of weaponry available have allowed soldiers to kill from a considerable distance, thus making the act of killing quite impersonal (Jones, 2000). This has allowed governments to utilise this advance in technology.

> The Germans took full advantage of this for the purpose of genocide in the World War II, although the mass bombing of German cities by the Allies and the use of the atomic bombs in Japan – if not genocide – at least demonstrated a willingness to engage in mass slaughter for the purpose of 'good' against 'evil'. (Jones, 2000:83)

In the concentration-camps individuals experienced in the performance of evil acts were in a position to socialise or adjust newcomers to the situation they found themselves in (Darley, 1992). However, even after this socialisation process had taken place many individuals still found the acts extremely stressful. Both the SS doctors and the men of the 101st Police Battalion utilised alcohol as a means to deal with the stress suffered (Browning, 1998; Lifton, 2000). A *Wehrmacht* neuropsychiatrist who treated large numbers of *Einsatzgruppen* personnel found "… that 20 per cent of those doing the actual killing experienced these symptoms of psychological decompensation" (Lifton, 2000:15). At a post-war trial it was described how some members of the *Einsatzgruppen* refused to obey orders, became drunk and suffered psychological illnesses. Even the HSSPF for anti-partisan warfare, Waffen-SS General *SS-Obergruppenführer* Bach-Zelewski, was hospitalised for stress-related issues as a result of the executions of Jews that he had directed, while a number of other high SS leaders also suffered from mental problems (Headland, 1992; Miller et al., 2006; Zukier, 1994). He was hospitalised from January to April 1941, when asked by his treating doctor Dr. Ernst Grawitz why he was under such strain Bach-Zelewski replied "Thank God I'm through with it. Don't you know what's happening in Russia? The entire Jewish people is being exterminated there!" (Miller et al., 2006:43)

SS-Obersturmbannführer Hartl gave evidence at his post-war trial that many of the soldiers in the killing units suffered a range of psychological repercussions ranging from impotence to mental derangement (MacLean, 1999b; Rhodes, 2002). This evidence of mental conflict can of itself be used to argue that members of the killing organisations were well aware that although their actions were officially sanctioned, they were not morally justifiable. Indeed, as Waller surmises, "… this perpetration-induced traumatic stress is consistent with how we expect ordinary, psychologically normal people to react to traumatic events outside the realm of ordinary experience" (Waller, 2002:69). In conclusion it is the case that obedience to orders that, embody or cause evil acts to be committed is an act of faith, that leaves the individual accountable and liable for the actions committed.

The SS mentality

The campaign in the East had begun with unspeakable harshness. We were all firmly convinced of the necessity of the battle, all believed in our leaders and in our own strength, and we were in no doubt that we would emerge victorious from this confrontation. (Weidinger, 1998:71)

These words of *SS-Brigadeführer* Otto Kumm give some insight into the mentality of the Waffen-SS upon their entry into Russia. It shows the belief that the soldiers of the Waffen-SS had in their own justification for the battle, the anticipated outcome of such, and their faith in the Nazi leadership. This view is reinforced by the comments of a soldier of the 3rd SS *Totenkopf* Panzer Division, Georg Kurpiers "We fought in the belief of the Führer, Volk and Vaterland" (Huffman, 2005:30).. In fact, of the SS members studied since the war, many have displayed a preference for monarchical or dictatorial forms of government, pride in their military achievements, and a high valuation of loyalty at the expense of justice or honour (Dicks, 1972; Kressel, 2002; Staub, 2002; J. Steiner, 2000). Interviews with SS concentration-camp officers after the war showed that they were "… enthusiastic about their role in creating a new world order and glad to do whatever was necessary…" to achieve such (Staub, 1989:132). This is also reflected in a study of Waffen-SS soldiers, which revealed that after the war the majority of those studied "… thought of their military past with satisfaction…" (J. Steiner, 1963:442). As one veteran of the *Leibstandarte SS Adolf Hitler* Division stated: "Back then we hadn't the slightest doubt about the rightness of our cause of the certainty of the ultimate victory. That was what we grew up with – at home, in the school, and in the Hitler Youth" (Bartov, 1992:113). This is how many of the SS soldiers justify the commission of atrocities; they were an elite who were capable of carrying out these crimes for the good of Germany.

In essence the end justified the means; this is how Himmler consecrated the actions taken by the SS, even if they involved criminality. Steiner had the following to say of his subjects, "… even if the costs had been known for playing these roles, the majority of the Waffen-SS, the military branch of the SS, would have still participated and had no regrets" (J. Steiner, 1963:442). The Waffen-SS morality was based on loyalty to the group, that being the *us* group. For those outside this group, the *them* group, contempt was held for their rights and privileges. This loyalty to the group can be referred back to my previous discussion about the devaluing of the victim and obedience to orders.

The Waffen-SS fostered an esprit de corps among their troops that enhanced both their obedience to authority and also their fighting ability. Indeed the esprit de corps fostered by the Waffen-SS allowed the soldier to see himself as a soldier of the Führer. In a post-war study it was noted that the "… elite SS divisions … had a larger hard core that other divisions of the army, so large as to embrace almost the entire group membership

Standard of the *Leibstandarte SS Adolf Hitler*

during most of the war – accounted for their greater fighting effectiveness"
(Shills et al., 1948:286). This hard core being politically, racially and ideologically committed to the Nazi cause. To further strengthen this core, officer candidates had to serve two years in the enlisted ranks before entering
the *Junkerschulen*. This helped to mould a bond between enlisted personnel and officers. The strength of the core of these divisions allowed them
again and again to be used where the fighting was fiercest with little worry
of them failing to carry out orders. It also allowed the divisions to be rebuilt
time after time when they were destroyed in battle. According to one Waffen-SS veteran the formation of the 9th and 10th SS Panzer Divisions in late
1943 depended on the fact that "... the young soldiers watched their

Unterführer and officers and listened to them, for these, mostly old soldiers of the Eastern Front, knew Russia and, with their war experience, formed the steel framework of the divisions" (Tieke, 1999:19).

Nipe argues that the Waffen-SS were not politically motivated but rather fought for their "... commander and their comrades, political ideals having scarce practical value in the daily life of the soldier..." (Nipe, 1996:268). Indeed it has been suggested that many volunteers for the Waffen-SS may not have been driven by a burning ideological need, but rather simply wanted to use the Waffen-SS for an alternative path to the military (J. Steiner, 1963; Weingartner, 1974). Many veterans such as Gerd Rommel (10th SS Panzer Division *Frundsberg,* also the son of Field Marshal Erwin Rommel), Eduard Janke (11th Panzergrenadier Division *Nordland*), Erwin Bartman (1st SS Panzer Division *Leibstandarte SS Adolf Hitler*) and Freidrich-Karl Wacker (16th SS Panzergrenadier Division *Reichsführer-SS*) claim they joined the Waffen-SS because of its status and favourable impressions they had formed by its pre-war parades, etc (Williamson, 1995).

In a post-war interview *SS-Obergruppenführer* Karl Wolff, Himmler's adjutant, stated that when he joined the SS he was told that "Well just as there was an elite guard in the Kaiser's time there is an elite guard now in the new movement and that is the SS, you should join the SS" (Bloomberg, 2000). To support this view there is considerable evidence that "SS members saw themselves as an elite..." (Staub, 1989:130). Werner Busse, a veteran of the *Frundsberg* Division, stated that "I choose to volunteer for the Waffen-SS because it was known to have a greater atmosphere of comradeship and also because it was an elite force, more dedicated to Germany's cause" (Williamson, 1995:22).

Wolfgang Filor, a veteran of the *Das Reich* Division, saw it as a great honour to join the Waffen-SS due to the stringent selection procedures in place in the early days of the organisation. In essence only the best human material was accepted (Halliley, 2003). Some volunteers, such as Johann Voss, recounted how on hearing of the Waffen-SS and its early war exploits and the supposed pan-European nature of the force from a young Waffen-SS friend of his he felt "... carried away by his enthusiasm anxious to hear more ... this ... version of the Waffen-SS and its pan-European dimension had a new and strong attraction" (Voss, 2002:27).

At the beginning of its life the SS was extremely selective about who was allowed to enter, with stringent screening in place in respect to physical ability and racial background (Birn, 1991; Keegan, 1970; Reitlinger, 1957; Wegner, 1990; Williamson, 1995). As has been previously noted, those joining the Waffen-SS could scarcely argue that they did not know they were joining an organisation that was based on racial, ideological and political ideals. As noted by Stein:

> Elite military formations with high standards of physical selection, aggressive leadership, and an esprit de corps supplied by either tradition or ideological indoctrination make extremely formidable adversaries. The early SS divisions possessed all of these qualities in abundance, and this fact is the key to an understanding of their combat performance. (Stein, 1966:59).

This loyalty manifested itself in the fact that Waffen-SS soldiers saw themselves as an elite and had a strong attachment to their unit. It is of interest then that one SS veteran gives the following insight into how they were able to commit atrocities, "Comradeship was everything. It gave us the mental and physical strength to do what others were too weak to do" (Staub, 1989:130). *SS-Obergruppenführer* Felix Steiner, commanded of the 5th *Wiking* Division, 3rd SS Panzer Corps, and at the end of the war the 11th SS Army. He gave this reasoning for the camaraderie among the Waffen-SS:

> An extensive interest in the welfare of the troops, and the cultivation of the feeling of comradeship increased the already close feeling of unit between all the ranks, and strengthened the spiritual unity of the troops, and the confidence between officers and men. (F. Steiner, 1947:9)

This loyalty was converted into blind obedience to the criminal directives and orders issued by Hitler and executed by the Waffen-SS. This loyalty to the inner group is still reflected in memoirs written today. *SS-Sturmbannführer* Ralf Tiemann, who served as chief operations officer in both the *SS Leibstandarte* and *Das Reich* Divisions, had this to say on comradeship in the Waffen-SS: "This chronicle should serve to quell any doubt that to this very day, despite all of the disappointment, demonisation and defamation of our great experience, that there is one thing that actively remained in us, the camaraderie." (Tiemann, 1998:7).

The Waffen-SS was seen as an elite. To this end Himmler and the SS went to great lengths to promote the successes of the Waffen-SS and idolised those soldiers who displayed the qualities valued by the SS in the face of the enemy. *SS-Unterscharführer* Fritz Christen was just one of the men put forward as an example of the Waffen-SS fighting spirit. On the 24th of September 1941 Christen was attached to the antitank detachment of the *Totenkopf* Division, which was fighting in Russia as part of Army Group North. Christen was cut off from his division and all of his comrades were killed. Despite this, when confronted by 15 enemy tanks Christen continued to fire his cannon and destroyed six of the attacking tanks. Christen continued to fight the Russians killing some 100 Russians and destroying 13 enemy tanks over a two-day period. He was awarded the Knight's Cross for this action and at that stage of the war was the first enlisted man and the youngest recipient of the award in the Waffen-SS (Schneider, 1993; Simpson, 1990).

The image promulgated by the Waffen-SS was that they were an elite who had to be hard on those who stood in the way of their objectives, but they also had to be harder on themselves. For this reason Himmler often went to great lengths to emphasis the sacrifice that the SS men were making by committing various atrocities. In a speech to a gathering of SS generals at Posen on the 4th of October 1943 Himmler had this to say about the extermination of the Jews:

> I mean the clearing out of the Jews, the extermination of the Jewish race ... Not one of all those who talk this way has witnessed it, not one of them has been through it. Most of *you* must know what it means when 100 corpses are lying side by side, or 500, or a 1000. To have stuck it out and at the same time — apart from exceptions caused by human weakness — to have remained decent fellows, that is what has made us hard.
>
> (Nuremberg Military Tribunal, 1946: Vol 5:251)

Himmler attempted to fortify himself and those called upon to conduct these killings by arguing that this was an onerous duty that only the most loyal and dedicated could be trusted to conduct. How successful Himmler was in this respect can be seen in the comments of an SS sergeant as to why he engaged in mass executions:

> The reason I did not say to Leideritz *(his commander)*[85] that I could not take part in these things was that I was afraid that Leideritz and others would think that I was a coward ... I did not want Leideritz or other people to get the impression that I was not as hard as an SS-Man ought to have been. (Klee et al., 1988:78)

In 1943 soldiers of the 9th SS Panzer Division *Hohenstaufen* were told to conduct themselves to the following ideals; "The inner affirmation of struggle, also under the most difficult conditions. The courage to face up to every eventuality without flinching. Determination in the face of all reverses" (Wegner, 1990:207). A member of the 4th SS Panzergrenadier *Polizei* Division wrote in a letter home describing this determination:

> With us now are the new replacements that have arrived. They are all splendid youths. With double the zeal we enter now on the training. If then the time for us is coming we will with fresh strength and the old fighting spirit set out to our new action. On the Eastern Front the hard battle of destiny rages further ... we remain hard and keep unshakably erect in and through this time and I am proud as well to be an SS officer. For us there is only one thing: To fight and to win. (Huffman, 2005:80)

It was this determination and toughness that allowed the Waffen-SS to be so resilient to the end of the war. *SS-Obergruppenführer* Eicke imbued in the *Totenkopf* Division with "... a potent mixture of intense commitment to the political goals of Germany, high unit morale and a healthy dose of pride in their toughness, which was carefully developed in the men of the original Waffen-SS divisions" (Nipe, 1996:126). In an order to this division, *SS-Obergruppenführer* Eicke succinctly outlined the hardness that he expected his troops to display on the Eastern Front:

> ... Officers, NCOs and men! You have had rich opportunities in hard hours to prove characteristics and physical hardness. I call on your hearts. Guard the belief and the corps spirit. Belief and spirit moves mountains. If you in the next weeks find things hard to handle, then think of it, that this hardness has been brought about by war. Hardness saves blood and educates the inner psychological discipline. But behind the hardness beats a warm sympathetic heart. There lives the comradeship. I ask for the full employment of your strength, ruthlessness in person and clear eyes for the political necessities. We are political soldiers of the Führer. We have the passionate belief in the Führer and the unshakable will for the Führer. If called for we are prepared to give the highest sacrifice. With this attitude we will win. Hunt on! (Huffman, 2005:93)

SS-Obergruppenführer Lothar Debes instructed the 6th SS Division *Nord* to display the following traits regarding leadership; "Leadership and formations must by all training not only be educated in combat techniques and hardship, but also in crisis to be versatile" (Debes, 1947:36). *Wiking* veteran Hendrik Verton recalled how:

> Because of our military education and ideals we could not afford to weaken, when confronted with an extreme situation in combat. We were not threatened with a court martial. The combustion which drove us to self sacrifice was psychological. We told ourselves "we must do it or all is lost". That motivation stood foremost with us in the Waffen-SS. (Verton, 2007:99)

This was the much vaunted hardness that the SS placed so much emphasis on. Indeed, Himmler would often praise the virtues of toughness and hardness in dealing with subhumans and the repugnant acts this involved for the soldiers. A series of SS pamphlets discussed SS culture and one was titled "Be Hard!" (Pruess Publishing, 2004b). An SS correspondent had this to say in relation to the military conflict in the East; "The realisation that only a hardness and ruthlessness towards one's own person shaken by nothing solves the military task, this realisation is the principle of this war. We must become even harder" (Pruess Publishing, 2004b:37). These ideals reflected the thinking of Hitler himself, his justification for atrocities being "… shrinking from violence showed moral weakness, while willingness to destroy showed moral strength" (Victor, 1998:91). After witnessing a mass execution Wolff recalls that Himmler gave the commanders of the execution squads the following speech:

> He could not relieve them of this duty, he could not spare them in the interests of the Reich, in this planned 1000 year Reich, in its first decisive great war since the takeover of power. They must do their duty. (Bloomberg, 2000)

In correspondence to Waffen-SS General Gottlob Berger, chief recruiting officer of the Waffen-SS, Himmler stated, "The occupied territories will be cleared of Jews. The Führer has charged me with carrying out this very difficult task. No-one can relieve me of the responsibility. I cannot allow myself the luxury of discussing it" (Krausnick et al., 1965:69). SS soldiers were extolled in SS pamphlets that "Bolshevism itself has taught us the lesson that there can be no half measures in this conflict. We have become steel hard …We know that fate is in our hands and we will master it" (Pruess Publishing, 2001:40). Indeed SS bureaucrats "… expressed the feeling that they had done a necessary wartime job with great conscientiousness and self-sacrifice" (Koehl, 1959:123). This need for hardness can be seen to spring from the fact that the Waffen-SS were political soldiers. As such they were involved in an eternal struggle, which required constant vigilance to protect Germany. This vigilance was necessary because the enemy was not clearly defined like that of a purely military soldier, the enemy could be external or internal. The distinction between peace and war was a grey one and civilian life all but disappeared for the SS soldier. This eternal struggle would take a harsh physical form in the conflict in Russia.

Difficult life conditions

The claim has been made that Germany was merely responding to the threat of a Russian invasion. Hitler's *Luftwaffe* adjutant, Von Below, recalled Hitler stating that "He thought it was likely that Russia would attack from the autumn of 1941 onwards ... Hitler stated that his decision to invade the Soviet Union in the spring of 1941 was final" (Von Below, 1980:69). Some Waffen-SS veterans still claim the above. For example, in the post-war history of the 1st Company *Leibstandarte SS Adolf Hitler* this argument is continued; "Can one attribute peace-loving intentions to the Soviet Union when it had already transferred 100 divisions to its western frontiers in autumn 1940, while on the German side there were only 35?" (Quassowksi, 1999:143). *SS-Brigadeführer* Karl Herrmann explained how the invasion of Russia came to his knowledge; "Peace and tranquillity, and the generous hospitality of the East Prussian population were suddenly and rudely shattered by the well-known Führer proclamation of 21 June 1941, with it Hitler opened our eyes to the necessity for this campaign" (Herrmann, 1947:1).

This type of thinking is important. It clearly allowed the soldiers of the Waffen-SS to see the Russians as the aggressors while they could envisage themselves as the protectors and defenders of the Reich. This in turn allowed them to blame the difficult life conditions they faced during the conflict on the Russians. The judges of the IMT rejected this argument of Russian aggression:

> It was contended for the defendants that the attack upon the U.S.S.R., was justified because the Soviet Union was contemplating an attack upon Germany and making preparations to that end. It is impossible to believe that this view was ever honestly entertained.

(The International Military Tribunal, 1946: Vol 1:215)

A meeting between top German generals, Halder and Brauchitsch, before the invasion concluded that Germany would be better off maintaining a friendship with Russia and that "Russian intentions ... posed no threat" (Megargee, 2000:103). Indeed the opinion of senior generals such as Field Marshal Von Rundstedt when interviewed after the war was that there was no threat of offensive action from Russia and certainly he saw no evidence of it as his forces pushed into Russia (Liddell Hart, 1975). As tensions between the two countries increased Stalin resisted the urges of his military chiefs to adopt plans for a pre-emptive strike against the build-up of German forces. The analysis of Colonel-General Halder, chief of staff of the German Army (OKH)[86] in 1941 would make any threat of attack seem unlikely as;

> Soviet policy up to then led Halder to consider a large scale offensive by the Red Army at the beginning of June 1941 to be "most improbable" and

> he regarded the deployments (of the Red Army) as defensive measures …
> As no aggressive intentions had been attributed to Stalin, Hitler and his
> military leaders were not disturbed by the ability of the Red Army to fight
> a war. (Forster, 1997:128).

It is generally accepted by military historians that the war on the Eastern Front was the scene of the worst atrocities that were seen during World
War II. It was a war that unleashed barbarity for a variety of reasons including:

> … physical survival and mental attrition, casualties and cohesion, dra-
> conian discipline and brutality, indoctrination and criminal policies simul-
> taneously constituted a part of the individual soldier's daily front-line
> experience, moulded his views and directed his actions. (Bartov,
> 1997:327)

The issue of difficult life conditions can produce the climate in which
mass atrocities such as genocide are more likely to develop and take place.
For this reason it is necessary to see what impact the physical fighting conditions themselves had on the propensity of soldiers to commit atrocities.
Bartov (1997) describes the demodernisation of the German Army as the
conflict progressed, where the armed forces began to suffer from a lack of
effective weapons and a manpower shortage. To deal with this lack of
replacements German infantry divisions were reduced from nine battalions
to six battalions. The infantry division in 1939 had a nominal strength of
17,734 men, while in 1943 the nominal strength was 12,772 men (Healy,
1993). This lack of replacements increased the stresses on combat soldiers
as;

> … The supply system reached breaking point. The men at the front had to
> make do with inadequate clothing, insufficient food provisions and
> extremely wretched accommodation facilities for long periods of time in
> the height of the Russian winter. All these factors combined to create an
> acute sense of crisis. Both physical and mental attrition were highly
> prevalent, and the incidence of illness and nervous breakdowns greatly
> increased. (Bartov, 1997:327)

SS General Max Simon succinctly outlined the manpower problem
after the war, "It was absolutely impossible to replace adequately the casualties of the Eastern campaign. The cadres of efficient NCOs of whom there
had been too few from the outset, were decimated a few months after the
start of the campaign, there was a lack of officers in all companies and battalions" (Simon, 1949:11). An example of the attrition suffered is that in the

first 12 months of the war the 4th Waffen-SS *Polizei* Division lost over half of its 14,588 men (Pierik, 2001).

From the very first months in the campaign the German forces suffered from a lack of manpower. By comparison the Russians, although sorely depleted after the losses of 1941, were able to mobilise a huge reserve of manpower and industrial resources. Indeed the fortunes of the respective armies were almost the converse of each other, even as the German Army began its numerical and qualitative decline, the Soviet Army was evolving into an organisation totally unlike that of even a year before. This disparity between the two forces was evidenced by the fact that:

> The Russian armoured formations were constantly improving in terms of the quality of leadership and the use of armour in battle. German combat quality began to decline after mid 1943, due to unreplaceable losses in trained and experienced men and officers, and the inability of Germany to produce sufficient numbers of tanks and assault guns. (Nipe, 1996:328).

This numerical advantage enjoyed by the Russians is clearly evidenced in the manner in which troops were sometimes deployed to attack. The Russian military made considerable use of the human-wave attack, in which waves of soldiers would charge towards the enemy line. Such tactics while successful on some occasions, were callous in the extreme – cruel to the extent that individual human lives became worthless. Soldiers of the 3rd SS Panzer Division *Totenkopf* were amazed during the initial fighting in June 1941 by the "... Russian infantry's continued suicidal charges..." (Sydnor, 1990:160). Former commander of the division, Max Simon, recounted that "If the first attack is repelled it is definitely certain that a second will follow and a third, fourth and so on, without the slightest change in the method of attack. Human lives play no role..." (Simon, 1953:11). *SS-Brigadefïhrer* Karl Herrmann commented on the Russian soldier; "The Russian soldier's clothing is scanty, and his personal equipment immaterial. No value is placed on his life. Since the casualty rate is considered immaterial the Russian soldier is driven without mercy into the heaviest fire. Once he has given his life he is simply dumped in a hole" (Herrmann, 1947:4).

The disparity between the two sides only increased as the Germans suffered a reduction in it's level of equipment while the Russians, with help from America and Britain increased its mechanisation (Healy, 1993; Jukes, 2003). This support helped to underline a theme espoused by many German soldiers including those of the Waffen-SS. The theme essentially being that they were engaged in an unequal struggle against a barbaric foe that was supported in every way by the other ally nations. As one Waffen- SS veteran stated:

> But the wave from the east rose and rose, and came implacably closer. It was thrown forward on tens of thousands of American trucks, and was fed by many millions of tons of American supplies. It had already crushed the outer bastions of Western civilisation against the East, and its cultural monuments. The fruits of Nordic-Germanic colonisers, after thousands of years of hard work, and after steadfast struggle against the barbaric, ravaging expeditions of the Asian hordes, had now been destroyed. (Hillblad, 2002:29).

This lack of manpower forced the Germans to utilise their combat units for long periods in the front lines without rest. This had dire results. The account of numerous German soldiers highlights that they suffered continuously from "... never getting enough sleep" (Schroder, 1997:314). Veteran of the *SS Leibstandarte* Division, Ralf Tiemann, describes the effect of this type of combat in a letter home from the Russian front in July 1943:

> Hard weeks lie behind my company. So hard, like I never experienced before in this war ... For days we were on the edge in enemy fire from every weapon. For four days and four nights we didn't leave the confines of our panzer. We had to stay awake the whole time. (Tiemann, 1998:61).

In other words, the Waffen-SS soldiers on the Eastern front were facing difficult life conditions and it was all too easy to blame the Russians for the difficulties they faced. It has been noted that sleep deprivation can have both psychological and physical effects on soldiers that can impair their performance both mentally and physically (Haslam & Abraham, 1987). This situation was also recognised by the German command. In a post-war interview General Rohricht stated that "On the Eastern Front the divisions never got a rest, and that became a debilitating factor" (Liddell Hart, 1975:257). It has been noted that constant exposure to combat without rest can lead to an increase in stress and a decrease in combat performance. *Das Reich* veteran Hans-Joachim Lindow describes how after the first winter in 1941 and the Russian counter-attacks before the gates of Moscow the stress of combat and retreat began to tell:

> The term retreat was dishonourable, it just wasn't done. And therefore for us it was if we had made a mess of it, as if we had done something wrong. We were finished, absolutely done for, right at rock bottom both psychologically and physically. (Halliley, 2003)

Studies have shown that after some 30 days in combat there is a noticeable decline in combat effectiveness. After some 100 days of intermittent combat non-effective behaviour became frequent (Manton, Wilson, & Braithwaite, 2000). Indeed "… physical fatigue is one of the most evident hardships of campaigning…" and can cause soldiers to become careless, take more risks and lower their performance and morale (Haslam et al., 1987:221). A medical consultant for the German Army stated that stress and other psychiatric symptoms were the result of living in terror, having little sleep and living in dirty and wet conditions (Haslam et al., 1987). During the fighting in the Demyansk pocket in 1942 a number of German divisions were trapped, including the *SS Totenkopf* Division. After a number of weeks of bitter fighting in atrocious conditions the acting commander of the SS division, Max Simon, wrote to the authorities in Berlin and stated "… that for the first time since the beginning of the war he had lost hope. The hardships of the Russian campaign, and the unbelievable suffering and sacrifices of the men … had simply become more then he could bear" (Sydnor, 1990:244).

The quality of the fighting troops had also been in steady decline as a result of the enormous casualties being inflicted on the Waffen-SS. The *Totenkopf* division was involved in 10 months' continuous combat until it was taken out of the front line in October 1942 with only some 6000 survivors (Nipe, 1996). When 281 soldiers from the division were later medically examined, an SS doctor found that "… about 30 per cent were not fit for further military service and resembled the concentration-camp inmates that he had become familiar with during a tour of duty in the camps" (Nipe, 1996:126). *SS-Brigadeführer*, Dr. Oskar Hock, stated that "The fighting power of the troops was naturally lowered because of the meagre fare. While no marked epidemics resulted, many soldiers suffered from skin diseases. This was contributed not only to poor nutrition, but also to the necessity of spending a lot of time in filthy field fortifications" (Hock, 1947:19).

During the recapture of Kharkov in 1943 the *Leibstandarte SS Adolf Hitler* Division endured three months of continuous fighting. In his postwar history of the division, operations officer of the division *SS-Obersturmbannführer* Rudolf Lehmann noted that at the end of this period the division had suffered some 167 officers and 4373 men as casualties, or 44 per cent of the division's strength, (Lehmann, 1990:194). The 2nd Waffen-SS Panzer Division *Das Reich* fought its way to within 16 kms of the Kremlin and entered the suburb of Lenino during the German drive on Moscow during 1941. But the human cost of achieving this was high, with some 60 per cent casualties or 7000 men being lost, losses that Germany was already struggling to replace (Sharpe & Davis, 2003; Williamson & Andrew, 2004a). This is clear evidence of the enormous physical cost of the campaign and the devastating effect it would have had on the survivors.

This continuous lack of, and turnover in, troops due to casualties, reduced the combat effectiveness of those troops available. The Waffen-SS troops faced difficult life conditions in the form of the climate, the ongoing combat without rest, the sheer distances involved, and perhaps most importantly, the realisation that they were not involved in a short campaign as in the West. Rather they were now involved in a long and bitter ideological struggle in a foreign country. As one veteran of the *Das Reich* Division stated, "Now it was clear to every one of us that this Russia would be a very hard nut to crack" (Gunther, 2004:101).

The nature of the terrain and fighting caused members of the Waffen-SS to realise that the war in the East set new and different standards than had been known previously. To deal with these difficult conditions the soldiers turned more to the Nazi ideology to seek reassurance that they were fighting a just and necessary cause and provide rationale for their suffering. The German soldiers found it difficult if not impossible to accept the climatic conditions and distances they found forced upon them during the Russian campaign. The soldiers of the Waffen-SS faced abhorrent weather conditions from freezing winters to scorching summers during their combat on the Eastern Front as evidenced by a number of unit histories (Husemann, 2003; Lehmann, 1990; Ullrich, 2002; Weidinger, 2002). *SS-Obergruppenführer* Lothar Debes served in the 6th and 10th SS Divisions before becoming the Waffen-SS commander in Italy (A. Munoz, 2001; Westwood, 2001). He offered the following insight into the conditions faced by the men on the northern Russian front:

> Operations in the Polar region are influenced by the long 20-hour day darkness in winter and the 23-hour a day daylight in summer, also by the climatic conditions of the particular area, which in the north is artic in character with areas of tundra and further south pass over into dense forests interspersed with lakes and swamps; these are factors which require diametrically opposite combat methods in winter and summer. (Debes, 1947:1)

Waffen-SS doctor Oskar Hock outlined the dangers faced by the Waffen-SS soldiers in the harsh winter climate:

> The troops were in general poorly equipped for winter warfare in Russia. There was an outright want of winter clothing, and especially felt boots. There were hardly enough fur coats available to supply the sentries. Therefore frostbite occurred in increasing measure, hands and feet being especially susceptible to it. (Hock, 1947:12)

Kurt Sametreiter, a member of the *Leibstandarte SS Adolf Hitler,* recounted the winter conditions during the campaign in Russia, "Minus 46 degrees, minus forty six degrees and no overcoat, more froze to death than were wounded … I often cried out for my mother" (Halliley, 2003). This lack of winter equipment led members of the Waffen-SS to obtain winter equipment from any source available. Heinz Maeger, a member of the *Leibstandarte* Division, outlines the lengths some would go to; "When Russians fell we rushed to get their uniforms off as quickly as possible before they got cold, so that we had something warm to put on" (Halliley, 2003). *Das Reich* veteran Hans-Joachim Lindow recalls soldiers' ears falling off in the freezing winter conditions (Halliley, 2003). Other soldiers of the Waffen-SS relate, however, that it was not only the cold that made life difficult.

> Almost every day we had to deal with grotesque situations. Here is one of many examples. Our marching group is enveloped in swirling dust clouds. The encircling dust, which constantly infiltrates every cut and gap in our uniforms, down to our boots, with a fine layer, envelops the entire column concealingly. (Fischer, 2004:68)

Jan De Wilde, of the SS Volunteer Legion *Flandern,* recalled how it was so cold that the ground froze:

> We needed explosives and grenades to dig graves for our fallen comrades. Also, in certain positions along the lines we would pile the dead bodies of Russian soldiers on top of each other and cover them with snow so that we could lay in some kind of protection since we couldn't dig trenches. (Brandt, 1998:51).

The fighting itself was different to that which the German soldier had encountered during the Western campaign. One veteran described the fighting as being "… not just tough, but brutal in the extreme, it was a relapse into complete barbarity" (Schroder, 1997:317). The gauge of how brutal the fighting was can be determined that during two weeks of non-stop attacks by Russian soldiers against soldiers of the SS *Totenkopf* division trapped in the Demyansk pocket in February 1942 less then 100 prisoners were reported taken (Sydnor, 1990:220). The harshness of the fighting soon became apparent to those involved. At Gusi near Leningrad on the northern end of the front, the Waffen-SS Freiwilligen Legion *Nederland*.[87] which was comprised of Dutch volunteers, was getting its first taste of this barbarity. A convoy was ambushed by Russian soldiers and,

> Six of the legionnaires cut off from the rest of the group were all shot down. Afterwards, at the sound of moaning, the Russians appeared. A couple of the Dutchmen died instantly from the head wounds they sustained, those that did not were finished off with bayonets and rifle butt blows ... These confrontations really summed up the problem surrounding the ideological war ethic on the Eastern Front. There was no room for romantic notions about the war and there was no reprieve. (Pierik, 2001:95)

It is my contention that these harsh physical conditions only added to the situational influences that allowed the Waffen-SS to commit atrocities. It is clear that the actions of the Waffen-SS derived from a combination of situation the soldiers found themselves in and the disposition of the individual soldiers themselves. To argue that either one cause or the other is responsible solely for the atrocities committed does not seem a plausible explanation. Rather an interactive approach of the acts committed provides the most robust explanation for understanding how ordinary men could commit such terrible atrocities.

Conclusion:

As I stated from the outset this book is an exploration of the Waffen-SS, and by necessity evil. The previous chapters have shown how the Waffen-SS actions came about from interactive causation, in that both situational and dispositional influences played a role. We have seen that the atrocities committed by the Waffen-SS cannot be isolated to either the influence of the situation or the effect of the personality of the perpetrator. As previously discussed, one could frame the policies of Himmler and the Waffen-SS command as a strategic evil (the situation) and the actions of the subordinates as tactical evil (the dispositions and actions of the individual). This can been seen by the fact that not only were atrocities implemented from the high command, but they were also instigated from the lower ranks on their own initiative. This is clearly evidenced by comments made by Waffen-SS General, *SS-Obergruppenführer* Erich Bach-Zelewski, in his reference to wild actions by subordinates and difficulties in controlling them. I have shown that the conditions on the Eastern Front were conducive for atrocities to occur from the bottom up and top down. This can be seen by the general nature of the criminal orders given and the specific criminal actions taken in response to them.

This book by necessity is also of concerned with the acts of evil that mankind is so capable of committing. So the obvious question that begs answering is were the actions of the Waffen-SS evil? To answer this question let me first say that it is obviously not possible to examine each and every individual atrocity and apply the definition to such. Rather, a broad organisational approach has been applied throughout this book. Secondly it is not easy to define what one means by evil, and I do not intend to discuss it at length. I have however read widely on the subject and from these writing I have distilled the following definition of evil acts.

An ***objective assessment***[88] needs to be carried out by looking for the following elements: ***an evil act can be said to consist of:***
A serious intentional act or omission;
Which causes severe mental or physical harm; and
This harm is unnecessary or disproportionate to any instigation or provocation.

Clearly it can be seen that the actions of the Waffen-SS were in fact intentional. That would seem beyond argument. That these actions caused serious harm is also beyond contention as evidenced by the millions of innocent people killed and the evidence of victims and perpetrators themselves. Perhaps the most contentious aspect of the application of the definition is in relation to the third part, that the harm was unnecessary or disproportionate to any instigation or provocation. The apologists for the Waffen-SS argue that the Waffen-SS was just part of Germany's armed response to the looming military threat of the Soviet Union. This allows them to argue that the conflict was a preventative action to avoid a greater threat, that being the invasion of Germany by Russia. I would argue that I have showed lucid evidence that this was not the case in 1941.

Certainly in a broad context I would argue that the brutal military campaign undertaken by the Waffen-SS was not in response to any provocation or instigation that would have justified such. Rather I would describe their actions as intentional. Their actions served no legitimate military goal, but rather an ideological one. This becomes even clearer when one considers the anti-partisan and *Einsatzgruppen* actions behind the front lines. Here it would seem obvious that the slaughter that was undertaken was at worst nothing less than the simple murder of innocents, at best it could be described as disproportionate to the military threat facing the Waffen-SS. Certainly the judges of the post-war trials saw the German response as d isproportionate and unwarranted. When one moves on to the actions undertaken in the concentration-camps it would seem that any defence of Waffen-SS actions there would seem to fail. The previous research has shown that there would be difficulty in raising any claim of provocation or necessity for the genocide that took place within this system.

The objective assessment reveals that the actions of the Waffen-SS in totality meet the requirements of my definition of evil. However I see this assessment as only the first step in determining if an act or acts are evil. There are other factors that contribute to an act being seen as evil. These factors can be called the *three emotive agents*. They include the *perceived senselessness of the act, the perceived innocence of the victim of the act, the uniqueness of the act.* There is a need to expand upon why these emotive agents can assist us in classifying why an act is evil.

When referring to the *senselessness* of the act we are suggesting that the evilness lies in the ability of the act to defy imagination and reason. In his discussion of primordial evil Katz (1988:288) examines a number of "cold-blooded" killers and suggests, "... the senseless nature of their killings creates a crisis of understanding". Evil events such as the holocaust and the recent tribal massacres in Rwanda instil a sense of the crime being incomprehensible. The justification, provocation or instigation of an act can provide us with some ability to understand the rationale or reason for the act. This allows us to place such acts within the confines of everyday life, thus we do not perceive the acts as evil. We can perhaps rationalise to some degree the murder of a prisoner by a soldier in a fit of rage. We find it hard to rationalise the brutal murder of young baby at a concentration camp.

We also take account of the *innocence* of the victim. It is this factor of innocence and the victim's lack of capacity to have caused justification, provocation or instigation for the act that can provide us with grounds for classifying acts as evil. Traditionally crimes that have involved innocent or vulnerable victims such as the young or old have raised widespread condemnation. Crime committed against victims such as this strike some kind of chord in society that demands our attention and raises feelings in us that these types of crimes are above the ordinary. Perhaps this can be explained by the insight given by author Lance Morrow:

> When I have asked Americans and Europeans to tell me the most evil act they could imagine anyone committing, they have almost always spoken of acts against children – torture, rape, and murder. It would be difficult, in their reading, to surpass in evil a father who a few years ago set fire to his eight-year-old son, not killing him but disfiguring him horribly. (Morrow, 2003:49)

This sense of evil can relate back to the innocence of the victim. The ICC (in Rule *145*) has also recognised that the circumstances of the victim (i.e. being defenceless) are influential when it comes to judging the gravity and punishment of a crime. The crimes of the SS against children would seem to easily fall into what we would term evil actions. Evidence was given by a camp inmate as to their treatment upon arrival at the concentration-camps:

All we could hear were the screams and we could see the pile of smoke coming out of the chimney of the crematoriums, and we also used some sort of a camouflage — that was in 1944; that was when the Hungarian Jews arrived — we used a music camouflage. At the time the children were burned on big piles of wood. The crematoriums could not work at the time, and therefore, the people were just burned in open fields with those grills, and also children were burned among them. Children were crying helplessly and that is why camp administration ordered that an orchestra be made by a hundred inmates and should play. They played very loud all the time... Without the orchestra they would have heard the screams of horror; they would have been horrible screams. The people two kilometres from there could even hear those screams, namely, that came from the transports of children. The children were separated from their parents, and then they were put to section III camp. Maybe the number of children was several thousand. And then, on one special day they started burning them to death. The gas chambers at the time were out of order, at least one of them was out of order, namely, the one near the crematorium; it was destroyed by mutiny in a special commando in August 1944. The other three gas chambers were full of the adults and therefore the children were not gassed, but just burned alive. When one of the SS people sort of had pity with the children, he took the child and beat the head against a stone first before putting it on the pile of fire and wood, so that the child lost consciousness. However, the regular way they did it was by just throwing the children on to the pile.

(Nuremberg Military Tribunal, 1946: Vol 5:663)

The aspect of *uniqueness* allows us to put acts that are above and beyond ordinary daily events into the higher category of wrongfulness. The judges at Nuremberg acknowledged that uniqueness of the acts of the Holocaust was one of the main factors in the creation of the category of crimes against humanity. This sense of the crime being unusual can display itself in the sadism of the act or the callous way in which the act is carried out. It should be noted here that while the act may not be unique or rare in absolute terms (e.g. Genocide or serial killers); the uniqueness of the act lies in the evilness of the act. By uniqueness I am referring to the ability of an event to create a sense of novelty and create a need to explain the rare or unexpected. In essence, the act can cause psychological shock upheaval or confusion in bystanders as to how such an act could be committed. Our moral conscience is shocked. As a society we tend to readily categorise as evil unique or expressive violence, as against instrumental violence. As previously mentioned, Rule *145* of the Elements of Crime of the *Rome Statute* specifically singles out crimes that involve a particular cruelty. I interpret this as unique actions above and beyond normal crimes.

We can see all three of these agents present in the actions of Waffen-SS Colonel, *SS-Standartenführer* Franz Ziereis. Ziereis was a soldier who was accepted into the Waffen-SS as a training officer and later rose to be camp commandant of the Mauthausen Concentration-camp (MacLean, 1999a; Waller, 2002)[89]. Upon arrival of new prisoners to the camp Ziereis "... would sometimes stand on a convenient vantage point from which to view a newly received transport and select random prisoners as targets for his own shooting practice" (Waller, 2002:7). These actions strike one as senseless in that the actions resulted in the death of human beings for mere target practice, the innocence of the victims is highlighted by the arbitrary manner in which they were selected for no apparent valid reason and last the very method of the crime makes it unique in nature. In short, the presence of the emotive agents allows us to more readily accept his actions as evil. While not all of these agents are present in every evil act, it is usually the case that at least one or more of the agents is present. The presence of one of these agents is the releaser that allows us to place the act in the category of *evil,* as above just being *bad*. The greater the degree one or any of these agents is present then the more prepared are we to label the act as evil.

I would argue that all three of the emotive agents are present in the actions of the Waffen-SS. The acts were *senseless* in that the vast majority of the atrocities or evil acts committed served no valid military purpose. They did not assist the Waffen-SS in achieving the military goals they had set. In fact there is clear evidence that the atrocities committed increased the resistance to the Waffen-SS. The actions were not based on being a functional part of the campaign to achieve a goal; rather I would suggest they were intentional acts committed to express and serve the racial and ideological goals of the Waffen-SS, and to a large extent the Nazis. In a military sense they were senseless, in fact the actions discussed only make sense when considered in the context of a genocidal campaign.

There can be no denying that the vast majority of victims of the Waffen-SS were *innocent* of any military justification for the actions taken against them. The Waffen-SS upon entry into Russia quickly engaged in an orgy of murder and slaughter of racial and ideological targets. That they knew these people were innocent is further reinforced when one considers how they attempted to conceal these acts behind the use of euphemisms that would bring these racial and ideological targets into the sphere of military targets. This has been clearly proved by a variety of evidence that I referred to in the previous chapters. While the Waffen-SS may have attempted to portray their victims as being deserving of their punishment, the facts do not support this.

Quite simply the magnitude and systematic way in which the Waffen-SS participated in the overall system of the terror that was the SS makes the evil acts committed by them *unique*. The fact that the SS system could kill millions of people contributes to its uniqueness. That the killing undertaken by the Waffen-SS was spread from the frontlines to hundreds of miles behind them shows the enormity of the undertaking. The Waffen-SS was involved not only in the military aspects of the SS state, but it was also heavily involved in the economic pillaging that the SS undertook. It was further implicated in the depraved features of the SS system such as the medical experiments. I would argue that the systematic actions undertaken by the Waffen-SS on the Eastern Front should be considered evil acts.

This book was guided by two main questions. The first major question concerned the Waffen-SS. Was the Waffen-SS an organisation that committed evil acts or simply just innocent soldiers doing their duty? This book has filled a large void in relation to examinations of the Waffen-SS and the horrendous acts they performed. There can be no doubt that from an organisational standpoint the Waffen-SS was at the forefront of committing what I have defined as evil acts in the name of the Nazi state. The second question was how and why do ordinary people commit acts of evil? The interactional causation model that I have proposed would seem the most comprehensive way to explain how evil actions can occur. The dichotomy of situation and personality being responsible for evil actions is a false one; this book has shown that the vast majority of evil acts are a combination of both the situation and personality.

This book has attempted to confront genocide, the crime of crimes, by describing and documenting the evil acts that the Waffen-SS committed, and then analysing and explaining why they happened by using the concept of evil. There will always be acts committed by ordinary humans against other humans that seem inhumane in the extreme. These are the acts that I believe society as a whole needs to classify as evil. Without this classification it would seem that true horror of what mankind is capable cannot be fully comprehended. The Waffen-SS were without doubt a remarkable fighting formation and in the annuals of history will be remembered for the military prowess they displayed. They should also be remembered by history for the unspeakable crimes they committed and role they played in the genocide of millions. Whilst they may have been ordinary men, they were not ordinary soldiers.

**Russian soldiers holding the captured battle standard
of the *Leibstandarte SS Adolf Hitler*.**

Glossary of Terms:

Term	Meaning
Abteilung	Section or detachment, usually used to describe a panzer detachment smaller than regimental size, roughly equal to a battalion.
Abwehr	Intelligence service of the German armed forces; taken over by the SS in 1944
Armee	An army or field formation of at least two corps
Armeekorps	An army corps or field formation of at least two divisions
Armeeoberkommando	Army headquarters or headquarters staff
Barbarossa	Code name for invasion of USSR
Freikorps	Free corps; illegal military formations composed largely of WWI veterans, active in post-war Germany
Führer	In general, leader or officer; specifically Hitler
Führerbefehl	Order issued by Hitler
Führererlass	Decree or edict issued by Hitler
Gebirgs	Mountain (i.e. division)
Heer	The Army
Heeresgruppe	Army group, field formation usually composed of at least two armies
Kampfgruppe	Battle group
Landwehr	Military reserve of men between 35 and 45
Lebensraum	Living space
Legion	Legion, military formation composed of foreigners serving in the German armed forces
Luftwaffe	German Air Force
Oberkommando des Heeres (OKH)	Army High Command
OberKommando Des Wehrmacht (OKW)	Armed Forces High Command
Ostland	Baltic States and White Russia
Reichsarbeitsdienst (RAD)	Reich Labor Service
Reichsgesetzblatt (RGBl)	Reich Legal Gazette
Reichswehr	German Armed Forces from 1920-1935.
Ritterkreuz	Knight's Cross
Sturmabteilung (SA)	Storm Troops; brown shirted militia of the Nazi Party
Volksdeutsche	Ethnic or racial Germans; persons of German blood but of non-German citizenship, considered by the Nazi Party as a part of the German "race" or Volk
Wehrmacht	The German armed forces (Army, Navy and Air Force)

SS and Waffen-SS Terms

Allgemeine SS	General SS; main body of pre-war SS, composed of part-time volunteers
Einsatzgruppe	Action group; special SS/SD execution team responsible for the massacre of persons dictated by Nazi racial and political policies
Einsatzkommando	Smaller component of an Einsatzgruppe
Freiwilligen	Volunteers
GEheime STaatsPOlizei	Gestapo, secret state police, a branch of the SS
Hitlerjugend	Hitler Youth
Kommandostab RFSS	Headquarters of the Reichsfuhrer SS while in the field
Konzentrationslager (KZ)	Concentration-camp
Kriminalpolizei (Kripo)	Criminal Police; part of the SS organisation
NationaliSozialistische Deutsche ArbeiterPartei (NSDAP)	National Socialist German Workers Party (Nazi Party)
Ordnungspolizei (Orpo)	Order Police; regular uniformed police, incorporated into the SS organisation
Panzergrenadier	Mechanised infantry
Reichsfuhrer SS (RFSS)	Reich Leader of the SS, specifically Himmler
Reichskommissariat fur die Festigung Deutschen Volkstrums (RKFDV)	SS agency for the "strengthening of Germanism"; primarily concerned with ethnic Germans
Reichssicherheitshauptamt (RSHA)	Main Office of Reich Security; SS agency headed by Heydrich, later Kaltenbrunner
SchutzStaffel (SS)	Protection Squad, Defence Corps; originally elite corps of the NSDAP, later all-inclusive designation for the components of the complex organisation headed by Himmler
Sicherheitsdienst (SD)	Security and intelligence service of the SS
Sicherheitspolizei (Sipo)	Security Police; component of the SS organisation
Standarte	SS or SA formation equivalent to a regiment
Totenkopfstandarten	Death's Head Regiments; armed SS formations created at the beginning of the war to handle special tasks of a police nature; disbanded in 1941, and personnel absorbed into the Waffen-SS
Totenkopfverbände (SSTV)	Death Head formations; armed full-time component of the SS during pre-war period, tasked with guarding concentration-camps and political prisons
Totenkopfwachsturmbanner	Designation for the Death's Head guard battalions of the Waffen-SS, which guarded concentration and extermination camps during the war
Verfügungstruppe (SSVT)	Militarised component of the SS in the pre-war period; direct predecessor of the Waffen-SS
Waffen-SS	Armed SS
Wirtschafts - und Verwaltungshauptamt (WVHA)	SS Main Economical and Administration Office; after March 1942 responsible for operation of concentration-camps

Dramatis Personae:

Soldiers of the *Totenkopf* Division

Erich Bach-Zelewski

Born in Pomerania on the 1st of March 1899, Bach-Zelewski served in the German Army during World War I. He joined the Nazi Party in 1930. In 1941 he was promoted to *SS-Obergruppenführer* in the Waffen-SS. Bach-Zelewski was placed in command of anti-partisan operations on the Eastern Front from 1942-1944 and was Himmler's special deputy for anti-partisan warfare.

Bach-Zelewski suffered from some psychological illness as a result of the effects of having to carry out orders associated with the extermination policies carried out in the east. He was responsible for the brutal suppression of the Warsaw uprising in 1944. He led various SS Corps until the end of the war. Bach-Zelewski gave evidence at the Nuremberg trials in regards to SS activities on the Eastern Front. He received a 10-year sentence; this sentence was later suspended however, he was arrested on other charges relating to offences prior to the war. Bach-Zelewski died in prison while serving a life sentence.

Gottlob Berger

Born on the 16th of July, 1896 at Gerstetten, Württemberg, Berger served as Himmler's main recruiting officer in 1939 and became head of the SS Central Office in 1940, but this only added duties of overseeing ideological training. His organisational abilities contributed to the amazing expansion of the Waffen-SS in World War II, but he also became ensnared in typical internecine fighting among the SS hierarchy.

Berger volunteered for army service at the outset of World War I and rose to the rank of first lieutenant in the infantry by the time of his discharge in 1919, having received several wounds and decorations of the Iron Cross first and second class. Joining the Nazi Party in 1922, he became a member of the SA and entered SS service in 1936. Training with the army brought him the rank of major in the reserve by 1938, but his initial rank upon entering the SS was colonel, based upon his SA service through 1933. His various duties on the SS staff centred on sport organisation and training. After the war, the Nuremberg Tribunal sentenced him to 25 years' imprisonment, of which he served 10 years, being released in 1951. He worked on the staff of the right-wing journal Nation Europa (Coberg), and died January 5, 1975 in his city of birth.

Wilhelm Bittrich

Born on the 26th of February 1894 Bittrich served in World War I with the army before becoming a pilot. He ended the war with several decorations. Bittrich served in the post-war army and trained German pilots in the Soviet Union from 1930 to 1932.

In 1932 he joined the Nazi Party and the SS. During the early years of the war he was in command of the Deutschland regiment and won the Knight's Cross on the Eastern Front while holding this command. He later took command of the 9th SS Panzer Division *Hohenstaufen* and led it during the battles on the Eastern Front and in Normandy. Promoted to *SS-Gruppenführer*, Bittrich was in control of the 2nd SS Panzer Corps at Arnhem where he decimated the Allied forces. Bittrich was praised for the compassion he showed to the paratroopers at Arnhem. He was also prepared to confront Himmler by allowing church services to be held in his command in defiance of standing orders. The French imprisoned him until 1954.

Josef "Sepp" Dietrich

Born on the 28th of May 1892, Dietrich initially worked as a tractor driver before World War I. During World War I Dietrich served in various artillery formations before ending the war as an NCO in one of the early tank formations. He was awarded the Iron Cross and several other awards.

Dietrich was commissioned in the German police while at the same time being politically active. He joined the Nazi Party in 1928 and in matter of days joined the SS. Dietrich developed close ties to Hitler by being his personal bodyguard and later commanding the *Leibstandarte SS Adolf Hitler*, the most famous Waffen-SS division.

Dietrich was promoted to *SS-Oberstgruppenführer* and eventually commanded the 6th SS Panzer army during the Battle of the Bulge. He was tried at Nuremberg and found guilty and sentenced to a period of imprisonment for the massacre of American prisoners.

Oscar Dirlewanger

Born on 26th of September 1895 Dirlewanger had an outstanding career as a military officer in World War I and was wounded several times and received several awards. He finished the war as a junior officer in an infantry division.

He joined the Nazi Party in 1922 and about this time received a Doctorate degree from the University of Frankfurt in economics. Dirlewanger later served in the volunteer Condor Legion during the Spanish civil war. He later returned to Germany and joined the Waffen-SS in 1940 after initially being prevented by a number of criminal allegations being levelled at him for moral crimes.

Dirlewanger was responsible for the formation and command of the Dirlewanger Sonderkommando, which principally operated as a security force on the Eastern Front during World War II. It consisted mainly of poachers, concentration-camp inmates, Waffen-SS and Army penal troops. The Sonderkommando was responsible for numerous atrocities and in February 1945 was formed into the 36th Waffen-SS Grenadier Division. It is thought that Dirlewanger died in 1945; however some uncertainty surrounds the circumstances of his death.

Theodor Eicke

Born on the 17th October 1892, Eicke served in infantry units throughout the World War I, earning the Iron Cross and several other awards and ending the war as an NCO.

After the war Eicke spent some time at technical college and in the police until his political views caused him to be ousted. Eicke joined the SS to give expression to his radical views in 1928. Eicke was then placed in control of the SS guards of the concentration-camp system and developed them into an efficient fighting force that was eventually the 3rd Waffen-SS *Totenkopf* Panzer Division. On the Night of the Long Knives Eicke was responsible for the shooting of SA chief Ernst Rohm.

During the war *SS-Obergruppenführer* Eicke was placed in command of the *Totenkopf* Division of the Waffen-SS until his death on the Russian front in 1943 after his observation plane was shot down by Russian troops.

Hermann Fegelein

Born on the 30th of October 1906 Fegelein spent some brief time in a German Army Calvary regiment in 1925 and later went on to join the Bavarian Land Police. He joined the General SS in 1933 and he progressed through the ranks in the Calvary units of the SS.

In 1940 he was accepted into the Waffen-SS. He commanded the SS Calvary brigade on the Eastern Front during 1941/42 where it took part in a number of mopping up operations and committed various atrocities. He reached the rank of *SS-Gruppenführer* and commanded the Waffen-SS 8th Calvary Division *Florian Geyer* for a time. He was appointed as Hitler's liaison officer for the Waffen-SS where he married Gretl Braun (sister of Hitler's mistress). On the 26th of April 1945 Fegelein deserted the Führer bunker in Berlin as the end of the war drew near. Hitler however noted his disappearance and had Fegelein located and arrested at his house by the SS. Upon learning of Himmler's attempts to make peace with the Allies Hitler sought a scapegoat and had the SS execute Fegelein.

Odilo Globocnik

Born on the 21st of April 1904, he joined the Austrian Nazi Party in 1931 and became a member of the SS in 1934. Between 1933 and 1935 he was arrested four times by Austrian authorities for his activities in the illegal NSDAP and for high treason. Altogether he spent 11 months in jail.

Globocnik soon volunteered for the Waffen-SS and served as a non-commissioned officer with the SS-Standarte *Germania* from March until November 1939, serving with distinction in the German invasion of Poland.

Reichsführer-SS Heinrich Himmler had not forgotten one of his most obedient servants: surprisingly enough, on November 9, 1939, Globocnik was appointed SS and Police Leader in the Lublin district of the General Government. After a disappointing party career, Globocnik now had a second chance in the ranks of the SS and the police. The following years proved what he was capable of.

On October 13, 1941, Globocnik received a verbal order from Heinrich Himmler to start immediate construction work on Belzec, the first extermination camp in the General Government. The construction of two more extermination camps, Sobibor and Treblinka, followed in 1942. All in all Globocnik was responsible for killing more than 1.5 million Polish, Slovak, Czech, Dutch, French, Russian, German, and Austrian Jews in the death camps of Operation Reinhard, which he organised and supervised. He exploited Jews as slave labourers in his own forced-labour camps and seized the properties and valuables of murdered Jews.

After Mussolini's downfall, Globocnik was transferred from the General Government to Friuli-Venezia Giulia in the German-occupied portion of Italy in September 1943 and was stationed in his home town of Trieste. He was appointed Higher SS and Police Leader of the Operation Zone of Adriatic Coastal Region. His main task there was combating partisans, but again, he played a leading role in the persecution of Italian Jews. With the advance of Allied troops, Globocnik retreated into Austrian Carinthia and finally went into hiding high in the mountains in an alpine hut near Weissensee, still in company of his closest staff members.

Tracked down and captured by the British on May 31, 1945, he committed suicide the same day in Paternion by biting on his capsule of cyanide.

Paul Hausser

Born on the 7th of October 1880 Hausser served in various units including the infantry and the Imperial Navy as an observer. Later during the First World War Hausser served on the General Staff and on other staff units. He was awarded the Iron Cross and numerous other awards. At the conclusion of World War I Hausser remained with the post-war army until he left the army in 1932 with the rank of Leutnant-General.

He later joined the SA and a short time later was recruited by Hitler to assist in solving training issues of the Waffen-SS. Hausser developed the training curriculum for the SS officer schools. He was later responsible for the formation of the first Waffen-SS division during the war in 1939. This division was later to become the 2nd Waffen-SS *Das Reich* Panzer Division. He was placed in charge of the 1st SS Panzerkorps. During the battle of Kharkov in 1943 he disobeyed a direct order from Hitler by retreating in order to save his men. He was promoted to the rank of *SS-Oberstgruppenführer* and went on to briefly command various army groups. He was a witness at Nuremberg and a strong advocate for former Waffen-SS soldiers.

Reinhart Heydrich

Born on March 7, 1904, Heydrich was an *SS-Obergruppenführer* in the SS. He was nicknamed The Butcher of Prague, The Blond Beast and Der Henker (German for the hangman).

Heydrich participated in the Freikorps when he was young. In 1922 he joined the navy; however, he was later dismissed for improper behaviour. His behaviour in court was apparently so disdainful that the court also rebuked him for insubordination. Heydrich was left with no career prospects. However, he remained engaged to von Osten, whom he married in 1931.

1931 was to be a turning point for Heydrich in another, far more important way. Himmler wished to set up a counter-intelligence division of the SS. Acting on a friend's advice, he interviewed Heydrich, and after a 20 minute test whereby Heydrich had to outline plans for the new division, Himmler hired him on the spot. In doing so Himmler also effectively recruited Heydrich into the Nazi Party.

Heydrich soon built up a fearsome reputation within the party, and in July 1932 his division took on the title of Sicherheitsdienst (SD). Later he became the boss of the *Reichssicherheitshauptamt (RSHA)* of which the SD, the Gestapo and the *Einsatzgruppen* were parts. Heydrich became one of the main architects of the Holocaust during the first years of World War II and chaired the Wannsee conference at which plans for the deportation of the Jews to extermination camps were discussed. In September 1941 he was appointed Protector of Bohemia and Moravia, replacing Konstantin von Neurath whom Hitler considered insufficiently harsh. During his role as de facto dictator of Bohemia and Moravia, Heydrich often drove around alone in a car with an open roof- a show of confidence in the occupational forces and their repressive measures in subduing the population.

On May 27, 1942 he was assassinated by a team of British-trained agents of the Czechoslovak Government in exile in London. Despite Himmler sending his best doctors, Heydrich died in agony in a Prague hospital at 4:30am on June 4 at the age of 38. The retaliation from the Nazis was savage; a stark warning to potential copycats. On June 10 all males over the age of 16 in the village of Lidice, 22 km north-west of Prague, were murdered a day after the town was burnt. Heydrich's eventual replacement was Ernst Kaltenbrunner.

After Heydrich's death, the first three "trial" death camps were constructed and put into operation at Treblinka, Sobibor and Belzec. The project was named Operation Reinhard in Heydrich's honour.

Heinrich Himmler

Born on October 7, 1900 Himmler was the commander of the SS and one of the most powerful men in Nazi Germany. As *Reichsführer-SS,* he led the SS, and all of its combined offices, and was one of the key figures in the organisation of the Holocaust. Born near Munich, Bavaria, Germany into a middle-class family, he was the son of a Bavarian schoolmaster and attended Landshut High School. After graduation, Himmler was appointed an Officer Cadet in 1918 and joined the 11th Bavarian Regiment for service in World War I. Shortly before Himmler was due for commissioning as an officer, however, the war ended and Himmler was discharged from the military without ever having seen any combat.

In 1919, a year after World War I had ended; Himmler began studying agriculture at a technical college in Munich. At the same time, he became active in the Freikorps, private armies of right-wing ex-German Army men resentful of Germany's loss of the World War I. Himmler in 1923, applied to join the Nazi Party, which was recruiting Freikorps members as potential members of the new Nazi stormtrooper units, known as the SA.

Between 1927 and 1929, Himmler devoted himself increasingly to his duties as Deputy-Reichsführer-SS. Upon the resignation of SS Commander Erhard Heiden, Himmler was appointed as the new *Reichsführer-SS* in January 1929. At the time Himmler was appointed to lead the SS, it numbered only 280 members, and was considered a mere battalion of the much larger SA. Himmler, himself, was only considered as an SA-Oberführer, but after 1929 Himmler simply referred to himself as the *Reichsführer-SS*.

By 1933, when the Nazi Party rose to power in Germany, Himmler's SS numbered 52,000 members and the organisation had developed strict membership requirements, ensuring that all members were of Hitler's Aryan "Herrenvolk" (i.e. master race). Now a *Gruppenführer* in the SA, Himmler next began a massive effort to separate the SS from SA control and introduced black SS uniforms, to replace the SA brown shirts, in the fall of 1933. Shortly thereafter, he was promoted to SS-Obergruppenführer und Reichsführer-SS.

Both Himmler, and another of Hitler's right hand men, Hermann Goring, agreed that the SA and its leader, Ernst Röhm were beginning to pose a threat to the German Army and the whole Nazi leadership of Germany itself. Röhm had strong socialist views and believed that although Hitler had successfully gained power in Germany, the real revolution had not yet begun, leaving some Nazi leaders with the belief that Röhm was intent on using the SA to administer a coup.

With some persuasion from Himmler and Goring, Hitler began to feel threatened by this prospect, and agreed that Röhm must die. Hitler delegated the task of administering Rohm's demise to Himmler and Goring, who, along with Reinhard Heydrich, Kurt Daluege and Walter Schellenberg, carried out the execution of Röhm and numerous other senior SA officials, in what became known as The Night of the Long Knives on June 30, 1934. The very next day, Himmler's title of *Reichsführer-SS* became an actual rank and he was appointed to the position while the SS became an independent organisation of the Nazi Party.

In 1936 Himmler had gained further authority as the SS absorbed all of Germany's local law enforcement agencies into the new *Ordnungspolizei*, considered a headquarters branch of the SS. Germany's secret police forces were also under Himmler's authority in the presence of the Sicherheitspolizei which would, in 1939, expand into the much larger Reichsicherheitshauptamt. The SS was also developing its military branch, known as the *SS-Verfügungstruppe*, which would later become known as the Waffen-SS. After the Night of the Long Knives, the *SS-Totenkopfverbände* had been given the task of organising and administering Germany's regime of concentration-camps and, after 1941, the extermination camps of Poland. The SS, through its intelligence arm the *Sicherheitsdienst* (SD), was charged with finding Jews, Roma, homosexuals and communists and any other culture or race deemed by the Nazis to be either Untermenschen (sub-human) or in opposition to his regime, and placing them in concentration-camps. Himmler now became one of the main architects of the Holocaust, using elements of mysticism and a fanatical belief in the racist Nazi ideology to justify the mass murder and genocide of millions of victims.

In 1944, Himmler was granted still further power as the result of a bitter rivalry between the *SicherheitsDienst* (SD) and the Abwehr, the intelligence arm of the *Wehrmacht.*

The involvement in the July 20, 1944 plot against Hitler of many of the Abwehr leaders, including its head, Admiral Canaris, prompted Hitler to disband the Abwehr and make the SD the sole intelligence service of the Third Reich. This increased Himmler's already considerable personal power. In late 1944, Himmler became commander of army group Oberrhein (Upper Rhine), which was fighting the oncoming United States 7th Army and French 1st Army in the Alsace region on the west bank of the Rhine.

Himmler held this post until early 1945, when he was switched to command an army group facing the Red Army to the East. As Himmler had no practical military experience as a field commander, he was quickly relieved of his field commands and appointed as Commander of the Home Army. At the same time, he was appointed as the German Interior Minister and was considered, by many, to be a candidate to succeed Hitler as the Führer of Germany.

By the spring of 1945 Himmler had lost faith in German victory, and came to the realisation that if the Nazi regime was to have any chance of survival, it would need to seek peace with Britain and the United States. Towards this end, he contacted Count Folke Bernadotte of Sweden at Lübeck, near the Danish border and began negotiations to surrender in the West. Himmler hoped that the British and Americans would fight their Russian allies with the remains of the Wehrmacht. When Hitler discovered this, Himmler was declared a traitor and stripped of all his titles and ranks. At the time of Himmler's denouncement, he held the positions of Reich Leader-SS, Chief of the German Police, Reich Commissioner of German Nationhood, Reich Minister of the Interior, Supreme Commander of the Volksturm, and Supreme Commander of the Home Army. Himmler next turned to the Americans as a defector, contacting the headquarters of Dwight Eisenhower and proclaiming he would surrender all of Germany to the Allies if Himmler was spared from prosecution as a Nazi leader. In a final example of Himmler's mental state at this point, he sent a personal application to General Eisenhower stating that he wished to apply for the position as Minister of Police in the post-war government of Germany. Eisenhower, however, refused to have anything to do with Himmler, and Himmler was subsequently declared a major war criminal.

Attempting to evade arrest, Himmler disguised himself as a member of the Gendarmerie, but was recognised and captured on the 22nd of May 1945 in Bremen, Germany, by a British Army unit. Himmler was scheduled to stand trial with other German leaders as a major war criminal at Nuremberg, but committed suicide in Lüneburg by swallowing a cyanide capsule before interrogation could begin. Feared by many, but respected by few, many historians have argued that Himmler was more made by those who worked under him rather than by his own designs. He was survived by his wife and daughter Gudrun, who still lives in Germany to this day.

Adolf Hitler

Born on the 20th of April, 1889, Hitler was the Führer (leader) of the National Socialist German Workers Party (Nazi Party) and of Nazi Germany from 1933 to 1945. In that capacity he was Chancellor of Germany, head of government, and head of state, ruling as a dictator.

A highly animated, charismatic and gifted orator, Hitler is regarded as one of the most significant leaders of world history. The military-industrial complex he fostered pulled Germany out of the post-World War I economic crisis and, at its height, controlled the greater part of Europe.

Hitler's attempts to create a Greater Germany, specifically the annexation of Austria and the invasions of Czechoslovakia and Poland, were one of the primary factors leading to the outbreak of World War II in 1939. The embrace of total war both by the Axis and Allied powers during this time led to the destruction of much of Europe. Hitler is almost universally held responsible for the racial policy of Nazi Germany, the Holocaust, and the death and displacement of millions occurring during his leadership.

Hoping to be the founder of a thousand-year Reich, he committed suicide in his bunker beneath Berlin with much of Europe, and especially Germany, in ruins around him and the Red Army closing in 1945.

Otto Kumm

Born in Hamburg on the 1st of October 1909 Otto Kumm began a career as a typesetter in his early years. He joined the SA in 1930 and then joined the SS in 1931.

He served in the *Der Führer* regiment in the early years of the war, before going on to become its commander in 1941. After working in a corps staff position Kumm was given command of the 7th SS Mountain Division *Prinz Eugen* in 1944. He surrendered to US forces at the end of the war.

Otto Ohlendorf

Born on the 4th of February 1907 Ohlendorf initially pursued a career as an economist and a lawyer. He joined the SS in 28th of May 1925 and rose to the rank of SS-Gruppenführer. In 1936 he accepted a position in the RSHA under the leadership of Himmler.

When Himmler organised the 4 *Einsatzgruppen* he gave command of group D to Ohlendorf, which conducted operations in the Ukraine while attached to the 11th Army (commanded by Von Manstein). During a 12-month period it is estimated that the group liquidated 90,000 people. After the war Ohlendorf was charged at Nuremberg and was part of the *Einsatzgruppen* case. He was found guilty and executed on the 7th of June 1951.

Jochen Pieper

Born in 1915 Pieper joined the SS-VT as a means of obtaining a career in the armed forces. His marks for school precluded him from becoming an officer in the army. He was accepted into the Leibstandarte-SS Adolf Hitler and was accepted for officer candidate school.

He went on to command various formations within the Leibstandarte-SS Adolf Hitler and rose to the rank of *SS-Standartenführer* commanding the 1st Panzer regiment of the Leibstandarte-SS Adolf Hitler. He was the youngest regimental colonel in the Waffen-SS. He is remembered for his role in the massacre of American Soldiers at Malmedy. He was brought to trial after the war and sentenced to hang. This was subsequently commuted and he was released from prison in 1956. He later went to live in France where in 1976 his house was burnt down and he was murdered.

Oswald Pohl

Pohl was born on the 30th of June 1892, in Duisburg-Ruhrort as the son of a blacksmith. In 1920 he was accepted into the Weimar Republic's new navy, the Reichsmarine. Pohl was transferred to Swinemünde in Poland in 1924.

One year later, in 1925, Pohl became a member of the SA, and then finally joined the re-founded NSDAP. He was appointed chief of the administration department in the staff of the Reichsführer-SS and given the rank of SS-Standartenführer on February 1, 1934, and began to influence the administration of the concentration-camps.

In June 1939, Pohl became chief of both the *Hauptamt Verwaltung und Wirtschaft* (main bureau [for] administration and economy, part of the SS) and the *Hauptamt Haushalt und Bauten* (main bureau [for] budget and construction, part of the Reich's ministry for the interior). On February 1, 1942, both institutions were combined into the *SS-Wirtschafts-Verwaltungshauptamt* (SS-WVHA, SS main bureau for economic administration) with Pohl in charge; among other things, the SS-WVHA was in charge of the organisation of the concentration-camps, deciding on the distribution of detainees to the various camps and the rental of detainees for forced labour until 1944.

Pohl was made *SS-Obergruppenführer* and general of the Waffen-SS on April 20, 1942. In 1944, Pohl was put out of charge of the concentration-camps, with the Rüstungsministerium (ministry of armament) overtaking; at the same time, the responsibility for construction was also taken away from the SS-WVHA. However, Pohl remained in charge of the administration of the Waffen-SS for the remainder of the war.

After the end of World War II, in 1945, Pohl first hid in Upper Bavaria, then near Bremen; nevertheless, he was captured by British troops on May 27, 1946. He was sentenced to death on November 3, 1947, by an American military tribunal after the Nuremberg trials for crimes against humanity, war crimes and membership in a criminal organisation, as well as for mass murders and crimes committed in the concentration-camps administered by the SS-WVHA he was in charge of. However, Pohl was not executed right away. In 1950, Pohl's book, Credo. Mein Weg zu Gott, (Credo. My way to God) was published with permission from the Catholic church that Pohl became a member of again. Pohl was hung at Landsberg Prison on June 7, 1951, but he maintained he was innocent to the end, claiming that he was only a simple functionary.

Max Simon

Born on the 6th of January 1899 Simon served as a corporal in Leib-Kürassier-Regiment. In 1919 he was a member of the Freikorps service in Silesia against the Poles. Between the wars he served as a sergeant in the Reichswehr in Cavalry Regiment 16. On the 1st of May 1933 he joined the SS. In 1934 he was assigned to the Concentration-camp Inspectorate. On the 9th of November 1934 he was appointed commander of the SS guard unit at Sachsenburg concentration-camp.

On the 10th of July 1937 he was appointed commander of *SS-Totenkopf-Standarte 1 Oberbayern*. Simon's unit was used for police duties (i.e., rounding up Polish Army stragglers and murdering political leaders, priests, intellectuals and Jews) during the invasion of Poland in the rear area of the advancing German Army. In 1943 he was the commander of *SS-Totenkopf* Infantry Regiment 1 of the *SS-Totenkopf* Division, where he saw combat in the Western Campaign of 1940 and in Russia from June 1941. He then commanded the Totenkopf Division for sometime on the Eastern Front. During 1943-44 he was commander of 16th SS-Panzer Grenadier Division *Reichsführer-SS* in Italy and Hungary. He finished the war as the commanding General, 13th SS-Army Corps on the Western and South-western Fronts.

A veteran of the pre-war concentration-camp system, Max Simon's name became linked to war crimes as early as 1943. In November of that year, a Russian military tribunal sentenced him to death in absentia for his alleged role in the killing of 10,000 Russian civilians in the vicinity of Kharkov in the summer of 1943. After the war, the British indicted Simon as a war criminal for his complicity in the September 1944 massacre of Italian civilians at Marzabotta (estimates ranged from 300 to over 2,000 dead) in reprisal for partisan activity. Following his interrogation in the United Kingdom, Simon returned to Italy where a British military tribunal sentenced him to death. The sentence, however, was later commuted, and Simon was released in 1954 from Werl prison in Germany.

In October 1955, a German court in Ansbach tried Simon for an incident that occurred in the German town of Brettheim on 7 April 1945. On that date, Simon ordered the court martial and hanging of three citizens of the town who had disarmed some local Hitler Youth members to keep them from fighting U.S. troops. Twice acquitted of the charge (the court ruled he had been following a legal order), Simon died before the start of a third trial.

Franz Six

Franz Six studied at the Realschule, graduated from the classical high school at Mannheim in 1930 and then matriculated at the University of Heidelberg where he specialised in sociology and political science, receiving the degree of doctor of philosophy in 1934. He then taught at the University at Koenigsberg (where he also took up the position of Press Director of the German Students' Association). In 1936 he received the doctorate from the University of Heidelberg, and became Dozent in the faculty of law and political science at Koenigsberg; later, he passed examinations for the Venia Legendi at the University of Leipzig. By 1938 he was Professor at the University of Koenigsberg, and by 1939, he had obtained the chair for Foreign Political Science at the University of Berlin and was its first Dean of the faculty for Foreign Countries.

Six became a member of the SA in 1932 and of the SS and SD in 1935. In SS he attained the grade of *SS-Brigadeführer*. On June 20, 1941 he was appointed Chief of *Vorkommando* Moscow. According to Six, the task of this Kommando was to secure the archives and files of Russian documents in Moscow when the German troops should arrive there. He arrived in Smolensk on July 25, 1941 and remained there until the latter part of August when he returned to Berlin. The *Vorkommando* Moscow was used in liquidating operations while under the command of Six. Further, that the seizing of documents in Russia was done not for economic and cultural purposes, but with the object of obtaining lists of Communist functionaries who had themselves become candidates for liquidation. Six was tried and convicted at Nuremberg. Sentenced to 20 years imprisonment in 1948, he was released in 1952.

Felix Steiner

Born in Prussia on the 23rd of May 1896 Steiner served in various infantry units during the World War I and rose to the rank of Oberleutnant. He received a number of awards and served in the post-war *Reichswehr*.

He joined the Nazi Party and the SA in 1934 and later joined the SS in 1935. He went on to command the 5th Waffen-SS *Wiking* division in 1940. He was later given command of the 3rd SS Panzerkorps. He went on to command various army groups with the rank of *SS-Obergruppenführer*.

He was given command of Army group Steiner in which Hitler placed his hopes for a last-minute respite from the Russian offensive on Berlin in 1945. Steiner refused to commit his men to such a futile offensive. He was a witness at Nuremberg. Steiner is credited with developing the assault tactics and reliance on heavy infantry firepower utilised by the Waffen-SS in small unit engagements.

Jurgen Stroop

Born on the 26th of September 1895. Stroop as a *SS-Brigadeführer* was placed in charge of the suppression of the Warsaw Ghetto uprising by the Jews in 1943. He was a SS and Higher Police leader and also a member of the Waffen-SS. This action resulted in the annihilation of the Jewish population after a fight lasting some 28 days. He was found guilty by an American War tribunal and sentenced to death. He was executed in Warsaw on the 8th of September 1951.

Karl Wolff

Born on the 13th of May 1900 Karl Wolff served as a lieutenant in World War I. Between the wars he held various business posts.

He joined the Nazi Party and the SS in 1931. In July 1933 he was appointed adjutant to Himmler. He was promoted to *SS-Obergruppenführer* in the Waffen-SS. Wolff assisted in the deportation of Jews to the Treblinka extermination camp. He was made HSSPF for Italy and surrendered to US forces there in 1945.

After the war he was initially tried by a German court and sentenced to four years imprisonment, but served only a week of his sentence. In 1962 he was again arrested and charged with the murder of 300,000 Jews at Treblinka. In 1964 he was found guilty and sentenced to 15 years jail. He was again released early after serving only seven years.

Appendix 1: Waffen-SS Rank Structure

Waffen-SS	German Army	British Army
Reichsführer-SS	Generalfeldmarschall	Field-Marshal
SS-Oberstgruppenführer	Generaloberst	General
SS-Obergruppenführer	General	Lieutenant-General
SS-Gruppenführer	Generalleutnant	Major-General
SS-Brigadeführer	Generalmajor	Brigadier
SS-Oberführer	Nil	Nil
SS-Standartenführer	Oberst	Colonel
SS-Obersturmbannführer	Oberstleutnant	Lieutenant-Colonel
SS-Sturmbannführer	Major	Major
SS-Hauptsturmführer	Hauptmann	Captain
SS-Obersturmführer	Oberleutnant	1st Lieutenant
SS-Untersturmführer	Leutnant	2nd Lieutenant

Appendix 2: Features of Waffen-SS Officers

Level of Education of Senior Officers (%)

Level of Education	Obergruppenführer - to Brigadeführer	Oberführer and Standartenführer	Total %
Elementary Schooling	6.6	27.5	21.3
Middle Schooling	35.5	29.7	31.4
Qualified to enter University	38.2	18.7	24.4
Tertiary Qualifications	19.7	24.2	22.9

Note: Sourced from Wegner 1990.

Denominations of Senior Waffen-SS officers (%)

Rank	Protestant	Catholic
Obergruppenführer – Brigadeführer/Oberführer	79.5	20.5
Standartenführer	82.9	17.1
Obersturmbannführer	76.1	23.9
Sturmbannführer	77.2	22.8
Totals	66.7	33.3

Note: Sourced from Wegner 1990. These figures are not indicative of later cancellations of church membership and the totals do not include those cases where denominations could not be determined.

Professions of Senior Officers of the Waffen-SS (%)

Profession	Obergruppenführer- to Standartenführer	Obersturmbannführer and Sturmbannführer
Army Officers	23.8	1.9
Army NCOs	8.7	8.8
Police Officials	14.7	11.4
Other Civil Servants	6.4	4.1
Academic Professions	21.9	3.8
Workers/Clerks	7.9	11.4
Farmers	3.4	5.0
Businessmen	15.8	18.0
Craftsmen	9.8	27.1
No profession given or unemployed	4.5	20.2

Note: Sourced from Wegner 1990. These figures were gained from CV's of SS Officers and often more than one occupation was given, hence the fact that individual military groupings will exceed 100%.

Appendix 3: Order of Battle of the Waffen-SS

No.	Name of Division	Type of Unit	Nationality of Unit
	**Waffen-SS Divisions at the close of WWII**		
1st	**SS Panzer Division** *Leibstandarte SS Adolf Hitler* SS-Panzergrenadier Regiment 1 SS-Panzergrenadier Regiment 2 SS-Panzer Regiment 1 SS-Artillery Regiment 1	Panzer	German
2nd	**SS Panzer Division** *Das Reich* SS-Panzergrenadier Regiment 3 *Deutschland* SS-Panzergrenadier Regiment 4 *Der Führer* SS-Panzer Regiment 2 SS-Artillery Regiment 2	Panzer	German
3rd	**SS Panzer Division** *Totenkopf* SS-Panzergrenadier Regiment 5 *Thule* SS-Panzergrenadier Regiment 6 *Theodore Eicke* SS-Panzer Regiment 3 SS-Artillery Regiment 3	Panzer	German
4th	**SS Panzergrenadier Division** *SS-Polizei* SS-Panzergrenadier Regiment 7 SS-Panzergrenadier Regiment 8 SS-Sturmgeschutz battalion 4 SS-Artillery Regiment 4	Panzergrenadier	German
5th	**SS Panzer Division** *Wiking* SS-Panzergrenadier Regiment 9 *Germania* SS-Panzergrenadier Regiment 10 *Westland* SS-Panzer Regiment 5 SS-Artillery Regiment 5	Panzer	German/Dutch/ Norwegian/Danish
6th	**SS Gebirgs Division** *Nord* SS-Gebirgsjager Regiment 11 *Reinhard Heydrich* SS-Gebirgsjager Regiment 12 *Michael Gaissmair* SS-Sturmgeschutz battery 6 SS-Artillery Regiment 6	Mountain Troops	German/ Hungarian/ Romanian
7th	**SS Freiwilligen-Gerbirgs Division** *Prinz Eugen* SS-Gebirgsjager Regiment 13 *Arthur Phelps* SS-Gebirgsjager Regiment 14 *Skanderbeg* SS-Sturmgeschutz battalion 7 SS-Artillery Regiment 7	Mountain Troops	German Volunteers

No.	Name of Division	Type of Unit	Nationality of Unit
	Waffen-SS Divisions at the close of WWII		
8th	**SS Kavallerie Division** *Florian Geyer* SS-Kavallerie Regiment 15 SS-Kavallerie Regiment 16 SS-Kavallerie Regiment 18 SS-Panzerjager battalion 8 SS-Artillery Regiment 8	Cavalry	German
9th	**SS Panzer Division** *Hohenstaufen* SS-Panzergrenadier Regiment 19 SS-Panzergrenadier Regiment 20 SS-Panzer Regiment 9 SS-Artillery Regiment 9	Panzer	German
10th	**SS Panzer Division** *Frundsberg* SS-Panzergrenadier Regiment 21 SS-Panzergrenadier Regiment 22 SS-Panzer Regiment 10 SS-Artillery Regiment 10	Panzer	German
11th	**SS Freiwilligen-Panzergrenadier Division** *Nordland* SS-Panzergrenadier Regiment 23 *Norge* SS-Panzergrenadier Regiment 24 *Danmark* SS-Panzer Battalion 11 *Hermann Von Salza* SS-Artillery Regiment 11	Panzergrenadier	Various Nationalities Volunteers
12th	**SS Panzer Division** *Hitlerjugend* SS-Panzergrenadier Regiment 25 SS-Panzergrenadier Regiment 26 SS-Panzer Regiment 12 SS-Artillery Regiment 12	Panzer	German
13th	**Waffen-Gebirgs Division Der SS (Kroatische NR1)** *Handschar* SS-Waffen Gebirgsjager Regiment 27 SS-Waffen Gebirgsjager Regiment 28 SS-Panzerjager Battalion 13 SS-Artillery Regiment 13	Mountain Troops	Bosnian Moslems
14th	**Waffen-Grenadier Division Der SS (Ukrainische NR 1)** Waffen-Grenadier Regiment Der SS 29 Waffen-Grenadier Regiment Der SS 30 Waffen-Grenadier Regiment Der SS 31 SS-Artillery Regiment 14	Grenadier	Ukrainians
15th	**Waffen-Grenadier Division Der SS (Lettische NR 1)** Waffen-Grenadier Regiment Der SS 32 Waffen-Grenadier Regiment Der SS 33 Waffen-Grenadier Regiment Der SS 34 SS-Artillery Regiment 15	Grenadier	Latvians

Waffen-SS Divisions at the close of WWII			
No.	Name of Division	Type of Unit	Nationality of Unit
16th	**SS Panzergrenadier Division** *Reichsführer-SS* SS-Panzergrenadier Regiment 35 SS-Panzergrenadier Regiment 36 SS-Panzer Battalion 16 SS-Artillery Regiment 16	Panzergrenadier	German
17th	**SS Panzergrenadier Division** ***Gotz Von Berlichingen*** SS-Panzergrenadier Regiment 37 SS-Panzergrenadier Regiment 38 SS-Panzer Battalion 17 SS-Artillery Regiment 17	Panzergrenadier	German
18th	**SS Freiwilligen-Panzergrenadier Division** ***Horst Wessel*** SS-Panzergrenadier Regiment 39 SS-Panzergrenadier Regiment 40 SS-Panzerjager Battalion 18 SS-Artillery Regiment 18	Panzergrenadier	German/Hungarian Volunteers
19th	**Waffen-Grenadier Division Der SS** **(Lettisches NR 2)** Waffen-Grenadier Regiment Der SS 42 *Voldemars Veiss* Waffen-Grenadier Regiment Der SS 43 *Heinrich Schuldt* Waffen-Grenadier Regiment Der SS 44 SS-Artillery Regiment 19	Grenadier	Latvian
20th	**Waffen-Grenadier Division Der SS** **(Estnische NR 1)** Waffen-Grenadier Regiment Der SS 45 Waffen-Grenadier Regiment Der SS 46 Waffen-Grenadier Regiment Der SS 47 SS-Artillery Regiment 20	Grenadier	Estonian
21st	**Waffen-Gebirgs Division Der SS** **(Albanische NR1)** *Skanderberg* Waffen-Gebirgs Regiment Der SS 50 Waffen-Gebirgs Regiment Der SS 51 SS-Artillery Regiment 21	Mountain Troops	Albanian
22nd	**Freiwilligen-Kavallerie Division Der SS** ***Maria Theresia*** Freiwilligen-Kavallerie Regiment Der SS 52 Freiwilligen-Kavallerie Regiment Der SS 53 Freiwilligen-Kavallerie Regiment der SS 54 SS-Artillery Regiment 22	Calvary	Hungarian Volunteers
23rd	**Waffen-Gebirgs Division Der SS** *Kama* **later to** **become Division Nederland** Waffen-Gebirgsjager Regiment Der SS 56 Waffen-Gebirgsjager Regiment Der SS 57 Waffen-Gebirgsjager Regiment Der SS 58 Waffen-Gebirgsjager Artillery Regiment Der SS 23 This division was disbanded in 1944 and renamed the 23rd Panzergrenadier Division *Nederland*	Mountain Troops	Bosnian Moslems/ later Dutch

No.	Name of Division	Type of Unit	Nationality of Unit
	Waffen-SS Divisions at the close of WWII		
24th	**SS Gebirgs Division *Karstjager*** Waffen-Gebirgsjager Regiment Der SS 59 Waffen-Gebirgsjager Regiment Der SS 60 Waffen-Gebirgsjager Artillery Regiment Der SS 24	Mountain Troops	Various Slavic Nationalities
25th	**Waffen-Grenadier Division Der SS (Ungarische NR1) *Hunyadi*** Waffen-Grenadier Regiment Der SS 61 Waffen-Grenadier Regiment Der SS 62 Waffen-Grenadier Regiment Der SS 63 SS-Artillery Regiment 25	Grenadier	Hungarian
26th	**Waffen-Grenadier Division Der SS (Ungarische NR 2) *Hungaria*** Waffen-Grenadier Regiment Der SS 64 Waffen-Grenadier Regiment Der SS 65 Waffen-Grenadier Regiment Der SS 85 SS-Artillery Regiment 26 This division never reached full divisional status.	Grenadier	Hungarian
27th	**SS Freiwilligen-Panzergrenadier Division (Flamische NR 1) *Langemarck*** SS-Freiwilligen Grenadier Regiment 66 SS-Freiwilligen Grenadier Regiment 67 SS-Freiwilligen Grenadier Regiment 68 SS-Artillery Regiment 27 This division was regimental strength only.	Panzergrenadier	Flemish
28th	**SS Freiwilligen-Panzergrenadier Division *Wallonien*** SS-Freiwilligen Grenadier Regiment 69 SS-Freiwilligen Grenadier Regiment 70 SS-Freiwilligen Grenadier Regiment 71 SS-Artillery Regiment 28 This division was regimental strength only.	Panzergrenadier	Flemish
29th	**SS Waffen-Grenadier Division Der (Russische NR 1) later to become the (Italienische NR 1)** This division was regimental strength only and was in existence for only a short time due to the unreliability of its personnel.	Grenadier	Russian/Italian
30th	**SS Waffen-Grenadier Division Der (Weissruthensche NR 1)** Waffen-Grenadier Regiment Der SS 75 Waffen-Grenadier Regiment Der SS 76 Waffen-Grenadier Regiment Der SS 77 SS-Artillery Regiment 30	Grenadier	Belorussians
31st	**SS Freiwilligen-Grenadier Division** SS-Freiwilligen Grenadier Regiment 78 SS-Freiwilligen Grenadier Regiment 79 SS-Freiwilligen Grenadier Regiment 80 SS-Artillery Regiment 31	Grenadier	German/Hungarian

Waffen-SS Divisions at the close of WWII			
No.	Name of Division	Type of Unit	Nationality of Unit
32nd	**SS Freiwilligen-Grenadier Division 30** *Januar* SS-Freiwilligen Grenadier Regiment 86 *Schill* SS-Freiwilligen Grenadier Regiment 87 Kurmark SS-Freiwilligen Grenadier Regiment 88 SS-Artillery Regiment 32	Grenadier	German
33rd	**Waffen-Kavallerie Division Der SS (Ungarische NR 3) later to become Waffen-Grenadier Division Der SS (Franzosische NR 1)** *Charlemagne* Waffen-Grenadier Regiment Der SS 57 Waffen-Grenadier Regiment Der SS 58 SS-Artillery battalion 33	Grenadier	French
34th	**Waffen-Grenadier Division Der SS** *Landstorm Nederland* SS-Freiwilligen Grenadier Regiment 83 SS-Freiwilligen Grenadier Regiment 84 SS-Artillery Regiment	Grenadier	Dutch
35th	**SS Polizei Grenadier Division** SS-Police Grenadier Regiment 89 SS-Police Grenadier Regiment 90 SS-Police Grenadier Regiment 91 SS-Police Artillery Regiment 35 This unit never reached divisional strength.	Grenadier	German
36th	**Waffen-Grenadier Division Der SS** Formed from the Dirlewanger SonderKommando, this unit never reached divisional strength.	Grenadier	Mixed
37th	**Freiwilligen-Kavallerie Division** *Lutzow* SS-Freiwilligen Kavallerie Regiment 92 SS-Freiwilligen Kavallerie Regiment 93 SS-Artillery Battalion 37	Grenadier	German
38th	**SS Grenadier Division** *Nibelungen* Consisted of instructors and cadets from the Bad Tolz officer training school, this unit never exceeded regimental strength and was in existence for about a month.	Grenadier	German

Note: By the end of the war many of these units did not represent the nominal strength of a normal Waffen-SS Division, which was usually between 15,000 to 20,000 men. The numbering of exact regiments, etc may be incorrect as during the war the numbering of various units was changed regularly. It should be noted that towards the end of the war many of the Waffen-SS divisions were divisions in name only and their actual strength was far below the theoretical strength of the typical division. The nationality of the units represents only the main country of origin of men in that unit. In most cases the officers and NCOs of the unit were of German extraction.

Appendix 4: Strength of the Waffen-SS

Date	Waffen-SS	Officer Corps
31st December 1937	16,902	757
31st December 1938	22,718	1203
1st May 1940	90,638	2453
1st December 1942	23,6099	9558
31st December 1943	501,049	Unknown
30th June 1944	594,443	15,722

Note: Sourced from Wegner 1990

Sources:

Arad, Y. (1987). *Belzec, Sobibor, Treblinka: The Operation Reinhard Death Camps* Bloomington: Indiana University Press.

Arad, Y., Krakowski, S., & Spector, S. (Eds.). (1989). *The Einsatzgruppen Reports: Selections from the Dispatches of the Nazi Death Squads' Campaign Against the Jews in the Occupied Territories of the Soviet Union July 1941-January 1943.* New York: Holocaust Library.

Arendt, H. (1963). *Eichmann in Jerusalem: A Report on the Banality of Evil.* New York: Viking Press.

Association of Soldiers of the Former Waffen-SS (Ed.). (1973). *When All Our Brothers are Silent.* Coburg: Nation Europa.

Ax, A. (1947). *Operations of the 15th Waffen-SS Grenadier Division - 1st Latvian (D-230).*Unpublished manuscript.

Bach-Zelewski, E. (1946). *The 14th SS Corps in November-December 1944 (B-252).*Unpublished manuscript.

Ball, H. (1999). *Prosecuting War Crimes and Genocide.* Kansas: University Press of Kansas.

Barkan, E. (2004). Individual versus Group Rights in Western Philosophy and the Law. In N. Branscombe & B. Doosje (Eds.), *Collective Guilt: International Perspectives*
Cambridge: Cambridge University Press.

Bartov, O. (1992). *Hitler's Army: Soldiers, Nazis and War in the Third Reich.* Oxford: Oxford University Press.

Bartov, O. (1997). A View from Below: Survival, Cohesion and Brutality on the Eastern Front. In B. Wegner (Ed.), *From Peace to War: Germany, Soviet Russia and the World, 1939-1941*. Oxford: Berghahn Books.

Bartov, O. (1999). Professional Soldiers. In The Hamburg Institute for Social Science (Ed.), *The German Army and Genocide: Crimes Against War Prisoners, Jews and Other Civilians, 1939-1944*. New York: New Press.

Bartov, O. (2001). *The Eastern Front 1941-1945, German Troops and the Barbarisation of Warfare* (2nd ed.). New York: Palgrave.

Bartov, O. (2003a). *Germany's War and the Holocaust: Disputed Histories*. London: Cornell University Press.

Bartov, O. (2003b). Seeking the Roots of Modern Genocide: On the Macro- and Microhistory of Mass Murder. In R. Gellately & B. Kiernan (Eds.), *The Spectre of Genocide: Mass Murder in Historical Perspective*. Cambridge: Cambridge University Press.

Bassiouni, M. (1999). *Crimes Against Humanity in International Criminal Law*. London: Kluwer Law International.

Baumeister, R. F. (1999). *Evil: Inside Human Violence and Cruelty*. United States of America: Freeman and Company.

Bender, R. J., & Taylor, H. P. (1971). *Uniforms, Organisation and History of the Waffen-SS: Volume 2* (Vol. 2). San Jose: R J Bender Publishing.

Bender, R. J., & Taylor, H. P. (1972). *Uniforms, Organisation and History of the Waffen-SS: Volume 3* (Vol. 3). San Jose: R J Bender Publishing.

Bender, R. J., & Taylor, H. P. (1975). *Uniforms, Organisation and History of the Waffen-SS: Volume 4* (Vol. 4). San Jose: R J Bender Publishing.

Berglund, B. R. (2000). All Germans are the same: Czech and Sudeten German Exiles in Britain and the Transfer Plans. *National Identities, 2*(3), 225-244.

Berkowitz, L. (1999). Evil is more than Banal: Situationism and the Concept of Evil. *Personality and Social Psychology Review, 3*(3), 246-253.

Birn, R. B. (1991). Austrian Higher SS and Police Leaders and Their Participation in the Holocaust in the Balkans. *Holocaust and Genocide Studies, 6*(4), 351-372.

Birn, R. B. (1997). Two Kinds of Reality? Case Studies on Anti-Partisan Warfare during the Eastern Campaign. In B. Wegner (Ed.), *From Peace to War: Germany, Soviet Russia and the World, 1939-1941*. Oxford: Berghahn Books.

Blandford, E. L. (1994). *Hitler's Second Army: The Waffen-SS*. Osceola: Motorbooks International.

Blass, T. (1993). Psychological Perspectives on the Perpetrators of the Holocaust: The Role of Situational Pressures, Personal Dispositions and Their Interactions. *Holocaust and Genocide Studies, 7*(1), 30-50.

Bloomberg, C. (Writer) (2000). World at War: Genocide [DVD]. In M. Darlow (Producer), *World at War*: Thames.

Bourke, J. (1999). *An Intimate History of Killing: Face to Face Killing in 20th Century Warfare*. Great Britain: Basic Books.

Bracher, K. D. (1969). *The German Dictatorship: The Origins, Structure and Consequences of National Socialism*. London: Penguin Publishing.

Brandt, A. (1998). *The Last Knight of Flanders: Remy Schrijnen and his SS-Legion "Flandern/Sturmbrigade Langermarck". Comrades on the Eastern Front 1941-1945*. Atglen: Schiffer Publishing.

Breitman, R. (1991). *The Architect of Genocide: Himmler and the Final Solution*. London: Brandeis University Press.

Brenner, K. (1947a). *The 6th SS Mountain Division "Nord" and its part in Operation "Nordwind": North Alsace 1 January to 25 January 45 (B-476)*.Unpublished manuscript.

Brenner, K. (1947b). *Sixth SS Mountain Division "Nord" in defence engagements in North Alsace from 26 Jan to 1 Mar 45 (B-586)*.Unpublished manuscript.

Browning, C. R. (1998). *Ordinary Men: Reserve Police Battalion 101 and the Final Solution in Poland*. New York: HarperCollins Publishers.

Buchler, Y. (1986). Kommandostab Reichsfuhrer-SS: Himmler's Personal Murder Brigades in 1941. *Holocaust and Genocide Studies, 1*(1), 11-25.

Buss, P., & Mollo, A. (1978). *Hitler's Germanic Legions: An Illustrated History of the Western European Legions with the Waffen-SS. 1941-1943*. London: MacDonald and Janes Publishing Limited.

Butler, R. (1978). *The Black Angels: The Story of the Waffen-SS*. Middlesex: Hamlyn.

Butler, R. (2004). *Hitler's Death Head Division: SS Totenkopf Division*. Barnsley: Pen and Sword Military Classics.

Carruthers, B. (Writer) (2001). The Waffen-SS: The Alibi for History [Video]. In B. Carruthers (Producer), *Voices from Hitler's Army*: Cromwell Productions.

Christensen, C. B., Smith, P. S., & Poulsen, N. B. (2003). *The Danish Volunteers in the Waffen-SS and Their Contribution to the Holocaust and the Nazi War of Extermination*.Unpublished manuscript, The Danish Centre for Holocaust and Genocide Studies.

Clark, A. (1965). *Barbarossa: The Russian-German Conflict 1941-1945*. London: Phoenix Publishing.

Combs, W. L. (1986). *The Voice of the SS: The History of the SS Journal "Das Schwarze Korps"*. New York: Peter Lang Publishing.

Coser, L. A. (1969). The Visibility of Evil. *Journal of Social Issues, 25*(1), 108-109.

Dallin, A. (1981). *German Rule in Russia: 1941-1945 A Study of Occupation Policies* (2 ed.). London: MacMillan Press.

Darley, J. M. (1992). Social Organisation for the Production of Evil. *Psychological Inquiry, 3*(2), 199-218.

Darman, P. (Ed.). (2004). *Great Battles of the Waffen-SS*. Kent: Grange Books.

Davies, N. (2003). *Rising '44: The Battle for Warsaw*. New York: Viking Press.

Day, E., & Vandiver, M. (2000). Criminology and Genocide Studies: Notes on what might have been and what still could be. *Crime, Law and Social Change, 34*(1), 43-59.

Debes, L. (1947). *Fighting of the 6th SS Mountain Division "Nord" in the Southern Sector of the Lapland Front, in the wooded and lake areas of Kiestinki. (D-182)*.Unpublished manuscript.

Degrelle, L. (1983). *Leon Degrell-Epic: The Story of the Waffen-SS*. Torrance: Institute for Historical Review.

Dicks, H. V. (1972). *Licensed Mass Murder: A Socio-Psychological Study of some SS Killers*. New York: Basic Books.

Dmytryshyn, B. (1956). The Nazis and the SS Volunteer Division "Galicia". *American Slavic and East European Review, 15*(1), 1-10.

Doerffler-Schuband, W. (1949). *Officer Procurement in the Waffen-SS (D-178)*.Unpublished manuscript.

Engel, G. (1974). *At the Heart of the Reich: The Secret Diary of Hitler's Army Adjutant* (G. Brooks, Trans.). London: Greenhill Books.

Ertel, H., & Schulze-Kossens, R. (2000). *Europaische Freiwillige Im Bild*. Coburg: Nation Europa.

Fest, J. C. (1970). *The Face of the Third Reich* (M. Bullock, Trans.). London: Penguin Publishing.

Fischer, T. (2004). *The SS Panzer-Artillery Regiment 1 Leibstandarte Adolf Hitler (LAH): 1940-1945*. Atglen: Schiffer Military History.

Fletcher, G. (2002). Liberals and Romantics at war: The Problem of Collective Guilt. (The Storrs Lectures). *Yale Law Journal, 111*(1), 1499-1574.

Forster, J. (1985). New Wine in Old Skins: The Wehrmacht and the War of "Weltanschauungen" 1941. In W. Deist (Ed.), *The German Military in the Age of Total War*. Dover USA: Berg.

Forster, J. (1997). Hitler Turns East-German War Policy in 1940 and 1941. In B. Wegner (Ed.), *From Peace to War: Germany, Soviet Russia and the World, 1939-1941*. Oxford: Berghahn Books.

Garrard, E. (2002). Evil as an Explanatory Concept. *The Monist, 85*(2), 320.

Gewirth, A. (2001). War Crimes and Human Rights. In A. Jokic (Ed.), *War Crimes and Collective Wrongdoing: A Reader*. Oxford: Blackwell Publishers.

Gilbert, F. (Ed.). (1950). *Hitler Directs His War*. New York: Award Books.

Gingerich, M. (1997). Waffen-SS Recruitment in the Germanic Lands: 1940-1941. *Historian, 59*(4), 815-831.

Glantz, D. M., & House, J. (1995). *When Titans Clashed: How the Red Army Stopped Hitler*. USA: University Press of Kansas.

Goldhagen, D. J. (1997). *Hitler's Willing Executioners: Ordinary Germans and the Holocaust*. New York: Random House.

Guderian, H. (1996). *Panzer Leader* (C. Fitzgibbon, Trans.). New York: Da Capo Press.

Gumz, J. (1998). German Counterinsurgency Policy in Independent Croatia, 1941-1944. *The Historian, 6*(1), 33.

Gunther, H. (2004). *Hot Motors, Cold Feet: A Memoir of Service with the Motorcycle Battalion of SS-Division Reich 1940-1941*. Winnipeg: J J Federowicz Publishing.

Gutman, I. (Ed.). (1990). *Encyclopaedia of the Holocaust*. New York: MacMillan Publishing Company.

Halliley, M. (Writer) (2003). Hitler's SS [Television series on the History Channel]. In G. Knopp (Producer).

Haslam, D. R., & Abraham, P. (1987). Sleep Loss and Military Performance. In G. Belenky (Ed.), *Contemporary Studies in Combat Psychiatry*. New York: Greenwood Press.

Hatheway, J. (1999). *In Perfect Formation: SS Ideology and the SS-Junkerschule-Tolz*. Atglen: Schiffer Publishing.

Headland, R. (1989). The Einsatzgruppen: The Question of Their Initial Operations. *Holocaust and Genocide Studies, 4*(4), 401-412.

Headland, R. (1992). *Messages of Murder: A Study of the Reports of the Einsatzgruppen of the Security Police and the Security Service 1941-1943*. Cranbury: Associated University Presses.

Healy, M. (1993). *Kursk 1943: The Tide Turns East*. Oxford: Osprey Publishing.

Heaton, C. (2001). *German Anti-Partisan Warfare in Europe 1939-1945*. Atglen: Schiffer Publishing.

Heer, H. (1999). Russia: Three Years of Occupation, 1941-1944. In The Hamburg Institute for Social Science (Ed.), *The German Army and Genocide: Crimes Against War Prisoners, Jews and Other Civilians, 1939-1944*. New York: New Press.

Heiber, H., & Glantz, D. M. (2003). *Hitler and His Generals: Military Conferences 1942-1945*. New York: Enigma Books.

Herrmann, K. (1947). *Advance of an SS Division (motorised) to Lake Ilmen: June-August 1941 (D-225)*.Unpublished manuscript.

Hilberg, R. (1980). The Significance of the Holocaust. In H. Friedlander & E. Milton (Eds.), *The Holocaust: Ideology, Bureaucracy and Genocide-The San Jose Papers*. New York: Millwood.

Hillblad, T. (Ed.). (2002). *Twilight of the Gods: A Swedish Waffen-SS Volunteer's Experiences with the 11th SS Panzergrenadier Division Nordland, Eastern Front 1944-45*. Solihull: Helion and Company.

Hock, O. (1947). *Experience in the Medical Services of a Motorised SS Division during 1941/42 in Russia. (D-186)*.Unpublished manuscript.

Hohne, H. (1969). *The Order of the Death's Head: The Story of Hitler's SS*. London: Penguin Books.

Holmes, R. (1985). *Acts of War: The Behaviour of Men in Battle*. New York: The Free Press.

Huffman, C. (2005). *The Waffen-SS Soldier in World War 2: Fanaticism, Everyday Life and the New Military History*. Unpublished Doctor of Philosophy dissertation, Georgia State University.

Husemann, F. (2003). *In Good Faith: The History of the 4 SS Polizei Panzer-Grenadier Division Volume 1, 1939-1943* (Vol. 1). Winnipeg: Fedorowicz Publishing.

Jones, S. (2000). *Understanding Violent Crime*. Buckingham USA: Open University Press.

Jukes, G. (2003). *The Second World War (5): The Eastern Front 1941-1945*. Oxford: Osprey Publishing.

Kaltenegger, R. (1995). *Mountain Troops of the Waffen-SS 1941-1945*. Atglen: Schiffer Publishing.

Keegan, J. (1970). *Waffen-SS: The Asphalt Soldiers*. Toronto: Ballytine Books.

Kellett, A. (1987). Combat Motivation. In G. Belenky (Ed.), *Contemporary Studies in Combat Psychiatry*. New York: Greenwood Press.

Klee, E., Dressen, W., & Riess, V. (Eds.). (1988). *The Good Old Days: The Holocaust as Seen by Its Perpetrators and Bystanders*. USA: Konecky and Konecky.

Knopp, G. (2002). *The SS: A Warning from History*. Gloucestershire: Sutton Publishing.

Koehl, R. L. (1959). Toward an SS Typology: Social Engineers. *The American Journal of Economics and Sociology, 18*, 113-126.

Koehl, R. L. (1962). The Character of the Nazi SS. *Journal of Modern History, 34*(3), 275-283.

Koehl, R. L. (1983). *The Black Corps: The Structure and Power Struggles of the Nazi SS.* Madison: University of Wisconsin Press.

Kraas, H. (1947). *The 12th SS Panzer Division Hitlerjugend in the Ardennes Offensive. (B-522)*.Unpublished manuscript.

Krausnick, H., Buchheim, H., Broszat, M., & Jacobsen, H.-A. (1965). *Anatomy of the SS State.* New York: Walker and Company.

Kren, G., & Rappoport, L. (1976). The Waffen-SS: A Social Psychological Perspective. *Armed Forces and Society, 3*(1), 87-103.

Kressel, N. J. (2002). *Mass Hate: The Global Rise of Genocide and Terror.* New York: Plenum Press.

Kumm, O. (1947). *1 SS Panzer Division, 7 SS Mountain Division. (B-168)*.Unpublished manuscript.

Kumm, O. (1995). *Prinz Eugen: The History of the 7th SS Mountain Division "Prinz Eugen".* Winnipeg: JJ Fedorowicz Publishing.

Landwehr, R. (1998). *Budapest: The Stalingrad of the Waffen-SS.* Bennington: Merriam Press.

Lehmann, R. (1990). *The Leibstandarte III: 1 SS Panzer Division Leibstandarte Adolf Hitler.* Winnipeg: JJ Fedorowicz Publishing.

Lepre, G. (1997). *Himmler's Bosnian Division: The Waffen-SS Handschar Division 1943-1945.* Atglen: Schiffer Publishing.

Levinson, S. (1973). Responsibility for Crimes of War. *Philosophy and Public Affairs, 2,* 244-273.

Liddell Hart, B. H. (1975). *The German Generals Talk: Startling Revelations from Hitler's High Command.* New York: Quill Publishing.

Lifton, R. J. (2000). *The Nazi Doctors: Medical Killing and the Psychology of Genocide* (2nd ed.). New York: Basic Books.

Littman, S. (2003). *Pure Soldiers or Sinister Legion: The Ukrainian 14th Waffen-SS Division*. 2003: Black Rose Books.

Longerich, P. (1997). From Mass Murder to the "Final Solution": The Shooting of Jewish Civilians during the First Months of the Eastern Campaign with the Context of the Nazi Jewish Genocide. In B. Wegner (Ed.), *From Peace to War: Germany, Soviet Russia and the World, 1939-1941*. Oxford: Berghahn Books.

Lower, W. (2002). "Anticipatory Obedience" and the Nazi Implementation of the Holocaust in the Ukraine: A Case Study of the Central and Peripheral Forces in the Generalbezirk Zhytomyr, 1941-1944. *Holocaust and Genocide Studies, 16*(1), 1-22.

Lozowick, Y. (1987). Rollbahn Mord: The Early Activities of Einsatzgruppen C. *Holocaust and Genocide Studies, 2*(2), 221-241.

Lozowick, Y. (2000). *Hitler's Bureaucrats: The Nazi Security Police and the Banality of Evil*. New York: Continuum.

Lucas, J. (1991). *War on the Eastern Front: The German Soldier in Russia, 1941-1945*. London: Greenhill Books.

Lucas, J., & Cooper, M. (1975). *Hitler's Elite: Leibstandarte SS 1933-1945*. London: Purnell Book Services.

Lumans, V. O. (1993). *Himmler's Auxiliaries: The Volkdeutsche Mittelstelle and the German National Minorities of Europe, 1933-1945*. London: The University of North Carolina.

Luther, C. W. (1987). *Blood and Honor: The History of the 12th SS Panzer Division "Hitler Youth" 1943-1945*. San Jose: R James Bender Publishing.

Mackenzie, S. (1997). *Revolutionary Armies in the Modern Era*. London: Routledge.

MacLean, F. L. (1998). *The Cruel Hunters: SS-Sonderkommando Dirlewanger. Hitler's Most Notorious Anti-Partisan Unit*. Atglen: Schiffer Publishing.

MacLean, F. L. (1999a). *The Camp Men: The SS Officers Who Ran the Nazi Concentration Camp System*. Atglen: Schiffer Publishing.

MacLean, F. L. (1999b). *The Field Men: The SS Officers Who Led the Einsatzkommandos-The Nazi Mobile Killing Units*. Atglen: Schiffer Publishing.

MacLean, F. L. (2001). *The Ghetto Men: The SS Destruction of the Jewish Warsaw Ghetto, April-May 1943*. Atglen PA: Schiffer Military History.

Maier, G. (2004). *Drama between Budapest and Vienna: The Final Battles of the 6 SS Panzer Armee in the East-1945*. Winnipeg: JJ Fedorowicz Publishing.

Mann, C. (2001). *SS-Totenkopf: The History of the "Death's Head" Division 1940-45*. Staplehurst: Spellmount Publishing.

Manton, J., Wilson, C., & Braithwaite, H. (2000). Human Factors in Field Training for Battle: Realistically Producing Chaos. In M. Evans & A. Ryan (Eds.), *The Human Face of Warfare*. Sydney: Allen and Unwin.

Matthaus, J. (1996). What about the "Ordinary Men"? The German Order Police and the Holocaust in the Occupied Soviet Union. *Holocaust and Genocide Studies, 10*(2), 134-150.

Megargee, G. P. (2000). *Inside Hitler's High Command*. USA: University Press of Kansas.

Messenger, C. (1988). *Hitler's Gladiator: The Life and Times of Oberstgruppenführer and Panzergeneral-Oberst Der Waffen-SS Sepp Dietrich*. Exeter: A Wheaton and Company.

Messenger, C. (Writer) (2002). Waffen-SS [Video]. In R. Walker (Producer), *Gladiators of World War II*: BBC Worldwide.

Metelmann, H. (2001). *Through Hell for Hitler*. Havertown: Casemate Publishing.

Meyer, K. (2001). *Grenadiers*. Winnipeg: JJ Fedorowicz Publishing.

Milgram, S. (1974). *Obedience to Authority*. New York: Harper Perrenial.

Miller, M., Schulz, A., & McCanliss, K. (2006). *Leaders of the SS and Police: Georg Ahrens to Karl Gutenberger* (Vol. One). San Jose: Bender Publishing.

Mollo, A. (1982). *To the Death's Head True: The Story of the SS*. London: Methuen London Limited.

Mooney, P. (2004). *Dietrich's Warriors: The History of the 3. Kompanie, 1st Panzergrenadier Regiment, 1st SS Panzer Division Leibstandarte Adolf Hitler*. Atglen, PA: Schiffer Publishing.

Morrow, L. (2003). *Evil: An Investigation*. United States: Basic Books.

Morton, A. (2004). *On Evil: Thinking in Action*. New York: Routledge.

Muhlberger, D. (1991). *Hitler's Followers: Studies in the Sociology of the Nazi Movement*. London: Routledge Publishing.

Munoz, A. (2001). *Waffen-SS Officer Roster: March 1st 1945*. New York: Axis Europa Books.

Munoz, A. J. (1997). *The Kaminski Brigade: A History 1941-1945*. New York: Axis Eurpoa.

Nafziger, G. F. (2001). *The German Order of Battle: Waffen-SS and Other Units in World War 2*. United States of America: Da Capo Press.

Narveson, J. (2002). Collective Responsibility. *The Journal of Ethics, 6*, 179-198.

Newman, L. S. (2002). What is a "Social-Psychological" Account of Perpetrator Behaviour? The Person versus the Situation in Goldhagen's Hitler's Willing Executioners. In L. S. Newman & R. Erber (Eds.), *Understanding Genocide: The Social Psychology of the Holocaust*. Oxford: Oxford University Press.

Nipe, G. (1996). *Decision in the Ukraine: Summer 1943 II SS and III Panzerkorps*. Winnipeg: JJ Fedorowicz Publishing.

Nipe, G., & Spezzano, R. (2002). *Platz Der Leibstandarte: The SS-Panzer-Grenadier Division "LSSAH" and the Battle of Kharkov January-March 1943*. Southbury: RZM Imports.

Noakes, J., & Pridham, G. (Eds.). (1988). *Nazism 1919-1945: Volume 3 Foreign Policy, War and Racial Extermination*. Exeter: University of Exeter.

Nuremberg Military Tribunal. (1946). *Trials of War Criminals before the Nuernberg War Crimes Tribunal under Council Control Law No.10*. Nuremberg: Nuremberg Military Tribunal.

Office of the United States Counsel for Prosecution of Axis Criminality. (1946). Nazi Conspiracy and Aggression. accessed 2003, from http://www.yale.edu/lawweb/avalon/imt/imt.htm#proc

Padfield, P. (1990). *Himmler: Reichsfuhrer-SS*. London: Cassell and Company.

Paetel, K. O. (1959). The Black Order: A Survey of Literature on the SS. *Wiener Library Bulletin, 12*(3-4), 34-35.

Peppers, D. A. (1974). War Crimes and Induction: A Case for Selective Nonconscientious Objection. *Philosophy and Public Affairs, 3*(2), 130-166.

Perrigault, J., & Meister, R. (2004). *Gotz Von Berlichingen: Normandie*. Bayeux: Heimdal.

Pierik, P. (2001). *From Leningrad to Berlin: Dutch Volunteers in the Service of the German Waffen-SS 1941-1945*. Soesterberg: Aspekt.

Ploetz, K., Schramm, E., & Hillgruber, A. (1960). *Geschitchte des Zweiten Weltkrieges: History of the Second World War*. Wurzburg: Ploetz Publishing House.

Poprzeczny, J. (2004). *Hitler's Man in the East: Odilo Globocnik*. Jefferson, North Carolina: McFarland and Company.

Pruess Publishing (Ed.). (2001). *SS Defender against Bolshevism: Die Schutzstaffel als antibolschewistische Kampforganisation*. USA: Preuss Publishing.

Pruess Publishing (Ed.). (2004a). *SS Culture Volume Twelve: Soldier*. USA: Preuss Publishing.

Pruess Publishing (Ed.). (2004b). *SS Culture Volume Two: Be Hard!* USA: Preuss Publishing.

Pruess Publishing (Ed.). (2005). *Bolshevism - Jewish Sub-Humanity: Bolschewismus-Judisches Untermenschentum*. USA: Preuss Publishing.

Quarrie, B. (1981). *Waffen-SS in Russia*. Tucson: Aztec Corporation.

Quarrie, B. (1991). *Lightning Death: The Story of the Waffen-SS*. Somerset: Patrick Stephens Limited.

Quassowksi, H. (Ed.). (1999). *Twelve Years with Hitler: A History of 1. Kompanie Leibstandarte SS Adolf Hitler 1933-1945*. Atglen: Schiffer Publishing.

Radzik, L. (2001). Collective Responsibility and the Duties to Respond. *Social Theory and Practice, 27*(3), 445-471.

Ratner, S. R., & Abrams, J. S. (1997). *Accountability for Human Rights Atrocities in International Law: Beyond the Nuremberg Legacy*. Oxford: Clarendon Press.

Read, A., & Fisher, D. (1992). *The Fall of Berlin*. New York: Da Capo Press.

Rees, L. (1999). *War of the Century: When Hitler fought Stalin*. France: Imprimerie Pollina.

Reitlinger, G. (1957). *The SS: Alibi of a Nation 1922-1945*. New York: Da Capo Press.

Rempel, G. (1980). Gottlob Berger and Waffen-SS Recruitment: 1939-1945. *Militargeschichtliche Mitteilungen, 27*(1), 107-122.

Reynolds, M. (1999). *Men of Steel: I SS Panzer Corps, The Ardennes and Eastern Front 1944-45*. Staplehurst: Spellmount Publishing.

Reynolds, M. (2002). *The Devil's Adjutant: Jochen Peiper, Panzer Leader*. Kent: Spellmout Limited.

Rhodes, R. (2002). *Masters of Death: The SS Einsatzgruppen and the Invention of the Holocaust.* New York: Alfred A Knopf.

Rikmenspoel, M. (1999). *Soldiers of the Waffen-SS: Many Nations, One Motto.* Winnipeg: J J Federowicz Publishing.

Ripley, T. (2000). *Steel Storm: Waffen-SS Panzer Battles on the Eastern Front 1943-1945.* Osceola: Motorbook International.

Ripley, T. (2003). *Wehrmacht: The German Army in World War 2 1939-1945.* London: Brown Reference Group.

Ripley, T. (2004). *The Waffen-SS at War: Hitler's Praetorians 1925-1945.* London: Zenith Press.

Ruter, C. F., & de Mildt, D. W. (2004). Nazi Crimes On Trial: German Trials Concerning National Socialist Homicidal Crimes (Justiz und NS-Verbrechen). 2004, from http://www1.jur.uva.nl/junsv/

Ryan, C. (1994). *The Last Battle: The Classic History of the Battle for Berlin.* New York: Simon and Schuster.

Scarre, G. (1998). Understanding the Moral Phenomenology of the Third Reich. *Ethical Theory and Moral Practice, 1,* 423-445.

Schaap, A. (2001). Guilty Subjects and Political Responsibility: Arendt, Jaspers and the Resonance of the German Question in Politics of Reconciliation. *Political Studies, 49,* 749-766.

Scheffler, W. (1985). The Forgotten Part of the "Final Solution": The Liquidation of the Ghettos. *Simon Wiesenthal Centre Annual, 2,* 31-51.

Scherzer, V. (2006). The Evolution of the Waffen-SS Brigades and Divisions 1939-1945: Entwicklung der Waffen-SS Brigaden und Divisionen 1939-1945: Scherzers Militaire Verlag.

Schiffer Publishing (Ed.). (2000). *SS Officer List: As of 30 January 1942 SS-Standartenführer to SS-Oberstgruppenführer.* Atglen, PA: Schiffer Publishing.

Schmidt, H. (2001). *SS Panzergrenadier: A True Story of World War II.* Pensacola: Hans Schmidt Publishing.

Schneider, J. W. (1993). *Verleihung Genehmigt-Their Honour was Loyalty: An Illustrated and Documentary History of the Knight's Cross Holders of the Waffen-SS and Police.* San Jose: R James Bender Publishing.

Schroder, H. J. (1997). German Soldier's Experiences during the Initial Phase of the Russian Campaign. In B. Wegner (Ed.), *From Peace to War: Germany, Soviet Russia and the World, 1939-1941.* Oxford: Berghahn Books.

Schulze-Kossens, R. (1982). *Militarischer Fuhrernachwuchs der Waffen-SS Die Junkerschulen: The Junkerschools-Officer Training in the Waffen-SS.* Osnabruck: Munin Verlag GmbH.

Segev, T. (1987). *Soldiers of Evil: The Commandants of the Nazi Concentration Camps.* Jerusalem: Domino Press.

Sharpe, M., & Davis, B. L. (2003). *Das Reich: Waffen-SS Armoured Elite.* Surrey: Ian Allan Publishing.

Shills, E., & Janowitz, M. (1948). Cohesion and Disintegration in the Wehrmacht in World War Two. *Public Opinion Quarterly*, 280-315.

Simon, M. (1949). *Experience gained in combat with Russian Infantry (C-058).*Unpublished manuscript.

Simon, M. (1953). *Soviet Russian Infantry and Armoured Forces. (P-077).*Unpublished manuscript.

Simpson, K. (1990). *Fighting Elites: Waffen-SS.* Hong Kong: Gallery Books.

Smith, P. S., Poulsen, N. B., & Christensen, C. B. (1999). The Danish Volunteers in the Waffen-SS and German Warfare on the Eastern Front. *Contemporary European History, 8*(1), 73-96.

Solarz, J. (2003). *Wiking: 1941-1945.* Warsaw: Wydawnictwo Militaria.

Staub, E. (1989). *The Roots of Evil.* New York: Cambridge University Press.

Staub, E. (2002). The Psychology of Bystanders, Perpetrators and, Heroic Helpers. In L. S. Newman & R. Erber (Eds.), *Understanding Genocide: The Social Psychology of the Holocaust*. Oxford: Oxford University Press.

Stein, G. H. (1965). The Myth of a European Army: Waffen-SS was a Tool of Nazi Imperialism. *Wiener Library Bulletin, 19*(2), 21-22.

Stein, G. H. (1966). *The Waffen-SS: Hitler's Elite Guard at War*. London: Cornell University Press.

Steiner, F. (1947). *Operations of the 5th SS Panzergrenadier Division "Wiking" at Rostov and the Maikop Oilfields. Summer 1942. (D-248)*.Unpublished manuscript.

Steiner, J. (1963). The SS Yesterday and Today: A Sociopsychological View. In J. Dimsdale (Ed.), *Survivors, Victims and Perpetrators: Essays on the Nazi Holocaust*. New York: Hemisphere Publishing.

Steiner, J. (2000). The Role Margin as the Site for Moral and Social Intelligence: The Case of Germany and National Socialism. *Crime, Law and Social Change, 34*(1), 61-75.

Stokes, L. D. (2002). From Law Student to Einsatzgruppen Commander: The Career of a Gestapo Officer. *Canadian Journal of History, 37*(1), 41-74.

Stouffer, S. A., Lumsdaine, A. A., Williams, R. M., Brewster Smith, M., Janis, I. L., Star, S. A., et al. (1949). *The American Soldier: Combat and its Aftermath: Volume 2* (Vol. 2). Princeton New Jersey: Princeton University.

Strachan, H. (2000). On Total War and Modern War. *The International History Review, 22*(2), 341-370.

Streim, A. (1997). International Law and Soviet Prisoners of War. In B. Wegner (Ed.), *From Peace to War: Germany, Soviet Russia and the World, 1939-1941*. Oxford: Berghahn Books.

Sydnor, C. W. (1973). The History of the SS Totenkopf Division and the Postwar Mythology of the Waffen-SS. *Central European History, 6*, 339-362.

Sydnor, C. W. (1989). On the Histography of the SS. *Simon Wiesenthal Centre Annual, 6,* 249-262.

Sydnor, C. W. (1990). *Soldiers of Destruction: The SS Death's Head Division 1933-1945* (8 ed.). Princeton: Princeton University Press.

Tec, N. (1993). *Defiance: The Bielski Partisans.* Oxford: Oxford University Press.

The International Military Tribunal. (1946). *Trial of the Major War Criminals before the International Military Tribunal: Nuremberg.* Nuremberg: The International Military Tribunal.

The United Nations War Crime Commission. (1946). Law Reports of Trials of War Criminals. accessed 2004, from http://www.mazal.org/Default.htm

Theile, K. H. (1997). *Beyond "Monsters" and "Clowns": The Combat SS. De-Mytholigizing Five Decades of German Elite Formations.* New York: University Press of America.

Tieke, W. (1999). *In the Firestorm of the Last Years of the War: II SS-Panzerkorps with the 9 and 10 SS-Divisions "Hohenstaufen" and Frundsberg".* Winnipeg: JJ Fedorowicz Publishing.

Tieke, W. (2001). *Tragedy of the Faithful: A History of the III (Germanisches) SS-Panzer-Korps.* Winnipeg: JJ Fedorowicz Publishing.

Tieke, W. (2004). *SS Panzer Brigade Westfalen.* Winnipeg, Canada: JJ Fedorowicz Publishing.

Tiemann, R. (1998). *Chronicle of the 7 Panzer Kompanie I SS-Panzer Division "Leibstandarte".* Atglen: Schiffer Publishing.

Trang, C. (2000). *The Florian Geyer Division.* Bayeux: Heimdal.

Trevor-Roper, H. (2000). *Hitler's Table Talk 1941-1944* (N. Cameron & R. H. Stevens, Trans.). New York: Enigma Books.

Trevor-Roper, H. (Ed.). (1964). *Hitler's War Directives 1939-1945.* London: Pan Books.

Tsouras, P. G. (Ed.). (1995). *Fighting in Hell: The German Ordeal on the Eastern Front*. New York: Ivy Books.

Ullrich, K. (2002). *Like a Cliff in the Ocean: The History of the 3 SS-Panzer-Division "Totenkopf"*. Winnipeg: JJ Fedorowicz Publishing.

Ungvary, K. (2005). *The Siege of Budapest: One Hundred Days in World War Two*. London: Yale University Press.

Van Sleidregt, E. (2006). Criminal Responsibility in International Law. *European Journal of Crime, Criminal Law and Criminal Justice, 14*(1), 81-114.

Van Sliedregt, E. (2006). Criminal Responsibility in International Law. *European Journal of Crime, Criminal Law and Criminal Justice, 14*(1), 81-114.

Verton, H. (2007). *In the Fire of the Eastern Front: The Experiences of a Dutch Waffen-SS Volunteer on the Eastern Front 1941-45* (H. Toon-Thorn, Trans.). Solihull, West Midland: Helion and Company Limited

Victor, G. (1998). *Hitler: The Pathology of Evil*. Washington: Brassey's.

Volkner, W. (2004). *Many Rivers I Crossed*. Dorset: W.Volkner.

Von Below, N. (1980). *At Hitler's Side: The Memoirs of Hitler's Luftwaffe Adjutant 1937-1945*. London: Greenhill Books.

Von Lang, J. (2005). *Top Nazi: SS General Karl Wolff-The Man between Hitler and Himmler* (M. Friedrich, Trans.). USA: Enigma Books.

Von Manstein, E. (1982). *Lost Victories: The War Memoirs of Hitler's Most Brilliant General* (A. G. Powell, Trans.). Novato: Presidio Press.

Voss, J. (2002). *Black Edelweiss: A Memoir of Combat and Conscience by a Soldier of the Waffen-SS*. Bedford: The Aberjona Press.

Vuksic, V. (2005). *SS Armour on the Eastern Front: 1943-1945*. Winnipeg: JJ Fedorowicz Publishing.

Waller, J. (2002). *Becoming Evil: How Ordinary People Commit Genocide and Mass Killing*. Oxford: Oxford University Press.

Wegner, B. (1985). "My Honour is Loyalty": The SS as a Military Factor in Hitler's Germany. In W. Deist (Ed.), *The German Military in the Age of Total War*. Dover USA: Berg.

Wegner, B. (1990). *The Waffen-SS*. Padstow: TJ Press.

Weidinger, O. (1998). *Comrades to the End: The 4th SS Panzer-Grenadier Regiment "Der Fuhrer" 1938-1945*. Atglen: Schiffer Publishing.

Weidinger, O. (2002). *Das Reich 1941-1943: 2nd SS Panzer Division Das Reich*. Winnipeg: JJ Fedorowicz Publishing.

Weinberg, G. (1994). *A World at Arms: A Global History of World War Two*. Cambridge: Cambridge University Press.

Weingartner, J. (1974). *Hitler's Guard: Inside the Fuhrer's Personal SS Force*. New York: Berkley Books.

Weingartner, J. (1983). Law and Justice in the Nazi SS: The Case of Konrad Morgen. *Central European History, 16*, 276-294.

Weingartner, J. (1996). War against Subhumans: Comparisons between the German War against the Soviet Union and the American War against Japan 1941-1945. *Historian, 58*(3), 557-573.

Weitz, E. D. (2003). *A Century of Genocide: Utopias of Race and Nation*. Princeton: Princeton University Press.

Westwood, D. (2001). The German Army 1933-45: The Waffen-SS.

White, E. B. (1990). Majdanek: Cornerstone of Himmler's SS Empire in the East. *Simon Wiesenthal Centre Annual 7, 7*, 3-21.

Wiggers, R. (1990). *Nuremberg and the Waffen-SS: An Analysis of the Charge of Organisational Criminality*. Unpublished Master of Arts dissertation, University of Ottawa.

Wilkins, B. T. (2001). Whose Trial? Whose Reconciliation. In A. Jokic (Ed.), *War Crimes and Collective Wrongdoing: A Reader*. Oxford: Blackwell Publishers.

Williamson, G. (1994). *The SS: Hitler's Instrument of Terror*. London: Segwick and Jackson.

Williamson, G. (1995). *Loyalty Is My Honour: Personal Accounts from the Waffen-SS*. London: Bramley Books.

Williamson, G. (2003). *Waffen-SS Handbook 1933-1945*. Great Britain: Sutton Publishing.

Williamson, G., & Andrew, S. (2004a). *The Waffen-SS (2): 6 to 10 Divisions*. Oxford: Osprey Publishing.

Williamson, G., & Andrew, S. (2004b). *The Waffen-SS (4): 24 to 38 Divisions, and Volunteer Legions*. Oxford: Osprey Publishing.

Williamson, G., & Vuksic, V. (2002). *German Security and Police Soldier 1939-45*. Oxford: Osprey Publishing.

Wilson, P. (2000). *Himmler's Cavalry: The Equestrian SS, 1930-1945*. Atglen: Schiffer Publishing Limited.

Windrow, M., & Burn, J. (1982). *The Waffen-SS*. Oxford: Osprey Publishing.

Wolfson, M. (1965). Constraint and Choice in the SS Leadership. *Western Political Quarterly, 18*, 551-568.

Wykes, A. (1974). *Hitler's Bodyguards: SS Leibstandarte*. United States: Ballantine Books.

Yerger, M. C. (1997). *Waffen-SS Commanders: The Army Corps and Divisional Leaders of a Legend. Ausberger to Kreutz* (Vol. 1). Atglen: Schiffer Publishing.

Yerger, M. C. (1999). *Waffen-SS Commanders: The Army Corps and Divisional Leaders of a Legend. Kruger to Zimmermann* (Vol. 2). Atglen: Schiffer Publishing.

Yerger, M. C. (2000). *SS-Obersturmbannführer Otto Weidinger: Knight's Cross with Oakleaves and Swords - SS Panzergrenadier Regiment 4 "Der Fuhrer"*. Atglen, PA: Schiffer Military History.

Ziegler, H. (1989). *Nazi Germany's New Aristocracy: The SS Leadership 1925-1939*. Princeton: Princeton University Press.

Zukier, H. (1994). The Twisted Road to Genocide: On the Psychological development of Evil during the Holocaust. *Social Research, 61*(2), 423-456.

Endnotes

[1] The term Waffen meant fighting or armed SS. The term SS was derived from the formation of protection squads or Schutzstaffeln. The Schutzstaffeln were protection squads set up by the Nazi Party in the 1930s for the protection of Hitler and other leading Nazis.

[2] Although the study of Stein would appear to be dated, it is still considered one of the most important studies to ever examine the Waffen-SS.

[3] Name for the combined German Army, Air Force and Navy during World War II.

[4] Mobile killing groups that followed the combat forces and operated behind the front lines carrying out "cleansing" operations.

[5] During the invasion of Russia codenamed Operation "Barbarossa" there were initially three main German Army Groups called North, South and Centre.

[6] These manuscripts will be referenced in the bibliography under the individual officer's name, e.g. Max Simon C-058.

[7] The term SA is referring to *SturmAbteilung* or storm troopers organised by the Nazi Party for protection against attacks by rival political groups. These troopers were also known as the Brown Shirts.

[8] Note that there is disagreement between researchers as to the strength of the Waffen-SS at the conclusion of the war. Suffice to say that the estimates of the strength vary between 500,000 to 900,000 soldiers.

[9] Militarised component of the SS in the pre-war period; direct predecessor of the Waffen-SS.

[10] It should be noted that some of these divisions were only of regimental strength, while others existed for only short periods of time. This is especially true of the divisions formed towards the end of the war.

[11] My italics and addition. Clearly here Hitler is comparing the Waffen-SS to the regular German armed forces.

[12] These formations included the premier or classic divisions of the Waffen-SS such as the *Leibstandarte SS Adolf Hitler* and the *Das Reich* Divisions.

[13] The main difference being that a Panzer Division had a Panzer Regiment on its establishment whilst a Panzergrenadier only had a Battalion on its establishment.

[14] This army consisted of the 1st SS, 2nd SS, 9th SS, 12th SS Divisions and other army units as at the 5th March 1945.

[15] Elite units of the German Armed Forces in World War II wore armbands bands on their uniforms denoting the name of their unit. For example the men of the *Leibstandarte SS Adolf Hitler* Division wore a armband on the left arm with the words *"Adolf Hitler"* woven into the band.

[16] Thus making them "old party fighters" and seemingly more aligned to the political and ideological ideas of the Nazi Party.

[17] The Berghof was Hitler's residence and headquarters situated in the Bavarian Alps.

[18] Hitler Youth – Division formed from youths from this movement.

[19] Hitler issued the Commissar Decree to the top military command of the German armed forces in 1941 stating that all political commissars of the Russian Army who were captured were to be eliminated. Hitler further stated that any soldier who undertook these actions would be pardoned for breaking international law and that the Russian soldier was not entitled to the protection of The Hague Convention as Russia had not taken part in it.

[20] The 1st SS Infantry Brigade (Motorised) was later used to form the Waffen-SS 18th SS Panzergrenadier Division *Horst Wessel.*

[21] Milgram's research involved submitting a group of students to an experiment in which the supervisor would require them to administer electric shocks to an unknown person. In reality the shocks were not delivered but the victims acted as if they were. Milgram found that most of his students were prepared to deliver the shocks to quite high levels if instructed to do so by the supervisor.

[22] FR case 491.

[23] Ungvary gives the strength of the garrison as some 44,000 (including some 11,000 wounded) at the time of the breakout and cites

some 700 German soldiers reached the German lines. He does not stipulate how many of these were from the Waffen-SS.

24 Stein puts the figure claimed at 20,000.

25 GDR case 1083.

26 Russian State Security service.

27 FR case 428.

28 FR case 486.

29 FR case 062.

30 FR case 428.

31 Note that Westwood has a different spelling for this officer's name. He has it as Wilhelm Breimaler, who was commander of the III battalion, 1st SS Mountain Regiment *Prinz Eugen* from the 31 July 1943.

32 Waldemar Fegelein was a *SS-Hauptsturmführer* in the brigade and the brother of the Brigade and later divisional commander Hermann Fegelein.

33 Note the Williamson lists only 22 awards for this division.

34 My italics and insertion.

35 The forbearer of the Waffen-SS *Florian Geyer* Calvary Division.

36 The term used to describe the General SS.

37 Dalmatia is a mountainous strip of land, in south-eastern Europe, lying almost entirely within Croatia.

38 This figure does not include temporary or substitute HSSPF leaders.

39 This unit would later form the 24th Regiment of the 11th Panzer-grenadier Division *Nordland*.

40 Note these figures differ from the figures quoted by Yerger, but the basic argument is unchanged.

41 This unit was used in July 1943 to form SS Panzergrenadier Regiment *Norge* of the 11th SS Panzergrenadier Division *Nordland*.

42 Of note is that other sources such as Yerger and Bender and Taylor do not list Fitzthum as being in command of any Waffen-SS units.

43 My italics and insertion.

[44] Case number IX, known as the *Einsatzgruppen* case.

[45] This figure is not exact as there is some difficulty in arriving at a precise number of victims listed in the reports, however, most sources state that at least 500,000 people had been murdered.

[46] Exact service details were unavailable for two Waffen-SS officers, so total equals 28.

[47] Note that figures for the total of those killed vary. The accuracy of the final figure is not the issue here, rather the approximate figure serves to illustrate the scale of the crime, which is the important point.

[48] Boch was investigated, but found not to have committed any crimes.

[49] 3rd SS *Totenkopf* Division.

[50] The *Volksdeutsche Mittelstelle* or VOMI, the organisation that ensured the privileges of ethnic Germans living outside the borders of the German Reich.

[51] *Sonderatkion* indication mass executions.

[52] Case IV before the Nuremberg Military Tribunal, commonly referred to as the Pohl case.

[53] Schulze changed his name after the war to Schulze-Kossens.

[54] Death's Head formations, armed full-time component of the SS during pre-war period, tasked with guarding concentration-camps and political prisons.

[55] FR case 223.

[56] Note that Maclean lists no Waffen-SS service for Kremer.

[57] Case number 1 before the Nuremberg Military Tribunal, also known as the Medical Case.

[58] Case Number 37, Volume VII.

[59] FR case 223.

[60] FR case 247.

[61] FR case 111.

[62] FR case 649.

[63] The massacre by Waffen-SS troops at a French village that occurred in 1944.

[64] Führer head quarters.

[65] International Criminal Court, put in place by the United Nations to combat crimes against humanity, genocide etc.

[66] My italics and insertion.

[67] Of these, two Waffen-SS officers were identified, but no accurate records re their Waffen-SS service could be located. As a result they have not been included in this analysis. Therefore the total for the analysis is 28 officers.

[68] Ostheer was the term given to the German forces fighting on the Eastern Front.

[69] The German equivalent of a home guard or people's army.

[70] A mass-produced antitank weapon in the form of a hollow charge grenade launcher that could be carried by one man.

[71] GDR case 1156.

[72] Commonly referred to as the Battle of the Bulge, which took place in December 1944 and was the last effort by the Germans to win on the Western Front.

[73] My insertion and italics.

[74] My insertion and italics.

[75] My insertion and italics.

[76] This regiment would later form part of the 8th Waffen-SS Calvary Division *Florian Geyer*.

[77] FR case 570 refers.

[78] The Reich Security Head Office, which included the Gestapo, Security Police and Criminal Police. The RSHA was responsible for the direct orders for the *Einsatzgruppen*.

[79] The Rome Statute is the legislation governing the operations of the ICC.

[80] My italics.

[81] My italics.

[82] My italics.

[83] My italics.

[84] Twelve officers committed suicide and five were executed after Russians and Yugoslav war crime trails.

[85] My insertion and italics.

[86] *Oberkommando des Heeres* (OKH) or Army High Command.

[87] This legion would go on to form the 23rd Waffen-SS Freiwilligen Panzer Grenadier Division *Nederland*.

[88] This objective assessment is based on the rules of acceptable behaviour that can be determined by the reading of such international agreements as the Geneva Conventions, The Hague Conventions and even the more modern statutes of the ICC.

[89] Note that Maclean in his study of camp officers does not indicate that Ziereis completed any active military service with the Waffen-SS.

Printed in the United Kingdom by
Lightning Source UK Ltd., Milton Keynes
140817UK00001B/106/A

9 781598 584455